Tracing the Untraceable Buddha

LETTER

Tracing the Untraceable Buddha

The Vipassana Meditator's Journey to Enlightenment

Uffe Damborg

Foreword by Joseph Goldstein

Just as, Paharada, the great ocean slants, slopes, and inclines gradually, not dropping off abruptly, so too, in this dhamma and discipline, penetration to final knowledge occurs by gradual training, gradual activity, and gradual practice, not abruptly.

Paharada Sutta

The road to Bodh Gaya is not level; there are mountain passes, valleys, rivers, precipices and so forth. No matter what your personal road is like, do not lose courage, but repeatedly relax loosely in non-dual awareness. If we practice like this one day, we will arrive in Bodh Gaya, which means we will attain enlightenment. If we do not set out on the road, we will never arrive.

Tulku Urgyen Rinpoche, *Vajra Speech*

Meditators, one thing is very helpful for the arising of the noble eightfold path. What one thing? Good friendship. When a meditator has a good friend, it is to be expected that he will develop and cultivate the noble eightfold path.

Kalyanamitta Sutta

Shambhala Publications, Inc.
2129 13th Street
Boulder, Colorado 80302
www.shambhala.com

Cover Art: "Sacred signs on the Buddha's footprint, late 8th-late 12th century"
Cambodian Credit: Private Collection/Bridgeman Images.
Cover Design: Victor Mingovits

9 8 7 6 5 4 3 2 1

First Edition

Printed in the United States of America

Shambhala Publications makes every effort to print on acid-free, recycled paper.

Shambhala Publications is distributed worldwide by Penguin Random House, Inc., and its subsidiaries.

LIBRARY OF CONGRESS CATALOGING-IN-PUBLICATION DATA
Names: Damborg, Uffe, 1944- author
Title: Tracing the untraceable Buddha: the vipassana meditator's journey to enlightenment / Uffe Damborg
Description: Boulder: Shambhala Publications, 2026. | Includes bibliographical references and index.
Identifiers: LCCN 2025033078 | ISBN 9781645473954 trade paperback
Subjects: LCSH: Theravāda Buddhism—Doctrines | Spiritual life—Buddhism
Classification: LCC BQ7230 .D36 2026 | DDC 294.3/444—dc23/eng/20251222
LC record available at https://lccn.loc.gov/2025033078

The authorized representative in the EU for product safety and compliance is eucomply OÜ, Pärnu mnt 139b-14, 11317 Tallinn, Estonia, hello@eucompliancepartner.com.

Contents

Foreword

by Joseph Goldstein

I first met Uffe Damborg in Bangkok in 1966 when I was in the Peace Corps and he was a freelance reporter for a Danish newspaper. We quickly became good friends, sharing our early interest in Buddhism. After the time together in Thailand, we both ended up in Bodh Gaya, India, where we met our first teacher, Anagarika Munindra—a meeting that was to set the direction for the rest of our lives.

Munindra-ji had just come back from nine years in Burma (now Myanmar), where he had practiced meditation under the guidance of the Venerable Mahasi Sayadaw, one of the great Burmese meditation masters and scholars of the last century. When Munindra-ji completed his meditation training, he then undertook an exhaustive study of the early Buddhist teachings as preserved in the Pali canon, Pali being a vernacular language in India at that time.

Uffe and I practiced meditation intensively for an extended period of time, and Munindra-ji's open-mindedness, simplicity, and extensive knowledge—both in practice and theory—inspired our dedication to intensive practice. In Buddhist countries, very often great teachers will emphasize either the scholarly approach to the teachings of the Buddha or the practice of meditation. Munindra-ji, following the example of his own teacher, was an expert in both, and he imbued Uffe and me with the importance and value of interweaving both elements of the teachings.

Both of us have now been back in the West for many decades, writing and teaching meditation, drawing on our years of study in India; and for Uffe, many more years of meditation in Sri Lanka and work as a psychotherapist in Denmark.

All of this is by way of introduction to his wonderful book, *Tracing the Untraceable Buddha: The Vipassana Meditator's Journey to Enlightenment*. What makes this book so extraordinary is how systematically Uffe details so many different aspects of the teachings. In reading the manuscript, I was struck by how deeply Uffe is following in the lineage of Munindra-ji and the Venerable Mahasi Sayadaw as he weaves together the profound insights of meditation with the extensive and comprehensive teachings of the Buddha. Besides those we may be familiar with, such as the four noble truths, the laws of karma and dependent origination, and the practice of compassion and loving-kindness, Uffe draws on the many subtle aspects of the teachings found in the Abhidhamma. This is the detailed analysis of the mind-body process, sometimes referred to as Buddhist psychology. By frequently quoting directly from the Pali canon, we are reminded again and again that this is a path of liberation, leading to nibbana, the highest peace.

Uffe has done a remarkable job of combining the depth and subtlety of the teachings with his training and understanding as a psychotherapist, all expressed with his heart-opening poetic sensibility. It is a rare accomplishment, and I highly recommend it for anyone interested in deepening their understanding of the Buddha's extraordinary path to awakening.

Joseph Goldstein
Insight Meditation Society
Barre, Massachusetts

Preface

This book is a review of the profound teachings about the bondage and liberation of the human mind according to Theravada Buddhism—concepts that for millennia have inspired South and East Asian cultures and in recent times have had an impact on the West's spiritual understanding of life. Buddhism sets itself apart from most other religions by openly claiming to be the result of human insight, not divine revelation. Buddhism includes some of the same existential questions other religions engage with, but the Buddha's teachings are unique in being without belief in a creator god.

However, I leave it to the reader to judge whether Buddhism is a religion or rather a pragmatic doctrine of a meditative investigation of the causes of human suffering and liberation from it. I was one of the young Westerners who in the sixties and seventies became fascinated by Buddhism, drawn to its approach to mindfulness and self-discovery that led to a deeper understanding of both personal and collective human experiences. I have written a book that I would have liked to have read back then, when I traveled in the East and subsequently spent eight years in monasteries in South and East Asia. It should have been a book about the Buddha's entire teachings presented in a coherent way, similar to how knowledgeable Eastern Buddhists like my later teacher and spiritual friend in India, Anagarika Munindra-ji, understood Buddhism—based on tradition and sources, but completely undogmatic, because his knowledge sprang from his personal experience. My approach in covering Buddhist teachings is greatly informed by this great teacher who was my teacher for nearly six years in Bodh Gaya in northeast India. After a lifetime of practicing, studying, and teaching the *vipassana* meditation techniques and Abhidhamma teachings that Munindra-ji introduced me to, it is my hope that my own experiential knowledge may be of benefit to others in their spiritual journey.

In addition to Munindra-ji, I owe a debt of gratitude to many people who have been an inspiration to me, including the monks I met during my long stays in monasteries and hermitages outside India and the lay Buddhists who were always so unreservedly helpful when I was traveling in Asia. A general thank-you also to all the Western Buddhists who joined in the journey to Bodh Gaya in one way or another. Thanks especially to Joseph, Maria, Katerina, Antonio, and Lawrence. In my gratitude, I dedicate my book to all these people.

Uffe Damborg

Notes for the Reader

When I use the term *Buddhism*, I am referring specifically to Theravada (the School of the Elders), the oldest existing school of Buddhism, unless otherwise noted. Although many Westerners may be more familiar with the later Sanskrit forms of certain Buddhist terms, I mostly use the older Pali forms—for example, *dhamma* and *nibbana*—because that is the language of the earliest Buddhist *suttas* that the Theravada lineage upholds. These terms are used in all authentic teaching when learning to meditate in Theravada Buddhist monasteries, which more and more Westerners travel to the East to be enriched by. Pali terms are therefore interesting and necessary to include and explain in an account such as mine, but note that the diacritics of language are omitted in this book. When reviewing the various English translations of the suttas, one often encounters differences in the translation of key terms, which I have had to harmonize in the quotations to support my chosen line of nomenclature. In some cases, to clarify what I consider important points, I use my own translations, which are mentioned in the notes. Many of the quotations from the Pali suttas are from translations by the Venerable Bhikkhu Bodhi, who has kindly allowed me to make minor modifications to certain terms. It is open-minded Buddhism, and I thank him for his graciousness. When Ven. Bodhi translates the Buddha addressing a group of bhikkhus, I typically replace the word *bhikkhus* with *meditators*. When suttas give generic examples of a meditator's practice, I frequently change masculine gender pronouns to feminine pronouns for inclusivity (and many of the Buddha's disciples were, after all, women). Other minor changes are indicated in the notes.

Tracing the Untraceable Buddha

Introduction

The Journey to Bodh Gaya

The Buddha's teachings were handed down orally to posterity for several centuries before they were ever written down. Therefore, a Buddhist scripture typically begins with the phrase "Thus have I heard." In Pali, the word for a student or disciple is *savaka*: a "hearer"—that is, a person who, in a bookless time, encountered the Buddha's teachings by hearing about them in depth. Although I had read books on the Buddha's teachings before meeting Anagarika Munindra-ji (1915-2003) in India, I became a savaka of this exceptional teacher, who taught according to a living meditative tradition that went straight back to the roots of Buddhism.

Munindra-ji was enormously generous with his wisdom. With the open hand of a Buddhist teacher, he gave everything to anyone who desired his spiritual friendship. Since he had a wonderful sense of humor and a tireless eye for the good in his fellow people, he attracted many Westerners who, around the late sixties, began traveling to India in search of spiritual inspiration and guidance. I'd heard a great many wonderful things about Munindra-ji when I was in a Buddhist monastery in New Delhi, and I decided to look him up. There weren't many Buddhist teachers in the homeland of the Buddha around that time. In fact, Munindra-ji was the first vipassana teacher in India since the destruction of Buddhist culture by the invasion of Muslim armies in the twelfth and thirteenth centuries C.E. Munindra-ji was born into the Barua clan, one of India's oldest Buddhist families, in Chittagong, East India. He spent many years as a monk in Burma and was a distinguished student of the renowned *vipassana* (insight meditation) master Mahasi Sayadaw in Rangoon, under whose guidance he attained "stream entry." Munindra-ji then studied canonical scriptures with some of the most renowned Pali scholars in the country. After returning to India in 1966, he lived as a layman and began teaching vipassana and Abhidhamma—that is, Buddhist meditative psychology—at the Burmese Vihara in Bodh Gaya, where I met him in 1968.[1]

One of the first things Anagarika Munindra-ji told me was that I had to learn to live with persistent immersion in presence, whether I was Christian, Buddhist, or atheist. When I requested to learn how to meditate from him, he didn't ask me to take refuge, which is the traditional declaration of allegiance to Buddhism. In fact, there was not a single ritual ever with Anagarika Munindra-ji in the six years I spent with him, mainly in the Burmese Vihara. Munindra-ji instructed his students directly in the noble eightfold path to the attainment of the "fruit of stream entry," which is the heart of Buddhist spirituality. That's how I got to know him.

Arriving in Bodh Gaya

If you arrived in Bodh Gaya by train from Calcutta or Varanasi, you would travel the last kilometers from Gaya by horse-drawn cart or cycle rickshaw. There could be congestion on the road. Bullock carts with colossally large, solid wooden wheels rolled down the road as if straight out of an ancient Buddhist scripture. Now and then, elephants would be seen working with timber in the shade of the neem and banyan trees on the banks of the Neranjara River that ran alongside the road. This was the landscape that the Buddha had spoken of as "a delightful park, a lovely grove with a flowing river that was clean and charming, with smooth banks. And nearby was a village for alms." That place was Bodh Gaya, where the thirty-five-year-old Siddhattha Gotama, more than 2,500 years ago, under the full moon in May, became a buddha, or "enlightened." Sitting in deep meditation under a blossoming fig tree and favored by the golden light of the Vesak full moon above him, Siddhattha won his goal, "the highest freedom of all bonds: *nibbana* (Skt. nirvana)." Upon enlightenment, his mind awoke to what posterity knows as the four noble truths, which sum up all his teachings. It was the deepest transformative meaning of these truths that I was on my way to learn about from Munindra-ji—as close to the source as possible, so to speak.

The village of Bodh Gaya is located about ten kilometers south of Gaya in the present state of Bihar in northeast India. Today it is home to several Theravada and Mahayana Buddhist monasteries. Popular Buddhism perceives the village as the spiritual center of the universe. It was a place with a concentrated atmosphere around the Mahabodhi Temple, a second-century stone temple that rises in front of a broad, crooked pipal tree, believed to be a cutting of a cutting of a cutting of the fig tree under which Buddha, "the Awakened One," awoke from the sleep of existence. The strangely geometric decorations of the temple's facades were remarkably reminiscent of modern abstract art and were presumably meant as a symbolic negation of all known references to the inscrutability of his enlightenment. Pilgrims from South and East Asia made their way to the village all year round, but especially in May-June, the month of Vesak, and the full moon of the Buddha's night of awakening, when the trade winds begin to blow and the tinkling of temple bells sprinkle through the village's plane trees. In the evenings, the pilgrims and rural villagers gathered around the flickering dung fires and the oil lamps of the open-stalled chai houses along the unpaved main street. Tibetan refugees dominated the village scene in winter, especially when the Dalai Lama stayed in the Tibetan monastery located in the center of the village.[2] On lunar days throughout the year, a four-meter-long ritual brass horn would blast from the roof of the monastery, emitting an extremely loud honking sound that brought to mind a foghorn over "the ocean of births and deaths," which Buddhists must cross to reach the "other bank"—that is, nibbana.

My First Meeting with Munindra-ji

Where the emerald-green waters of the rice paddies ended, I caught sight of the first magnificent monastery building in Bodh Gaya. It was the Burmese Vihara. I opened the wrought-iron gate and stepped into a lush tropical garden enclosed by high, whitewashed walls. The grinding sound of the wooden wheels on the road outside sharpened the silence inside the garden. And the sparkling clarity of the running water, mixed with the laughter of the village women at the stone well farther away, suddenly surprised me. Out there along the wall, a man squatted in a white lungi in a silent listening circle of rickshaw wallahs. With a round, tonsured head and rimless glasses, he looked like a younger version of Mahatma Gandhi. As he spoke, he gracefully moved his hands with great presence, like those of a sitar player. When I came closer, I noticed his strong eyes and warm, disarming smile. And now I no longer wondered about his presence and its great impact on the respectful listening circle that squatted around him. Anagarika Munindra-ji was the rickshaw wallahs' teacher. He was also teacher to the village children who flocked around him everywhere he went and to the many pilgrims from all over Southeast Asia who came to Bodh Gaya all year round. A multitude of people knew, sought out, and rejoiced in Munindra-ji, who always had something uplifting to say about the Buddha's teachings and the path to liberating the mind that everyone could understand.

Around that time, Munindra-ji increasingly spent his time teaching a handful of Westerners. He offered them a rare opportunity to be with an authentic *kalyana mitta*, a "good spiritual friend," which is the term for a teacher in Theravada Buddhism. The *Dhammapada*, one of the most beloved scriptures in Theravada, says that when you find a good friend, you should "travel together, / Delighted and mindful, / Overcoming all dangers."[3] This is exactly what some of the travelers to Bodh Gaya did back then when they met Anagarika Munindra-ji.

After my first meeting outside the Burmese monastery, I thought of Upaka, the wandering philosopher who was the first person the Buddha spoke to after his enlightenment in Bodh Gaya. There was something alluring about the Enlightened One, whose face shone with a golden purity like the full moon. This led Upaka to ask if the Buddha was a god. The man with the beaming face denied this. So, was he an angel? He denied that too. In his confusion, Upaka then asked if the Buddha was a spirit. He got the answer that he was neither a god nor an angel nor a spirit but someone awakened (buddha) from the slumber of existence, a slumber that Upaka was still deep in because, instead of using this unique opportunity to learn about the greatest mystery of existence, Upaka shook his head skeptically and went on his way.

When I first met Munindra-ji surrounded by the rickshaw wallahs outside the Burmese Vihara, I was drawn to his presence in the same way, but fortunately I wasn't slumbering so deeply that I went on my way with a shake of my head. For me, it was the end of a journey that I had gradually come to realize was taking me in the wrong direction. I had been on a long existential journey without knowing what I was looking for, other than knowing that I was looking. I had traveled many thousands of miles overland and written newspaper articles along the way from North Africa, the Middle East, South and East Asia for more than three years. One day I realized I needed to change the destination to a journey deep into my mind. Everyday life with Munindra-ji was like an encounter with the Buddha's urging: "Here are the roots of great trees and desolate places for meditation. Be persistent. Don't waste time." Although they weren't exactly the words Munindra-ji said every day, he taught me the deep meaning of those places in my mind.

Munindra-ji talked about dhamma incessantly. He rarely engaged in small talk or discussed personal matters, but he always listened deeply. He delighted in discovering something fresh in each moment, often responding with his warm, infectious laughter. He was very skilled at mirroring the individuality of his students, encouraging them to meditate in "their own way," as he said. He repeatedly said that you were your own lamp; experience was your best teacher. In everyday life in the vihara, we noticed how caringly and heedfully Anagarika Munindra-ji accommodated each of us with his ability to guide meditators past every stumbling block on the path. Everyone in the vihara was influenced by his luminous presence, and every day became a meaningful immersion in the present that completely changed the direction of my life.

The Source of the Mindfulness Wave

Munindra-ji possessed a rare blend of expertise in that he was well read in the Pali canon of Buddhism and was also a meditation master who imparted a timeless teaching on the liberation of the mind. His teaching style went beyond rituals, and theories were based on the direct experience of his own enlightenment. Like an *Abhidhamma-acariya* (teacher of the Abhidhamma), Munindra-ji could nerd out about the smallest detail of this very comprehensive system of meditative psychology for which Burmese Buddhism is particularly famous. But at the same time, he had a completely sober and distanced attitude toward dogmatics. After a long talk, he could suggest with his disarming laugh that you simply forget all about "what is in the books" and instead investigate matters yourself in your meditation. This was entirely in line with the Buddha's famous speech in the *Kalama Sutta* about the pragmatism of the teaching and its ideal that the Buddhist meditator, at the end of the day, is her own best teacher.

In her book *Living This Life Fully*, the biographer Mirka Knaster shows that Munindra-ji was one of the grandfathers of the mindfulness wave in the West. He exerted an enormous influence on the spread of so-called pure insight meditation (*suddha vipassana*), a method popularized in the twentieth century mainly by Burmese meditation teachers but based on the ancient *Satipatthana Sutta*. Many of the Western vipassana teachers working in the West today are influenced by his simple, timeless, and self-empowering way of communicating the Buddha's teachings.

Spiritual Urgency and Compassion

Sometimes Munindra-ji summed up the Buddha's teachings with a single term: *appamada*. This concept can be translated as "earnestness," in the special sense of the persistent application of practice with spiritual urgency (*samvega*) associated with intensive meditation on a retreat. It was because of appamada that the Buddha achieved enlightenment under the Bodhi tree. And the last thing he told his disciples before he passed away was that they must strive for liberation with precisely this mentality. The concept of appamada, with its special emphasis on urgency, reflected Munindra-ji's enormously concentrated energy. Once, under Mahasi Sayadaw's tutelage in Rangoon, Munindra-ji had sat for sixteen hours in the full lotus position, absorbed in meditation on an excruciating pain in his knee before the pain passed. Once, when a confused tourist in Bodh Gaya asked him about the departure time of the next bus to the station town of Gaya, Munindra-ji answered the question as if it were about the search for absolute truth—to the great amusement of everyone, including the tourist.

According to Munindra-ji, a sustained, absorbed presence in the present moment was a potential opening for insight into the absolute, the deathless, nibbana. To emphasize the important point, he liked to tell an anecdote about a group of monks who were practicing vipassana within the rain forest. The story went like this: One of the monks was attacked by a tiger and called for help. Half of the poor monk's body was already in the tiger's jaws when one of the monks tried to console him with the cry, "Be deeply present in being eaten by a tiger, venerable sir!" At this point in the account, Munindra-ji closed his eyes as if in meditation and repeated a Mahasi Sayadaw-like mental note in a low, monotone voice: "Being eaten by a tiger. Being eaten by a tiger!"[4] And then he burst into his hearty laugh that made everyone laugh along with him.

As the tiger of old age, disease, and death attacked Munindra-ji, he began to lose his teeth. His students in the West pressed to be allowed to pay for his teeth to be fixed, but Munindra-ji refused. He said he wanted to explore old age and the decay of the body to the utmost, so he could die with a still deeper balance of mind and wisdom. After losing all his teeth, he died at his brother's home in Calcutta in 2003.

In my view, the anecdote about the necessity of sustained deep presence with an attacking tiger is an easily understood definition of a spiritual practice that is not so easy. It is based on neither faith nor speculative philosophy nor simply a religious view of life but on the necessity of one's deepest investigation of the truths of life called the dhamma-faring (*dhamma-cariya*). The four noble truths of Buddhism clarify how the transience of everything leads to suffering, dissatisfaction, and anguish (*dukkha*) when this basic condition is neglected and the dhamma traveler clings to notions of immutability. The Buddha declares that on the journey to liberating the mind, everything must be "directly understood"—that is, personally experienced moment after moment. Buddhist spirituality springs from this personal insight into the incessant changeability of existence and its consequences for the traveler's self-perception, sensations, and life history. These are the kinds of realizations that not only break the mind's attachment to suffering and ignorance but also foster empathy for everyone who endures such conditions. The compassionate attitude was the other side of Munindra-ji's ideal of appamada. From the beginning, when he was teaching vipassana, Munindra-ji also taught his students *metta* (loving-kindness meditation), which deepens the development of emotional empathy and compassion. He possessed these virtues to such an admirable degree that he was also of enormous importance for the spread of the knowledge of metta meditation in the West.

It was a gift to be with a teacher who lived as he taught. Originally there were six or seven Westerners in the Burmese Vihara in Bodh Gaya, and we spent several years with Munindra-ji. We all became deeply engaged in the open-ended course, as Munindra-ji called it, which was to completely change our lives. We sat in meditation for eight to twelve hours every day, and in deep silence we practiced walking meditation on the monastery's roof terrace or in the large garden, far into the night, between sitting meditation. There were no rituals, no formalities, no rules, no fixed daily schedule other than the sound of the Burmese gong, whose vibrating ore sound meant breakfast or lunch. By his example, Munindra-ji conveyed the ideal of stream entry as a profound source of inspiration that created a unique atmosphere in the monastery.

What was also fortunate for me was my friendship with the American vipassana teacher Joseph Goldstein, whom I had come to know a few years before when we were twenty-one years old. We first met at a Buddhist lecture in Bangkok and later lived the better part of six years together with Munindra-ji in Bodh Gaya. If mindful friends are essential for the development of the path, as the Buddha and Munindra-ji often pointed out, then Joseph's wise presence and his fine sense of humor were a perfect inspiration for the journey.

My Account

In the years since I left Bodh Gaya, the parables, metaphors, and anecdotes from the traditional Buddhist texts that Munindra-ji used in his teachings have served as mnemonic keys to his teaching and the many conversations I had with him. There are two concise images that come to mind. The first is the simile of the great ocean from one of the Buddha's sermons: "Just as, Paharada, the great ocean, slants, slopes, and inclines gradually, not dropping off abruptly, so too, in this dhamma and discipline, penetration to final knowledge occurs by gradual training, gradual activity, and gradual practice, not abruptly."[5] This is the pregnant image of the nature of spiritual development that gradually changes your orientation in life. In Buddhism, which is not a doctrine of faith, there are no leaps into the ten-thousand fathoms of faith and no revelations. Insight is something that needs to be developed and worked for with appamada. In fact, in Pali, the word *development* (*bhavana*) means "meditation."

The second image, from the oldest commentaries, is the concept of "the minor stream-enterer" (*cula-sotapanna*). A minor stream-enterer is someone who struggles with the ups and downs of their meditative practice and is destined for enlightenment, following the map to nibbana based on the early tradition of Buddhism and the way Anagarika Munindra-ji taught. The minor stream-enterer is like the traveler to Bodh Gaya depicted in this book's second epigraph:

> The road to Bodh Gaya is not level; there are mountain passes, valleys, rivers, precipices and so forth. No matter what your

> personal road is like, do not lose courage, but repeatedly relax loosely in non-dual awareness. If we practice like this one day, we will arrive in Bodh Gaya, which means we will attain enlightenment. If we do not set out on the road, we will never arrive.[6]

The minor stream entry leads to what Munindra-ji called the major stream entry, which is the portal to the mind's irrevocable liberation in Buddhist spirituality. It was the path that the Buddha declared to have found as a path from ancient times inside the rainforest—it is the path that flows toward full enlightenment. The minor stream entry is the initial entry into the stream of this path. Any serious meditator can achieve this state of mind, and my goal with this book is to inspire it.

The reader for whom I have written the book might be someone like the traveler I was in my twenties. Not necessarily someone traveling in the East but rather an individual embarking on a spiritual journey. The sequence in which I present the central concepts reflects the narrative structure I have chosen for this inner journey. To begin, both literally and symbolically, I introduce the reader to the Buddha's own journey to Bodh Gaya. Following this, I explore Buddhism's oldest teachings on karma, perception, the ethical freedom of will, and the mind's bondages, conditioning, and defilements caused by egocentricity and ignorance. These concepts are presented to deepen the reader's understanding of the subtlety of the liberation project of the four noble truths. Subsequently, the book delves into the map of the noble eightfold path, especially the foundations for right mindfulness and right concentration in the way these concepts are used in connection with instruction in vipassana on a retreat. All thirty-seven factors that lead to enlightenment are explained individually before being summarized within the overarching framework of the four noble truths. Then I show how the gradual realization of the truths defines the minor stream entry that leads to the fruition of stream entry through the insights (*nanas*) in vipassana. Along the way, there is a detailed instruction in and explanation of paranormal memories of past lives, which are an integral aspect of authentic Buddhism that is often treated superficially in Western literature. In the final chapter, I draw on fascinating accounts of the Buddha and the founding of the monastic order from the Vinaya Pitaka that are less known to Western readers in general.

The Buddha emphasized the importance of finding a spiritual guide for the journey to Bodh Gaya—someone whose inspiring example can illuminate the path of practice, much like Munindra-ji did for me. In an era when many Westerners gather bits and pieces of Buddhist teachings from apps and the internet, the third epigraph serves as a timeless reminder of the value of true spiritual companionship: "Meditators, one thing is very helpful for the arising of the noble eightfold path. What one thing? Good friendship. When a meditator has a good friend, it is to be expected that he will develop and cultivate the noble eightfold path."[7]

My spiritual friendship with Anagarika Munindra-ji and the transformative years I spent with him are a testament to this truth.

As I am also a psychologist, I sometimes refer to concepts from Western psychology, which will hardly be difficult for the attentive reader to distinguish from Buddhism. But whatever shortcomings and errors there may be in my account are due only to me.

1 | The Thus-Arrived, Tathagata

The Buddha's name was Siddhattha Gotama. According to the lunar Indian calendar, the future Buddha was born into the Sakya clan during the Vesak full moon in Lumbini, south of the lower Himalayas. He achieved enlightenment at the age of thirty-five under the golden light of the Vesak full moon in Bodh Gaya, south of the Ganges River. And he died at the age of eighty under the clearing of the Vesak moon between two tall sal trees in Kusinara, southeast of Lumbini, north of Benares.[1]

Siddhattha Gotama grew up in North India in the fourth-fifth centuries B.C.E., in the transitional period between the decline of Vedic cult teachings and the individualization of spiritual life—a time that parallels the emergence of philosophy in ancient Greece. A new way of thinking emerged that was more about the individual. It is the seed of modern self-awareness, expressed in the Greek philosopher Heraclitus's anti-authoritarian statement: "I researched myself."[2] It may not sound like much today, but in the sixth century B.C.E., it was a groundbreaking thought both in India and Greece.

The Buddha's Existential Attitude

But the Buddha was not a philosopher. His contemporaries perceived him as a *samana*, a practitioner of a specific discipline in India's spiritual tradition. Like other samanas of his time, the Buddha's meditative teaching instructs seekers to find answers to the great questions of existence for themselves. The Buddha shows a way but isn't a savior figure. He consistently emphasizes that liberation of the mind cannot be achieved on behalf of others. This existential perspective is often expressed through the idea that the meditator is both bound and freed by her own actions.

Siddhattha Gotama's awakening or enlightenment (*bodhi*) wasn't revealed to him or bestowed upon him by the grace of a god. The Buddha didn't believe in a creator god or anything that could *not* be verified by experience. Enlightenment, which is the source of his teachings and is expressed as the four noble truths, isn't a mystical experience for which he doesn't know the psychological and causal prerequisites. Before his enlightenment, he was determined to achieve "what can be attained by manly strength, energy, and exertion."[3] He developed such a thorough understanding of the causal processes that lead to the liberation of the mind that the formulation of his teaching is the first example of process thinking in the history of ideas.

The Footprints of the Buddha

When the Buddha talks about himself in the Pali suttas, he often uses the epithet Tathagata, meaning "one who has thus arrived," to emphasize that he is neither a philosopher nor a savior but a guide for others. Others should follow him by using the same meditative techniques that he practiced. In this sense, the four noble truths are "a footprint of the Tathagata,"[4] and becoming enlightened is possible for every human being who follows in his path.

The Tathagata had intuitively grasped the truth of the "thusness" (*tathata*) of existence. This refers to his deep understanding of the three universal characteristics: Everything is impermanent and constantly changing (*anicca*); life involves suffering (*dukkha*) because of this constant change; and for the same reason, there is no permanent "self" or "soul" (*anatta*).[5] He is "thus-gone" as a result of enlightenment, which gives him an unshakable awareness and realization of this "thusness." He can no longer fall back into the illusion of an unchanging self, I, or soul, which is why the scriptures claim that the Tathagata is "untraceable."[6]

It was this paradoxicality that I set out to trace on my journey to Bodh Gaya. What was meant by the Buddha's "untraceability"? And how was it to be understood that the noble eightfold path was the Buddha's footprint when it had led to precisely his tracelessness? To get a glimpse of real understanding, I had to follow those footprints.

How He Discovered an Ancient Path

The Buddha taught that the four noble truths were universal and timeless, and the tathagatas of the past followed this path to the irrevocable liberation of the mind.

"Suppose, meditators, a man wandering through a forest would see an ancient path. An ancient road traveled upon by people in the past. . . . So too, meditators, I saw the ancient path, the ancient road traveled by the perfectly enlightened ones of the past."[7]

But what, then, does this path traveled by the awakened ones of old consist of?

"It is just this noble eightfold path; that is, right view, right intention, right speech, right action, right livelihood, right effort, right mindfulness, and right concentration."[8]

The noble eightfold path is the fourth of the noble truths, and it is for all practical purposes from here that the tracks and the paradoxical "tracklessness" of the Tathagata must be followed.

The Mnemonic Ball of Yarn

In themselves, the four noble truths form a single so-called *sutta* (thread), which is an easy-to-remember template in the system of the oral transmission of the Buddhist scriptures before they were written down.[9]

The first noble truth is about dukkha, the fundamental suffering that everyone experiences in life. It is a part of being human, because our body and mind are subject to changes and conditions that ultimately lead to death.

The second noble truth is about the self-created suffering that arises through a disorienting "desire-thirst" for unchangeability, especially in our self-perception—that is, our urge to hold on to things, states, and relationships that we want to remain unchanged. But because everything in life changes, we create suffering and loss when we try to hold on to what cannot be held. This suffering depends on how we respond, moment by moment, to the ever-changing nature of life.

The third noble truth is about letting go of this "thirst" by developing a deep understanding of why we think and act as we do. We come to see that we cling to change and create pain we could have done without. We come to understand how we can change our ways of being in the world by cultivating wisdom based on awareness, equanimity, and compassion.

The fourth noble truth is about the noble eightfold path into the mind's connections and depths to achieve clarity and enlightenment. It is a meditative method for understanding the first three noble truths, leading to the mind's liberation from self-created suffering and a stance of resilient detachment from the universal suffering inherent in life.

The four noble truths arise psychologically in each moment of developed states of insight meditation. But each of the truths also functions as an independent sutta that connects the theorem with other mnemonic threads. The noble eightfold path thus includes a sutta for each of the eight links. The right view—which is the first link of the path—activates intuitive direct understanding (*abhinna*) of the four noble truths, which bind together the meaning of all the other threads in the insight process. The eighth link—right concentration—consists of the guidance in the various levels of concentration (*jhanas*) and their subcategories, the five links of absorption. The seventh link of the path—right mindfulness—contains the guidance in the four foundations of mindfulness. The sixth link of the path consists of guidance in the four right efforts that are necessary for meditative development. And so on. Just a handful of theorems are mentioned here, the suttas of which branch out further into the structure of the teaching system.

Apart from being the footstep of the Tathagata, the four noble truths are a mnemonic "ball of yarn" from which the entire Buddhist teaching system can be deciphered by the knowledgeable "listener" (*savaka*) who has listened to and memorized those teachings and validated their truths by meditative experience.

The Map and the Land

The noble truths include two levels of understanding. One is the theoretical level—my exposition of the four noble truths is obviously an immediate example. At this level, it is important to study the map of the country before traveling. The map also includes the literary-designed discourses in the sutta collection (Sutta Pitaka) with various biographical episodes as the frame narrative for the Buddha's speeches around the Ganges plain.

The second level is the journey itself, based on the personal experiences and encounters of the land. It is the immersion in the intuitive direct understanding (*abhinna*) of the four noble truths in the meditator's own life, when she lingers in concentrated introspection of the mind. At this level, the first link of the path, right view, is defined as the realization of dukkha, the understanding and elimination of the cause, and the clear awareness of the meditative path that has led the traveler here.

As the Buddha explains, "O meditators, just as a man in the gloom and darkness of the night, at the sudden flashing up of lightning, would with his own eyes recognize the objects: so, the meditator sees, according to reality, 'This is dukkha, this is the origin of dukkha, this is the extinction of dukkha, and this is the path leading to the extinction of dukkha.'"[10]

In this light, the paradoxical footprints of the Buddha become personalized for the meditator. If Buddhism only contained a "map" and not a land, and therefore was only a theory, the teaching would be merely a kind of combined philosophy and psychology, which with a little goodwill could be pieced together from theories in the West's own culture—albeit from much later periods. But the insight-meditative understanding of the four noble truths is a unique, concrete destination—and a place where the traveler from the West has never been before.

2 | Samana Gotama and His Self-Narrative

What we know of the Buddha's historical life and *how* he discovered this profound ancient path is based on accounts he tells in several almost identical suttas. These accounts are what a modern psychologist would call his self-narrative—that is, the personalized story that, time and again, a person tells others and themselves about their own perception of their life, albeit with slight variations each time depending on who the listeners are.

Siddhattha was likely neither a prince nor heir to a world empire, as depicted by the fantastic legend *Nidana-Katha* that a thousand years later was attached to the canon. But there can be no doubt that he was the son of a wealthy family. We thus hear him tell, in a completely different tone from the overexposed legend, that his father owned three houses, one for each of the North Indian seasons.

There were lotus pools with blue, white, and red lotuses to please the little Siddhattha, and life was splendid on the surface:

> I used no sandalwood unless it came from Kasi and my head-dress, jacket, lower garment, and upper garment were made of cloth from Kasi. . . . While in other people's homes, slaves, workers, and servants are given broken rice together with sour

> gruel for their meals, in my father's residence they were given choice hill rice, meat, and boiled rice.[1]

One of the touching passages in this narrative is Siddhattha's reflections in early youth on the impermanence of life:

> Amid such splendor and a delicate life, it occurred to me: "An uninstructed worldling, though himself subject to old age, not exempt from old age, feels repelled, humiliated, and disgusted when he sees another who is old, overlooking his own situation. Now I too am subject to old age and am not exempt from old age. Such being the case, if I were to feel repelled, humiliated, and disgusted when seeing another who is old, that would not be proper for me." When I reflected thus, my intoxication with youth was completely abandoned.[2]

On the same occasion, Siddhattha had thoughts of the sight of a sick person, at which the healthy person who is ignorant feels disgust, although he himself may become sick. It is therefore unworthy to feel this way, concluded Siddhattha: "When I reflected thus, my intoxication with health was completely abandoned."[3] Siddhattha had ended these thoughts by reflecting on the sight of the corpse, from which the average ignorant person turns away depressed and disgusted. But even this is undignified because they can be sure of dying themselves. "When I reflected thus, my intoxication with life was completely abandoned."[4]

Siddhattha's Disenchantment and Liberation

Siddhattha's great consciousness of death from his boyhood later became the deeply challenging existential theme of his teachings. In the suttas, the images of the old, the sick, and the corpse appear repeatedly. They are sometimes called divine messengers who remind people of the inevitable. Very often, the Buddha also uses the concepts of birth, old age, illness, and death as a metaphor for the insight into momentary change (*anicca*) of all phenomena, as developed in vipassana (insight meditation). These metaphorical figures of speech are frequently used in formulations of the following kind: "A meditator thus understands aging-and-death, its origin, its cessation, and the way leading to its cessation."[5] This meditator experiences intuitively the consequences of impermanence, moment by moment. One such consequence is that each moment is imbued with some degree of suffering—because things change, we either lose what we want to hold on to or something comes our way that we don't welcome. Another consequence is the absence of a core self—since we are always in flux, there is no stable entity we can pinpoint and identify as "me." The overarching understanding of "decay and death" consists of such moments, and these insights are deepened in connection with one's life history, which is brought to consciousness with unusual clarity in deep insight meditation. When the disciple Ananda asks the Buddha what intuitive insight into how it really is (*yathabhuta*) leads to, he is told that it leads to disillusionment and the fading away of clinging to thoughts, feelings, and sensations; and that disillusionment and fading away of clinging lead to liberation of mind.[6]

The spiritual goal of freeing the mind from the suffering, dissatisfaction, and anguish associated with an existence of loss and changeability is the great spiritual theme of the Buddha's teachings. It is a theme that is as old as humanity itself, but the Buddha's insightful meditative understanding of it as a liberation doctrine is unique.

The Story of the Renunciation, Asceticism, and Enlightenment

At the age of twenty-nine and challenged by his very keen awareness of the brevity of life, Siddhattha Gotama leaves his homeland south of the foothills of the Himalayas to live as a wandering seeker of truth on the plain of the Ganges. This he talks about in this way:

> Then I considered thus: "Why, being myself subject to birth, do I seek what is also subject to birth? Why, being myself subject to aging, sickness, death, sorrow, and defilement, do I seek what is also subject to aging, sickness, death, sorrow, and defilement? Suppose that, being myself subject to birth, having understood the danger in what is subject to birth, I seek the unborn supreme security from bondage: nibbana. Suppose that, being myself subject to aging, sickness, death, sorrow, and defilement, having understood the danger in what is subject to aging, sickness, death, sorrow, and defilement, I seek the unaging, unailing, deathless, sorrowless, and undefiled supreme security from bondage: nibbana.
>
> Later, while still young, a black-haired young man endowed with the blessing of youth, in the prime of life, though my mother and father wished otherwise and wept with tearful faces, I shaved off my hair and beard, put on the yellow robe, and went forth from the home life into homelessness."[7]

Siddhattha then narrates how he becomes a disciple of two *munis* (yogis) in the subcultural environment of the Ganges plain. He learns to master the jhanas (exquisite states of meditative absorption described in chapter 7) to such an extent that his teachers will share the leadership of their sects with him. But Siddhattha rejects this because, unlike the munis, he does not see the jhanas as transcendental enlightenment. Then he leaves the teachers to seek his own way to the incomparable peace of mind.

Many of Buddha's disciples were, like him, accomplished yogis in the common Indian meditation tradition, which fundamentally consists of breath meditation and other meditations with a simple structure suitable for the development of samadhi (concentration). In Buddhism this meditation system is called *samatha bhavana* (development of mental calm), which leads to the jhanas that Buddha learned from the munis. The noble eightfold path that Buddha declares to have found by himself branches out from samatha bhavana, and Siddhattha rejected it as a path to true enlightenment.

> Still in search, meditators, of what is wholesome, seeking the supreme state of sublime peace, I wandered by stages through the Magadhan country until eventually I arrived at Uruvela, at Senanigama. There I saw an agreeable piece of ground, a delightful grove with a clear-flowing river with pleasant, smooth banks and nearby a village for alms resort. I considered: "This is an agreeable piece of ground, this is a delightful grove with a clear-flowing river with pleasant, smooth banks and nearby a village for alms resort. This will serve for the striving of a clansman intent on striving." And I sat down there thinking: "This will serve for striving."[8]

He has these thoughts on the day of the full moon night of Vesak in Bodh Gaya, where he achieves enlightenment. We can imagine how the disillusioned Siddhattha sat under the tree in a state of highly advanced samadhi, no longer believing that mere absorption in mental one-pointedness could lead to his goal, and beginning to investigate the stream of his consciousness in profound detachment—just letting thoughts and impressions flow by like leaves drifting with the current in a quiet river.

The Indian Concepts of the Life Cycle

The Buddha related to, but of course also differed from, the common Indian life notion of the cycle of rebirths (*sangsara*, "turning around"), which is associated with meditation and karma.

The great philosophical problem in Buddha's India was the idea that the individual's soul or self was estranged by the entanglement in causal activities of karma (Pali, *kamma*, "activities") that kept sangsara turning.[9] This estrangement was believed to lead to repeated reincarnations of a core self (*atman*) at different stations of existence in the cycle of rebirth and thus the repeated abandonment to the vicissitudes of existence, loss, suffering, and death.[10] But according to the Buddha, the perception of the mind's unchanging core self is an illusion that is the very cause of existential estrangement and anguish. According to Buddhist teachings, the self's continuously changing stream of becoming is trapped and entangled in the cycle of rebirth and karma *precisely* because of an insatiable craving for a permanent core self, which is projected into as many life-historical fragments as the deluded craving clings to, and this is a cause of much suffering. Finding a realistic solution to the distortions of ignorance and craving was therefore the great challenge of Siddhattha's search for truth.

From my window in the Burmese Vihara, I could see the pink and slate-gray mountains where, according to the accepted chronology, Siddhattha had practiced ascetic exercises with five apostate disciples of one of the munis before arriving in Bodh Gaya. It made me think that the sutta just quoted, the *Sutta on the Noble Quest*, was spoken to a gathering of monks in a hermitage outside the Anathapindika Monastery in Savatthi, the capital of Kosala, as encouragement for their own noble pursuit of enlightenment. This sutta is notable for omitting Siddhattha's period of asceticism, maybe because it was of no interest to the listeners, who were already on the proper meditative path. The Buddha does mention his period of asceticism in several other suttas, especially when the listeners are themselves practitioners of asceticism.

Thus, it was—for example, in the *Great Sutta to Saccaka*[11]—spoken to the Jain Saccaka and others in the Great Grove in Vesali, in the Land of the Free Clans, where the Mahavira, the historical founder of Jainism, was born and raised and where his strongly ascetic teachings flourished.[12] In the Buddha's formulation of his teaching as *the Middle Way*, asceticism is one of a pair of extremes to be avoided; the other extreme is hedonism. But with the description of the enthusiasm that Siddhattha had manifested as an ascetic, he attracted the attention of the ascetics and made them receptive to his objections to the usefulness of asceticism. Many ascetics, especially followers of Mahavira, were thus won over to the meditative path of the Buddha's teachings.

And the well-to-do son Siddhattha had carried out the classic mortification of the flesh, the fast, to the extent that his backside became like a camel's hoof, his ribs jutted out as gaunt as the crazy rafters of an old roofless barn. According to the Buddha's own recollection preserved in the suttas, he was so skinny that "if I wanted to touch my belly skin I encountered my backbone."[13] He had also experimented with methodically stopping his breathing and had come close to dying from it. However, he didn't experience the joy of liberation that had been the goal of all these bizarre efforts. In a state of deep despair, his thoughts turned to the memory of a joyful day when, as a boy, he had rested in the shade of a rose tree. In a moment of bliss, the unusually mature boy had experienced a sense of unity like the first jhanic absorption. This memory inspired the disheartened ascetic to try meditation once again. He began eating normally, despite the disapproval of his ascetic companions, and eventually left them to seek peace of mind on his own.

According to this version of the self-narrative, it was only then that he arrived at Bodh Gaya. The narrative culminates in Siddhattha's realization of the four noble truths during the final watch of the night as he sat beneath the fig tree. The fourfold formulation of this insight, as previously mentioned, serves as the most comprehensive mnemonic thread in the Buddhist teaching system, connecting all the core principles of the teaching. The story of his journey from boyhood to enlightenment, including his ultimate insight into the four noble truths, is recounted by the Buddha many times in the canon—sometimes with, and sometimes without, the account of his realization of the futility of asceticism.

The Buddha is the religious founder who speaks most openly about himself, more frequently and in greater detail than others, but always with a teaching purpose when addressing disciples or debating with wandering philosophers and followers of other sects. As a result, we know a great deal about the key phases of Siddhattha's life and the transformation of his mind following his enlightenment at Bodh Gaya. He typically concludes the story of his enlightenment with a reflection on the four noble truths, which he intuitively grasped at Bodh Gaya—and it is difficult to imagine a more profound and meaningful self-narrative.

The Buddha elaborates on the four noble truths throughout his life in his speeches and for the instruction of the followers who follow in his footsteps. His description of his enlightenment is unusual in its concrete detail.

> I directly knew as it actually is: "This is suffering"; I directly knew as it actually is: "This is the origin of suffering"; I directly knew as it actually is: "This is the cessation of suffering"; I directly knew as it actually is: "This is the way leading to the cessation of suffering"; I directly knew as it actually is: "These are the influxes"; I directly knew as it actually is: "This the

> origin of the influxes"; I directly knew as it actually is: "This is the cessation of the influxes"; I directly knew as it actually is: "This is the way leading to the cessation of the influxes."
>
> When I knew and saw thus, my mind was liberated from the influx of sensual desire, from the influx of (misperceived ego-) becoming, from the influx of ignorance. When it was liberated, there came the knowledge: "It is liberated." I directly knew: "Birth is destroyed, the holy life has been lived, what had to be done has been done, there is no more coming to any state of being."[14]

The irreversible extinction of the *asavas*, the "influxes," is the negative formulation of Buddhism's psychological liberation project. The asavas consist of the three unwholesome conditions: ignorance, desire-thirst, and hatred, which lead to the bondage of the mind. The Enlightened One was often simply called One Who Is Free from the Inflows (*khinasava*). All the Buddha's enlightened disciples were *khinasava*, freed from the mind's clouding influxes of ignorance, "thirst," and hatred. They had thus eliminated the fetters that, in the grand scheme of things, were binding on the cycle of rebirths, sangsara. They had eliminated the misperceived genesis of a core self, which is the pivot in sangsara's perception processes. In this way "birth" had been eliminated in both contexts, and an end to suffering had been achieved. The repeated statement, "I knew it directly," is a mnemonic phrase that highlights the personal and experiential nature of the truth of the Buddha's understanding.

3 | The Core Teaching About Non-Core Self

Sitting in meditation at the foot of the fig tree in Bodh Gaya under the Vesak full moon, Siddhattha Gotama eventually found what he was seeking, nibbana, "the deathless" (*amata*). The transcendental realization of "the deathless" is beyond the flow of consciousness, thoughts, feelings, and sensations—and the insight irreversibly seals the paradoxical realization that there is no immutable subject (*atta*) in the flowing mind for whom the insight of enlightenment is for.

> Just as, meditators, in the autumn, when the sky is clear and cloudless, the sun, ascending in the sky, dispels all darkness from space as it shines and beams and radiates, so too, when the perception of impermanence is developed and cultivated, it eliminates all sensual lust, it eliminates all lust for (ego-) becoming, it eliminates all ignorance, it uproots all conceit "I am."[1]

Anatta, Non-Self

The understanding of *anatta*, which means "non-self" or "non-soul," is the key to the Buddha's unique teaching. It is also undoubtedly the part of the teaching that is most misunderstood in the West and the most difficult to explain because it is a meditative insight. On the one hand, anatta is a historically conditioned concept that refers to the negation of the flourishing notions of the soul (or the self) that is not relativized by causality and immutability. The Buddha classifies this notion under "view of eternity" in the discussions with other teachers. It refers to the lack in consciousness of an unchanging core of identity, self-essence, or substance in the religious and classically philosophical sense. The father of psychoanalysis, Sigmund Freud, has very clearly formulated this dominating concept on behalf of the European intellectual tradition, thus "normally, nothing is more certain for us than the feeling of our Self, of our own Ego. The 'I' seems to us to be independent, and to form a unity and to be clearly delineated against everything else."[2] Freud was the first, with great consequence, in the cultural circle of the West to see through this naïve notion of the psyche by demonstrating the conditioning of the self, the I, or the ego by unconscious processes. I use these terms here as synonyms for the dominant assumption of an autonomous and unchanging agent as the bearer of consciousness. The Buddha's teachings present all theoretical variants of this basic notion of an immutable core identity as a conceptual illusion and perceptual hallucination. The concept of an unchanging core self that rationally and sovereignly exercises supremacy over itself, or should do so, is a deeply entrenched way of perceiving the individual in Western culture. But with sustained meditation practice, according to the Buddhist teachings, we begin to see that it is only a construct—one without substance.

Non-Core Self

The primary criterion for the Self with a capital *S* is, according to the Buddhist definition, that it must be an unconditioned core that exercises sovereign supremacy over itself and therefore not be at the mercy of the relativizing conditions of causality and impermanence. *Anatta* refers to the reality (thusness) of precisely a relativized, conditioned, and composite self in an incessant "stream of becoming" (*bhava-sota*). It is a process self that only comes into being through its dependence on a multiplicity of both conscious and unconscious conditions. This compounded, ever-changing self is without a core (*sara*) of permanence, without a core of happiness, without a core of self.[3] Of course, this doesn't imply that the coreless process self doesn't experience great joy—for example, in the sublimely peaceful absorptions of samadhi (*jhana*)—but it depends precisely on the conditions, because joy is not a core of the self.

In other words, the Buddha initiated a revolution in psychology a few millennia before Freud, albeit from different angles and with drastically different consequences, but with the same conclusion: *The ego is not master in its own house.* But where Freud wanted to strengthen the ego, the Buddha provided an insightful meditative path to understand the illusion of the master ego and irreversibly eliminate the desire for it.

To Take Refuge in Oneself

The concept of the self is thus used by the Buddha in two basic senses that mustn't be confused. *Atta* (self) is both a noun and a pronoun and means "self" and "oneself," which the Buddha uses in reference to himself and others. The enlightened disciple is precisely a person who, through his realization of anatta, developed themselves (that is, developed the small-*s* self). He has won liberation from influxes of ignorance and desire that project hallucinations of the ego into the changing objects of the mind and thus binds consciousness to the anguish associated with bondage to the changeable. The meditator who strives to develop the process self in order to dismantle the distortions of ignorance is therefore recommended to withdraw from the distractions of pulverizing everyday life in order to immerse himself and live "as an island unto himself . . . with no other refuge"[4] while introspecting the mind intensively to understand it *as it is*. This is a recurring guide to insight meditation in the suttas. Thus, it is evident that the Buddha alternates effortlessly between a language of absolute truth—there is no self—and a language of relative truth—there is a changing, conditioned, and developing process of oneself or self. In general, in the analysis of the Abhidhamma, all formulations are strictly in terms of absolute truth, while utterances of both relative and absolute truth are found in the Buddha's instructions in the suttas.

The Path in the Middle

Different notions of the principle of cause and effect (the law of karma) are associated with these concepts of the self. The metaphysicians of the Upanishadic teachings—a strain of philosophical-spiritual discourse that was developed around the time of the Buddha—thus believed that the immortal self or soul (Skt. *atman*) was reflected in all the phenomena of the world, whose causal and changing forms of appearance must be an illusion (Skt. *maya*).[5] The perception of the phenomenal world as an illusion, in turn, made it impossible for these "seers" to understand the processes of the mind with the psychological realism so characteristic of early Buddhism. According to the Buddha's teachings, the changing, composite, and causal forms of appearance of phenomena are real phenomena (*dhammas*). They are "thus" (*tatha*), and they are the very field for developing the insights necessary to free the mind from ignorance of the self as a coreless stream.

> This world, Kaccana, for the most part depends upon a duality—upon the notion of existence and the notion of nonexistence.

> But for the one who sees the arising of the world as it really is with correct wisdom, there is no notion of nonexistence in regard to the world. And for one who sees the cessation of the world as it really is with correct wisdom, there is no notion of existence in regard to the world.[6]

The insight into the "stream of becoming" avoids the ontological extremes of being and nonbeing because "with a stream of continuity there is neither identity nor otherness. For if there were absolute identity in a stream of continuity, there would be no forming of curd from milk. And yet if there were absolute otherness, the curd would not be derived from milk. And so too with all causally arisen things."[7] Just as milk doesn't turn into wine but only into yogurt and butter and so on, so too the conditioned self flows from state of mind to state of mind in an identical process. The story that the Buddha so often narrates about himself takes place in an identical process, which is *his* life. But the process mustn't be confused with being an unchanging *essence*, a self, an atman, a supreme static agent, or an unchanging narrator of the narrative. The self is only a concept in the story—and not a separate narrator's grasp of it.

The Pragmatism of the Teaching

Even though the Buddha's teaching addresses the notion of transmigration across lives common in Indian spirituality, and even though the teaching also includes a method for paranormal recollection of past lives (as we shall see later), the Buddha also speaks of the cycle of rebirth as a metaphor for the core-self illusion, the moment-to-moment genesis of the misperception of ego in the causal processes of the mind.

In the famous sutta on the pragmatism of the teaching, the Buddha urges his listeners only to have confidence (*saddha*) in what their experience can verify. The sutta is addressed to the Kalama clan, whose members were not all convinced of the concept of rebirth. And the Buddha admits that belief in the cycle of rebirth is not necessary to overcome the suffering of one's present life. He goes on to reason that, since his teachings bring happiness in this present life, the practitioner is better off regardless of whether there are future lives. If there is rebirth, then practice will reduce their suffering in future lives. If there are no future lives, nothing will be lost, since the practitioner can secure the highest possible happiness in this very life.[8] In other words, whether past and future lives exist has no bearing on the pursuit of liberation in this present life. But in addition to noting this pragmatic attitude, we must also deal further with the Buddha's teaching's variant of the sangsara notion. In fact, one cannot fully comprehend the Buddha's theoretical formulation of the four noble truths if it is not seen in the larger context of the notion of the cycle of rebirths. The notion of a coreless stream of consciousness that passes on from existence to existence is a pure expression of the non-self doctrine. Anagarika Munindra-ji's way of teaching vipassana was in every way characterized by this understanding, which is often downplayed or completely ignored in Western books on Buddhist meditation.

The Five Aggregates That Are Subject to Clinging

Then who "turns round" in sangsara? The mind can be conscious at various levels of knowledge, of which intuitive, personal, direct knowledge of the basic condition of existence of immediate changeability and what follows from this insight leads alone to transformative understanding of the four noble truths. Just like a flame that travels from one wick to another (and in principle on to a third, etc.) isn't an unchanging core in motion but a ceaselessly changing process, so in the individual stream of consciousness there is no immortal soul or unchanging self-identity going round in the cycle of rebirths. At any given time, from moment to moment in sangsara, as well as from one life to the next, a human being is neither quite the same nor an entirely different person as before and after this unique moment.[9] In addition to being the seat of the cognitive functions, consciousness, according to this view, has the function of "relinking" (*patisandhi*) each preceding and subsequent process of perception in "the stream of consciousness" (*vinnana-sota*). This relinking function happens at every moment, and the relinking across lives is only different in intensity and not in nature when compared to the transition between two successive processes of consciousness in daily life. In both cases, *subconscious moments of becoming* (*bhavanga-citta*) flow between the conscious perception processes, creating coherence between the past and the present.[10] When Sati, the fisherman's son, asserts in a discussion with the Buddha that consciousness is a unit and that it is the very same consciousness that rushes on from moment to moment and from life to life, the Buddha draws his attention to the momentarily dependent arising, relativization, and conditioning of consciousness.[11] Consider, for example, the process of sight:

> In dependence on the eye and forms, eye consciousness arises. The meeting of the three is contact. With contact as condition, feeling comes to be; with feeling as condition craving; with craving as condition, clinging; with clinging as condition, (misperceived ego-) becoming. . . . This, meditators, is the origin of the world (*loko*).[12]

And thus also for the other perception processes, because "without a condition, there is no origination of consciousness."[13] And "the world" in this context is the illusion created by the unenlightened of a separate, unchanging existence as a core self or ego in the stream of consciousness. Each moment in the stream of consciousness, a set of five aggregates (*khandhas*)—or rather, five "aggregates that are subject to clinging"—arises, changes, and ceases. These five aggregates—matter (*rupa*),[14] feeling (*vedana*), perception (*sanna*), formative karma activities (*sankhara*),[15] and consciousness (*vinnana*)—operate to create the illusory sense of a core self when being clung to. These summaries are useful in the context of instruction in vipassana, and the theorem of the five khandhas is the mnemonic classification most often used by the Buddha for this purpose.

The Dhammas

However, dhamma (Skt. *dharma*) is the most comprehensive concept in the Buddha's teachings. A dhamma is a phenomenon precisely as its thusness is perceived in insight meditation. You may well be aware of a mental object—for example, a feeling or thought—but if you don't perceive the momentary changeability of the phenomenon, you don't see the feeling as a dhamma. In this state, ignorance easily projects the delusions "This is mine, I am this, this is my self" into the obscured dhamma.

According to modern phenomenology, a phenomenon is, grossly said, that which immediately manifests itself for perception. But according to Buddhist understanding, it must be added that a dhamma is not what immediately appears to a non-meditative awareness but what appears for perception only in samadhi-immersed states of consciousness.[16] All these dhammas are *sankhara-dhammas* (process phenomena) except for the transcendental *nibbana-dhamma*, which is referred to as "the deathless." The sankhara-dhammas are subject to the three universal marks (*tilakkhana*):[17] The dhammas are (1) momentarily impermanent (*anicca*), (2) potentially or actually painful or at least unsatisfactory (*dukkha*), and (3) coreless (*anatta*). Additionally, they arise dependent on specific conditions, both general and personal (*idappaccayata*).

When the process self or a compounded phenomenon manifests functions and qualities over time, it is due to "repetition conditioning" (*asevana-paccaya*) of the compositions on which the phenomenon depends for its continuous becoming in the flow. The stream of impermanency (*anicca-sota*) in this subtle and dynamic sense is the field of insight meditation that investigates all phenomena (*dhammas*) as *empty*. Not because phenomena don't exist but because they are always in a process of becoming—they never finally arrive—and this process of becoming is dependent upon myriad impermanent conditions that are *also* without a core of self, essence, or substance. The meaning of emptiness (*sunnata*), which is a somewhat negatively laden word in Western ears, refers just to the absence of this core. "Thusness" (*tathata*) has the same meaning but perhaps a more experiential ring.

The Stream of the Universal Norm

Dhamma as a phenomenological concept varies in meaning from a universal norm for all phenomena to the perception of one single phenomenon (one dhamma), such as a thought or feeling, being personally and directly understood in vipassana. The stream of the universal norm (*dhamma-sota*) is the overall regularity of impermanency and causality. At the macro level, the norm means that because our present universe has arisen, it is in a continuous process of mutability and, like everything else, will end one day.

On the micro level, this universal regularity is intuitively seen mirrored in the changing and conditional nature of every phenomenon. The flow of mental and physical phenomena arises and ceases as individual dhammas continuously, from moment to moment, in causal processes in the meditator's stream of consciousness. Insight meditation is about intuitively understanding, seeing into, and relating to these dhammas as dhammas and not as self or ego, thus experiencing that there is no dhamma at all to cling to. This is the beginning of the liberation of the mind's "turning round" in sangsara.

The Buddha's Dhamma

Both as a single phenomenon lasting one moment and as the norm for the infinity of universes,[18] *dhamma* also means "the teaching of the Buddha," which is the teaching on dissatisfaction and suffering associated with the stream of becoming in time, veiled by the misperceiving "thirst" for immutability in the changeable, which can only end in anguish. But the Buddha's dhamma is also the uplifting doctrine that teaches to dismantle the desire-thirst that fuels the cycle of suffering. The Buddhist spiritual practice the dhamma-faring (*dhamma-cariya*) is the term for this journey on the noble eightfold path to the incomparable freedom of mind. And in the grand context of this liberation project, the Buddha's dhamma includes the transcendental nibbana-dhamma that is not a dhamma in the sense mentioned heretofore, because this dhamma is "not-born, not-become, not-made, not-compounded"; it is therefore possible to "escape from . . . the born, become, made, and compounded."[19] The direct understanding of nibbana-dhamma is enlightenment, and this is one dhamma that is difficult to account for except as a negation of what it is not. So, for the time being, it suffices to state that all other dhammas except this one are compounded, impermanent, and conditioned phenomena. They are empty of a core self. They are just *thus*.

By letting go of the mistaken belief in a fixed essence within all dhammas, the mind becomes free from attachment. In this state free from clinging, consciousness ultimately flows toward the vast ocean of nibbana-dhamma.

4 | Karma, Perception, and the Ethical Freedom of Will

One day, the historical time span for the dispensation (*sasana*) of the Buddha's teachings will end because of the inexorable nature of the universal norm. This happens when the last remnants of Buddhism's scriptures and monasteries are blown away like dust in the wind. But even though the stream of the teaching of the universal norm ceases as a spiritual tradition, the stream of the universal regularity of mutability and causal connection of course continues across the stream of universes. Eventually conditions are such that a new historical dispensation from another buddha arises. Thus the Buddhist teaching is discovered anew again and again as worlds constantly arise and cease.

However, it was not the prospect of the end of the universe that I focused on in the meditation in my *kuti* (meditation hut) in the monastery garden in Bodh Gaya. Instead, I investigated the process characteristics of each phenomenon, moment by moment, in my thoughts, feelings, states of mind, and sensations, and saw in each object that "an arising is seen, a vanishing is seen, and its alteration while it persists is seen."[1]

I began to understand in my life history, which most of my meditations revolved around, that in this stream there was only the thusness of phenomena. For this reason, the flowing and conditioned process self can never truly become itself in the absolute sense of self, which is the disoriented longing of the illusorily separated individual—the longing that urged me to embark upon the long journey to the East.

One of the first things you become very aware of when you start meditating is your mind's programming, its conditioning of life-historical events, and your reactions to experiences as far back as your memory goes. You may have been out of touch with such events for a long time or perhaps you become fully aware of them for the first time in deep samadhi. Either way, you begin personally and directly to understand the causal processes of the mind—the conditioning connections between the past and the present—and the universal lawfulness of mental conditioning.

In the West, it is taken for granted that the ancient Greeks were the first to develop empirical theories of causality that replaced ancient mytho-magical explanations of the events of existence. But probably earlier than anyone else in the ancient world, the pre-Buddhist yogis had a demythologized understanding of causality, especially perceived in inner-psychic processes during deep meditation. The early yogis dubbed this perception of causality "the law of karma," and different spiritual traditions posited numerous variants of this law that strongly influenced the Indian culture's understanding of life. In its broadest sense, the Sanskrit term *karma* (Pali, *kamma*)—meaning "action," "activity," or "doing"—is the Buddha's teaching on the importance of people's intentional actions in primarily shaping their inner lives.

Karma Conditioning of the Mind

The Buddhist understanding of karma is concretely linked to the consciousness process (*citta vitthi*). This process involves two phases: the passive receptivity of an object in the initial phase of perception and the subsequent karma phase with a proactive response to the object.

The deeper you delve into the mind, the clearer you intuitively see the connection between what you have actively done over time with intention (karma) on the levels of thought, speech, or body and the effects of these actions on your own mind, whether shortly or long after, in the receptive phase of perception, regardless of whether you desire the effect or not. Therefore, Buddha speaks of "beings [as] owners of their actions . . . heirs of their actions; they originate from their actions, are bound to their actions, have actions as their refuge."[2]

In two ways, sentient beings "inherit" the moral and psychological consequences of their actions (karma), according to Buddha: first, as "fruits of action" (*kamma-vipaka*) in the subsequent receptive phases of perception processes; and second, accumulated in the unconscious as a *decisive supporting condition* for the further development of the ethically corresponding action pattern in a new karma phase.[3] For example, the past accumulation of acts of generosity forms a supporting condition for the development of generosity in future karma phases. The meditator naturally learns to meditate by developing the meditative processes that accumulate the conditions for concentration, mindfulness, and insight into the mind. The very concept of meditation, *bhavana*, in Pali literally means "more becoming"—and *development* is a modern term for that.

The Ethical Freedom of Will

The perception of the ethical freedom of will is fundamental to understanding the Buddha's teaching on karma. It's the volition to choose between wholesome or unwholesome karmic activities. This freedom is the crux of karma, which implies that karma, in a strict sense, is always an expression of a volitional *response* and not a deterministic *reaction* to the situation being acted upon. The Buddha declares, "It is volition, meditators, that I call kamma, for having willed, one acts by body, speech, and mind."[4]

According to the theorem of the perception process, the ethically free choice is exercised in the first moment of the proactive karma phase in the process of perception. This moment of consciousness is karmically "nonoperative" (*kiriya*), meaning that the moment is an ethically unconditional constituent of the perception process. It functions only to choose between wholesome or unwholesome conditions in response to a perception's receptive phase,[5] whereas one of the functions of volition (*cetana*) is that actions "accumulate" in the mind.[6] For significant actions, there will be fruit effects both immediately following perception processes and at any later time.

The distinction between the choice of actions that develop mental states leading to either bondage or liberation of the mind is the foundation of the Buddha's teaching on karma. It is in this sense that the Buddha asserts that one is bound by oneself and liberated by oneself. Since the notion of a creator god is an illusion, humans create the conditions for their liberation through the ethically free choice of the right actions. This is a fundamental understanding in Buddhist teaching.

The Ethical Freedom of Volition

To understand the karma conditioning process of the mind, it is important to distinguish between the two phases of perception and their different qualities of formative activities (*sankhara khandha*).[7] They are either actively forming—that is, determining the karma phase in the present—or they are passively formed in the receptive phase—that is, already determined by a past karma.

According to the Abhidhamma, all actively forming activities in the karma phase are volitions—for example, generosity, the level of attention, energy, buoyancy of perception, and concentration. They all actively form the response to a perceived object. But it is this specific *sankharo*, the volition per se (as pointed to in the quote above), that coordinates the activities and directs them toward a goal on the plane of thought, speech, or body.

The Ethical Roots of Karma

A wholesome karma phase is determined by three root conditions. They are non-craving, non-hatred, and liberating knowledge. In the unwholesome karma phase, the corresponding root conditions are craving, hatred, and ignorance. Unwholesome and wholesome roots (*mula*) act as conditions in the karma phase of the unenlightened. In the specific biographical context, the root conditions are nuanced in many ways on the plane of the body, speech, and mind for action. The state of generosity is a nuance of the root conditions of non-craving and knowledge, whereas the adverse state of stinginess is nuanced by the root conditions of craving and ignorance. The state of compassion is based on knowledge and non-hatred, while aversion is based on ignorance and hate, and so on.[8] Many more examples are reviewed in later chapters.

Although there is overlap between Buddhism's moral teaching and conventional morality, it is important to note that Buddhism's moral teaching, as reflected in the law of karma, is primarily the teaching about the actions that lead to the bondage or the liberation for the acting mind. However, there are also secondary effects on the surroundings, which I will return to.

You Can Do It

When Munindra-ji was quite young, his family arranged a marriage for him, which he rejected because he wanted something else for his life. And Munindra-ji made other significant decisions. He participated in initiatives that successfully reclaimed for the Buddhists the most sacred monument in Buddhism, the Mahabodhi Temple in Bodh Gaya, after the temple had been in the possession of a Hindu landlord for centuries. Munindra-ji took on the task of being the first administrator and overseer of the temple complex, which he managed to make function after centuries of neglect. This was a project that demonstrated something about his idealistic efficacy. But after five years in Bodh Gaya, he suddenly chose to travel to Burma. There was great pressure on him to stay, but nothing could make him change his mind. He wholeheartedly chose to immerse himself in the study and practice of Buddhism in Burma. He returned as the very competent vipassana teacher I met later, who had a significant impact on the spread of vipassana to the West.

It was not surprising that Munindra-ji always encouraged others to follow their hearts in decision-making and to take advantage of the opportunity in the vihara to immerse themselves, explore the mind, and not give up. "You can do it," he often said with a warm smile after a guidance session.

Fatalism and Spiritual Passivity

The ethical freedom of the will to choose the path to the liberation of the mind is a cornerstone of the Buddha's teaching. If an action from the past led to an absolutely determined reaction in the present, everything would be predetermined in human life. It would be futile to try to change anything through actions on the body, speech, or mind. It would be impossible to develop the noble eightfold path in response to an unwholesome fruit object and thus break the object's conditioning of the mind. Some of the philosophers in the time of the Buddha, however, had a fatalistic view of the law of karma, or they denied its operation altogether, but the Buddha of course had to reject these views.

> There are, meditators, three sectarian tenets which, when questioned, interrogated, and cross-examined by the wise, and taken to their conclusion, will eventuate in non-doing. What are the three?
>
> There are, meditators, some ascetics and brahmins who hold such a doctrine and view as this: "Whatever this person experiences—whether pleasure, pain, or neither-pain-nor-pleasure—all that is caused by what was done in the past."
>
> There are other ascetics and brahmins who hold such a doctrine and view as this: "Whatever this person experiences—whether pleasure, pain, or neither-pain-nor-pleasure—all that is caused by God's creative activity."
>
> And there are still other ascetics and brahmins who hold such a doctrine and view as this: "Whatever this person experiences—whether pleasure, pain, or neither-pain-nor-pleasure—all that occurs without a cause or condition."
>
> Meditators, I approached those ascetics and brahmins who hold such a doctrine and view as this: "Whatever this person experiences—whether pleasure, pain, or neither-pain-nor-pleasure—all that is caused by what was done in the past?" Then I said to them: "In such a case, it is due to past deeds that you may destroy life, take what is not given, indulge in sexual misconduct, speak falsehood, utter divisive speech, speak harshly, indulge in idle chatter; that you might be full of longing, have a mind of ill will, and hold a wrong view.
>
> "Those who fall back on past deeds as the essential truth have no desire to do what should be done and to avoid doing what should not be done, nor do they make an effort in this respect . . . and even the personal designation 'samana' could not be legitimately applied to them."[9]

In continuation of this discussion, the Buddha states that when actions are assumed to be caused by a creator god or to be causeless, then the individual is placed in the same situation as just outlined. "These, meditators, are three sectarian tenets which, when questioned, interrogated, and cross-examined by the wise, and taken to their conclusion, will eventuate in non-doing."[10]

Supporting Conditions

However, as already pointed out, not all causes are karma causes. For example, many events happened for Munindra-ji that supported the important choices he made. When Burma's first prime minister, U Nu, visited Bodh Gaya, he noticed the idealistic and initiative-driven Munindra-ji. Very magnanimously, U Nu invited him to Burma to study Abhidhamma and vipassana. This contributed to Munindra-ji's decision to leave Bodh Gaya. Without U Nu's invitation and financial support, it is uncertain whether Munindra-ji would have given up his important role as administrator of the Mahabodhi Temple at that time. In the perspective of the law of karma, it strikes me as an obvious example of how "supporting conditions" enable and enhance the development of karma and fruit, in the same way that earth, air, warmth, and water enable a seed's germination and growth into a plant and flowering. But the supporting causes must never be confused with being the seed or the plant that grows up. Supporting conditions are active in many contexts in our lives. There are causes that support the activation of karma and the ripening of the fruit without these causes being karma or the fruit of karma.[11]

To understand the teaching of karma, one must therefore distinguish in the receptive phase of perception between what is, strictly speaking, karma fruit and what is a supporting condition for the maturation of the fruit. In Munindra-ji's case, there was a great accumulation of wholesome karma in his mind that matured into fruit when U Nu invited him to Burma. In this situation, Munindra-ji's decision to travel was supported by his accumulated good karma and U Nu's invitation. But Munindra-ji's choice to travel was ethically free and an expression of new karma.

Karma, in Summary

In summary, karma is what one intentionally does in the proactive phase of perception directed at what happens to one in the receptive phase. During the perception of a significant object, the process is often repeated numerous times, thereby creating reflection for the attention's choice of a wholesome or unwholesome response to the object. When karma activities accumulate unconsciously, it is like potentially forming activities waiting for an opportunity to later form the receptive phase of perception or to support a chosen development of an ethically corresponding pattern in the karma phase.

The definition of karma fruit is the inevitable causal conditioning, programming, and conditioning of one's mind by one's own actions. However, the maturation of the karma fruit is also supported by the objective conditions in the external situation that happens—but external circumstances have nothing to do with the karma cause.

Effects of Other People's Actions on Oneself

To state another case: Different people will perceive the objective incident of a burglary in their home in different ways. This is because the burglary is only a supporting condition for *the way* the wronged person perceives the burglary during the receptive karma fruit phase of her perception. According to the law of karma, what *happens* to the perceiver is *the meaning* of the objective event in the receptive phase of perception. This meaning is conditioned by the way she has previously perceived and responded in ethically similar situations; this is the fruit of her past karma. Perhaps she breaks down or reacts with anger, gallows humor, or extreme feigned indifference. There are many ways to perceive an infringement, and it is most often experienced very personally because of the infringed person's karma from the past, which ripens in the situation. Even if the objective situation is instigated by another person and, in this case, a complete stranger's volition. However, the objective event—the burglary—has nothing to do with karma other than the thief's own.

If the thief's objective action is mistaken for being the victim's karma fruit and not merely a supporting condition for it, the misunderstanding implies that *the reason* for the burglary is the victim's actions in the past. This is equivalent to mistaking the climatic conditions for the seed that germinates. It also implies that the poor thief must be predestined to commit the wrongdoing, because free will is an illusion. This fatalistic interpretation of the law of karma is completely contrary to the Buddha's teaching.

Conditioning as Common Suffering

When the objective conditions are pleasant, we often do not notice the potential suffering of surrendering to conditioning as a life condition, in contrast to when the conditions are unpleasant and the surrender is evident—for example, when we are subjected to other people's unwholesome actions. But conditioning is a common lawfulness of life in sangsara and a variant of dukkha, which in this context is expressed as *conditioning suffering* (*sankhara-dukkhata*).[12]

Suffering arising from conditioning also involves being subject to experiencing the effects of one's own karma from the past, although it doesn't cancel one's moral ownership of karma.

Conditioning suffering is either potential or actual in all processes of body and mind phenomena. Common conditioning suffering is one of two main motivations for the Buddhist to desire liberation from the bondage of sangsara. The other motivation is liberation from the potential or actual suffering in impermanence. Both variants of dukkha are manifestations of the coreless dhammas and what follows from surrendering to the general and impersonal conditions of processes.

Old Age, Illness, and Death

In the same way, old age, illness, and death are surrendering to general conditions of dukkha rather than the fruit of specific karma, at least not the fruit of any other karma, the first cause of which is lost in the primordial mists. The fact is that "birth is suffering [dukkha], aging is suffering, illness is suffering, death is suffering, union with what is displeasing is suffering; separation from what is pleasing is suffering . . ." as the Buddha declared in his first sermon.[13] By recognizing that these conditions are universal invites us to cultivate a deeper understanding of our shared humanity and inspires a compassionate response toward ourselves and others facing the inevitable trials of life.

In a sutta, the Buddha lists many illnesses that flourished in his time, which he did not consider effects of karma.[14] Other objective conditions, including climatic changes resulting in drought and famine, are mentioned in the commentary to this sutta. But the way all these objective conditions are immediately perceived in the receptive phases of people's perception is conditioned by the fruit of the previous karma of the perceiver. The response to this in the present karma phase of perception is the development of new karma that accumulates in the mind for the future. That is how sangsara "turns round."

The Scope of the Law of Karma

At the popular level in the East, the law of karma has often been a source of speculative explanations about causes for everything objectively between heaven and earth. For the sake of simplicity, I am ignoring here the popularizing epic representation in the legendary writings (especially in the Jataka tales in Khuddaka Nikaya), which presents the law of karma in colorful anecdotes with morally edifying points for popular understanding. In this popularized understanding of karma, a burglary in your home would be presented precisely as the fruit of the fact that *you* had committed a burglary at the thief's house in a previous life. You are being repaid precisely with the same coin in a strict one-to-one relation. This perception is not uncommon at the popular level in Buddhist countries, but as explained, it is not in accordance with the essential karma psychology. The network of inner and outer causes for the maturation of a person's karma fruits is said in the suttas to be of such extensive complexity that an attempt to understand all the causes is categorized by the Buddha as one of the "inconceivable matters."[15]

By recognizing the limits of our understanding of the law of karma, we develop a deeper respect for its complexity, moving beyond the simplistic notion of retribution to embrace a more realistic perspective on ethical action and its far-reaching impacts. This helps us gain a clearer perspective on how our actions influence the interconnected web of life in ways that are often hard to grasp but can significantly affect both ourselves and others. Even so, it is still possible to understand that an event caused by another person's free will is not the karmic result of our own past actions but rather a contributing factor to its unfolding. Additionally, we always have the ethical choice in the present moment to respond in a way that is either helpful or harmful.

The Psychological Subjectivity of the Law

As a rule of thumb, the perception of the law of karma is developed by the meditator with insight into the law's conditioning of her own life history. In vipassana, the meditator comes to understand that this lawfulness is about how her specific actions, conditioned by the wholesome or unwholesome roots, bind her to suffering or liberate her from suffering in this life. And that is regardless of the suffering the meditator has otherwise been exposed to because of the general conditions in the cycle of rebirths. In other words, it is important to emphasize the primary psychological and subjective nature of the Buddhist concept of karma, in that for now, the death and rebirth processes are set aside, even though the accumulation of karma in one lifetime ultimately serves as a condition for a new existence. This topic will be revisited in chapter 15. For now, it is sufficient to note that a person's rebirth into a specific family within a specific cultural setting initially sets the path for certain objective events and conditions that one is likely to encounter. However, according to the Buddha, it does not eliminate the subjective perception of the fruits of karma that are brought to maturity in the receptive phases of perception. Nor does it eliminate the range of free will in the proactive phase for different ways of relating to what happens.

The Course of Meritorious Action

As noted before, the Buddha mentions a list of ten actions in an unwholesome karmic process that lead to suffering. Many suttas also mention ten wholesome actions of the opposite process.[16] On the karma plane of the body, they include the formative activities of loving-kindness (*metta*), generosity (*dana*), and blameless sexual conduct. On the plane of speech, they include those formative activities that, according to one's knowledge, are conciliatory (rather than slanderous), mild instead of vexatious, wise instead of muddled, and in accord with the truth. On the plane of the inner mind, they include thoughts that are free of desire-thirst, rooted in loving-kindness, and grounded in right views, including the recognition that there is a conditional effect on one's mind, either binding or liberating; that will is ethically free to choose. This also includes the understanding that the notion of the unchanging ego, the immutable self-identity, the core self, is an illusion that, as a motive for action, is a source of suffering. When right speech and right action are referred to as path links in the moral section of the noble eightfold path, the path link of right livelihood is added, which entails earning a living without harming others. It is also worth mentioning that Buddhism's attitude toward sexuality is free from the moralistic idiosyncrasies that are so common in religions. There are no other sexual norms in Buddhism for laypeople than a *sila*, a moral prescription or guideline that concerns abstaining from sexuality that harms others.[17] However, in the broader sangsaric perspective, sexuality is considered as a fetter to the cycle of rebirths.

This guide is intended for the layperson who, at the outset, isn't intent on developing the noble eightfold path as a meditative practice but will settle for blameless living in the cycle of rebirths for the time being. This, too, is commendable. The accumulations of such a karma course will be a supporting condition for a possible later meditative effort, in which case blameless sexual conduct will include celibacy for the duration of the retreat. From this perspective, the redirection of sexual energy, known as sublimation, is a crucial foundation for sustained and in-depth exploration of the mind.

Moral Fear and Shame

In the choice between wholesome or unwholesome roots, attention is guided by the activities of *intuitive fear* (*otappa*) and *intuitive shame* (*hiri*), which the Buddha calls "the moral pillars of the world."[18] These forming activities act as a bulwark against anything unwholesome and safeguard the development of wholesome karma patterns. Moral intuition of shame is based on the individual's self-respect, which prevents her from acting in ways she would be blamed for by people whose moral judgment she trusts, while moral fear is based on the intuitive orientation to the consequence of an unwholesome action for herself and others.[19] In other words, intuitive fear and shame constitute the karma activities of conscience. Hiri and otappa always co-arise in wholesome states and with the experiential confidence (*saddha*) as a strong incentive to act in accordance with the ethical orientation of the wholesome states of mind.

Insight Meditative Karma

When the freedom of choice in the karma phase is the subject of focused reflection, volitions are expressed as conceptualized intentions (*chanda*). A special category of spiritual intentionality (*dhammachanda*) orients the mind toward the karma actions of the noble eightfold path.

When the mind's immersed in vipassana, the intuitive level for the path's first link, right view, is activated—that is, the personal, direct understanding of the mind's thusness. This insight is rooted in a constellation of the wholesome root conditions that activate karma that is "neither dark nor bright and which leads to a result which is neither dark nor bright—it is karma that leads to the elimination of karma."[20] This is the powerful vipassana-karma, which extinguishes all binding influxes (*asava*). The influxes cease irrevocably when they are fully understood in a life-historical and *buddho*-meditative sense—that is, in the intuitive understanding of the three universal characteristics: momentary change, dukkha, and no-core self—and thus the understanding that there is nothing at all to cling to in sangsara. By realizing the nature of existence as impermanent in this subtle sense, we can cultivate an unwavering tranquility amid life's fluctuations. The ultimate fruition of karma, which is neither light nor dark, culminates in the transcendental nibbana that irrevocably seals off this liberation.

5 | Ignorance, Desire-Thirst, and Hatred

Munindra-ji was also an Abhidhamma-acariya with the profound Abhidhamma culture of the Burmese monastic order in his baggage. In Burmese Buddhism, there is a strong tradition of using the Abhidhamma in connection with vipassana. The Abhidhamma is based on a systematization of the theorems from the Buddha's teachings and constitutes one-third of the Pali canon. In the suttas, these theorems are presented as guidelines for meditation with some psychological analyses, while the Abhidhamma contains only the analyses but in much greater detail. The Abhidhamma includes a model of eighty-nine types of consciousness, fifty-two mental factors or aspects of states of consciousness, and twenty-eight elements of matter. Their interrelations in the dhamma stream (of consciousness and phenomena) are illuminated not only with the formal twelve relations in dependent origination (in 144 variants) but also according to a finely woven model of twenty-four general relations (*paccaya*) between the dhammas. In this way, the Abhidhamma expands both the analytical and synthetic methods from the suttas' understanding of dhammas as impermanent, conditioned, and coreless process phenomena.

Munindra-ji was known for his in-depth analyses, but what truly made him remarkable was his pragmatic approach. He emphasized that Buddhism is not just a theory but a practice that requires personal experience and insight. With his warm and engaging teaching style, he reminded his students that Buddhism is a "come-and-see-for-yourself" teaching; it is a world that must be experienced and understood through one's own practice. Munindra-ji managed to inspire his students to explore this world with diligent curiosity and a reminder that Buddhism is about connecting to truths through the direct experience of them.

Obscured Luminosity of Mind

Munindra-ji often quoted Buddha on the understanding that our minds were originally "luminous" but were obscured by the accumulation of unwholesome karma. The Buddha pointed out that although the obscuration may challenge us, it also holds the potential for great inspiration to explore the mind. When we begin to understand the extent of the obscuration, we will, with spiritual necessity, engage in the work of liberating the mind. It is the illusion of the ego that has shackled and darkened the light. However, Buddha does not explain *how* or *when* the luminous purity of the mind was originally obscured. He asserts only that there is no known beginning to ignorance and desire.

This is yet another "inconceivable matter" for understanding. Just as the precisely branching effects of karma, it is pointless to speculate about this.[1] But when he is asked about the first cause of ignorance and desire-thirst, he states that even if the first cause is not known, the specific causes of ignorance and desire-thirst in perception here and now can be known and therefore overcome. It is therefore important to understand the nature of these specific causes.

All unwholesome actions will accumulate in the mind as defilements (*kilesas*) and in patterns of "latent negative tendencies" (*anusayas*). These defilements and patterns support and reinforce the momentum of unwholesome actions in the karma phase and mature as fruits in the receptive phase of perception. In contrast, the forming activities that crystallize from the wholesome roots accumulate as "mental merit" (*punna*) and form the basis for the development of the noble eightfold path.

The fundamental anusayas are the mind's three deeply rooted dispositions for craving after pleasant object-stimulus, aversion to unpleasant object-stimulus, and negligence of neutral object-stimulus. Another dominant anusaya often mentioned by the Buddha is the tendency for assertiveness of ego-referential viewpoints. However, there are as many specific anusayas as there are defilements, which through repeated actions form character traits such as doubt, impatience, arrogance, self-assertion, and jealousy.

The Distortions of Ignorance

In the process of perception, the original brilliant purity of consciousness is dampened by the root condition of ignorance, which obscures the sensation, thought, or feeling in the same way a cloud shadows the moon and hides it, according to the fifth-century commentator Buddhaghosa.[2] Basically, ignorance is expressed as a lack of attention to the object's thusness. A synonym for ignorance, *adassana*, means "not seeing." When the mind is *ignoring* reality and not seeing thusness, objects are obscured by four types of distortions (*vippallasa*).[3] These distortions can be transcribed as "hallucinations" in the case of perceptions and "illusion" when it comes to thinking based on those perceptions.

The first distortion is the obscuration of permanence (*nicca-vippallasa*) of the object. The continuity of obscured perceptions of momentary changeability overlaps with static impressions as a result. The second distortion is the misconception of objects as a source of pleasure; the changing of pleasure causes some sort of dissatisfaction or anguish (*dukkha*), which is properly understood in vipassana. As a third distortion, the object is obscured by the attraction in what is precisely not attractive, which is a variant of the source of anguish but specifically in relation to the mutable body. The fourth obscuration is the distortion of the core self (*atta-vippallasa*) in what is increasingly deepened in insight as a conditioned process self without an unchanging core or agent, no matter how deep into the flow the intuition penetrates.

Distortions only arise in unwholesome states of mind. The wholesome states, which are free from the misperception of an ego, unfortunately are generally not sufficiently prominent to intuitively understand the object's "thusness," at least not continuously, unless awareness is anchored in samadhi.

Desire-Thirst and Grasping

While ignorance veils the object's thusness, desire-thirst—including its variant, hatred—is the activity that manipulates the obscured object. There are several Pali synonyms for desire-thirst (*tanha*), often labeled as craving for sensory pleasures, craving for (ego-)becoming (*bhava*), and craving for non-becoming. In any case, the desire-thirst is like a thief waiting in the darkness behind the door in the karma phase of perception. It follows that attention's clinging (*upadana*) to the object can be compared to the thief's hand stretching out in the dark[4] and grasping the obscured object, whether it be a thought, feeling, mental state, or sensation in the receptive phase of perception.

And desire-thirst "has the characteristic of grasping an object, like birdlime (lit. 'monkey lime'). Its function is sticking, like meat put in a hot pan. It is manifested as not giving up, like the dye of lamp-black. Its proximate cause is seeing enjoyment in things that lead to bondage."[5]

Clinging to the object holds the mind in the grip of misperceived ego reference. Hatred, which is the negative aspect of craving, expresses aversion and condemnation to push the object away with the binding effects of egocentric actions that arise from ignorance and craving. Ignoring the object is an expression of clinging to indifference.

When the meditator blocks insight into the nature of constant change by clinging to a thought, feeling, or state of mind with the belief "This is mine, I am this, this is my self,"[6] it is always driven by the misperceptions that the object is unchanging and unconditional, at least in that moment, while consciousness is attached to it. The first belief, "This is mine," is driven by craving. The second belief, "I am this," is driven by conceit, which is a variant of the first misperception. The third belief, "This is my core self," arises when deluded thinking begins to develop narratives about these two basic misperceptions. The patterns of clinging form the development of a distorted ego in the unenlightened mind.

The Fetter of Wrong View About the Self

Consciousness develops theories, opinions, and notions based on erroneous perceptions of a core self as being embedded in the five aggregates that are subject to clinging. For example, the person perceives that the body *is* the self, or that the body possesses the self, or that the body is *in* the self, or that the self is in the body. This is also true for the other four aggregates: perception, feeling, karma activities, and consciousness. In this way, twenty variants of the self-embedding point of view, designated *wrong view of the self* (*sakkaya-ditthi*)[7] arise, structuring the unenlightened narrative about herself and raising many difficult questions over time:

> "Was I in the past? Was I not in the past? What was I in the past? How was I in the past? Having been what, what did I become in the past? Shall I be in the future? Shall I not be

> in the future? What shall I be in the future? How shall I be in the future? Having been what, what shall I become in the future?" Or else she is inwardly perplexed about the present thus: "Am I? Am I not? What am I? How am I? Where has this being come from? Where will it go?"
>
> When she attends unwisely in this way, one of six views arises in her. The view "self exists for me" arises in her as true and established; or the view "no self exists for me" arises in her as true and established; or the view "I perceive not-self with self" arises in her as true and established; or the view "I perceive self with not-self" arises in her as true and established; or else she has some such view as this: "It is this self of mine that speaks and feels and experiences here and there the result of good and bad actions; but this self of mine is permanent, everlasting, eternal, not subject to change, and it will endure as long as eternity."[8]

The conviction of an unchanging core in the self (*sakkaya-ditthi*) for whom all these speculations are about and the clinging of consciousness to this narrative construction is the first of ten fetters (*samyojana*) to the cycle of rebirths and misconceptions of ego, which is eliminated by the insights of vipassana, as we shall see later.

The Fetter of "I Am" Conceit

One of the last barriers to achieving full enlightenment is the fetter "I am" conceit (*asmimana*), which arises from a sticky identification with the five aggregates of mental and physical components, in comparison with other people. As a result of arrogance, the person imagines, for example, that they possess greater knowledge, abilities, or beauty than others—or that they should. They may perceive themselves as superior due to factors such as family background, social status, education, or race. There are no limits to what phantasmagorical comparisons with others can revolve around in relation to their body, feelings, perceptions, karma activities, and consciousness (the five aggregates).

The complex dynamics of asmimana illustrate how suffering in social interactions can be shaped by layers of arrogance, deeply embedded in distorted perceptions of personal values. The core of the concept of conceit is the "I am more valuable" delusion (superiority complex) (*atimana*), which paradoxically draws its energy from its counterpart, the "I am less valuable" delusion (inferiority complex) (*omana*). This opposition is further maintained by the "I am equally valuable as others" delusion" (*mana*), which reflects a too-sensitive preoccupation with being equal to others. These are all states in which the mind is misconceiving, "I am thus/the object." The interlinked emotions between the states span a wide spectrum from narcissistic self-assertion, haughtiness, vanity, and megalomania; to the dishearteningly low self-esteem of feelings of inferiority, self-condemnation, and discouragement; to the anxious and touchy sense of equality as reinforcing conditions for the entire scale of this fetter.

While sakkaya-ditthi is a conceptual belief that structures the narrative of the life-historical episodes in the person's self-perception—and the comparison with others is certainly an essential part of the fuel in this narrative—the activity of comparison itself stems from a deeper level of ignorance and desire. It is likely because the self-process was developed relationally and belongs to an earlier and more primitive level of social awareness than the narrative of the self's separateness. According to the teachings of liberation, the fetter of delusion is therefore only weakened and not eliminated when the fetter concerning the core self's conceptual sphere of imagination is eliminated. The fetter of "I am" conceit is eliminated only at the very end, before the full enlightenment, according to the doctrine of liberation.

From a modern perspective, the interpersonal scenarios of this fetter seem to flourish today in the competitive societies of the West, with their shrill circumstances for individualism and perfectionist culture. But the fact that the link was perceived by the Buddha a couple of millennia ago as a very dominant obstacle to human happiness is certainly very thought-provoking too.

Other Specific Defilements

Many other defilements distort the purity of mind as mentioned in the suttas and the Abhidhamma—for instance, stinginess (*macchariya*), in which greed is dominant in misconceiving "the object is mine." Stinginess is defined as all forms of pettiness characterized by the reluctance to share possessions, success, influence, and knowledge with others. *Issa*—envy and jealousy's hatred of other people's happiness and prosperity—is another complex emotion that, in addition to ignorance and desire-thirst, is rooted in hatred. Issa also means gloating—that is, the hatred-joy at others' adversity—and an aversion-induced preoccupation with finding fault with others. Issa and macchariya are often mentioned in the suttas. They are not independent fetters but belong to the fetters of hatred and craving, respectively, and are interesting examples of specific Buddhist emotions that require several Western concepts to define. Many other unwholesome formative activities have, due to ignorance and desire-thirst, obscured the mind's pristine purity: pretense, disloyalty, stubbornness, deceitfulness, harsh sexuality, and so on. When the root condition of hatred is added, the pattern activates—among other things—unwillingness, aversion, aggression, condemnation, mockery, vindictiveness, and other forms of wickedness. Intolerance, shame, guilt, irritation, impatience, embarrassment, and regret are also based in this pattern of root conditions. Anxiety and sadness are interestingly perceived as forms of aversion; and grief is seen as aversion directed toward clinging to the pain of a loss.

As a result of the repetition of unwholesome actions and identification with them, the meditator accumulates impurities as ingrained tendencies or binding character traits that gather in the optics of the illusion about the separated core self (*sakkaya-ditthi*) in the unliberated mind. The lists of unwholesome activities do not represent an exhaustive description of the unenlightened mind but are examples of some impurities that could appear in vipassana where they are included in the practice of the third foundation of mindfulness of mental states as mental states.

The meditator in vipassana can analyze the activities as she pleases if she does not identify with the thoughts, because it is only the intuitive understanding of the impurities as egoless dhammas that liberates the mind from them. It is precisely within the scope of intuition in vipassana to investigate the life-historical implications of such dhammas. In handling difficult emotions, the meditator learns intuitively how to identify emotions and uses the repetition of mental notes to let go of the emotions—for instance, *Anger, anger.* This correct use of mental noting proves highly effective in addressing difficult emotions during vipassana practice in the learning phase (see p. 119). Additionally, meditating on emotions and understanding their personal significance fosters a deeper sense of self-compassion and empathy.

General Unwholesome Activities

There are formative karma activities that arise in *all* "ego-obscured" states, which underline the condition of suffering in unwholesome states of mind. One is restlessness, which creates an imbalance between the pattern-forming activities—for example, in connection with asmimana or sakkaya-dithi—and attention, concentration, energy, feeling, and perception. According to

Abhidhamma, the restless mind is like a heap of ashes that is hit by a stone, causing the ashes to scatter in all directions. The greater the restlessness and confusion, the better the conditions are for "moral fearlessness" (*anotappa*) and "moral shamelessness" (*ahiri*), which are the forming activities of the unscrupulous drive of unwholesome action on the planes of body, speech, and thought. Moral fearlessness applies to the consequences of the action for oneself and others, and shamelessness concerns the initiation of the unwholesome action because of the actor's lack of self-respect.

Summary of Conditioning of the Mind

According to the dhamma-faring, the three unwholesome root conditions—their contaminating influxes (*asava*), their ongoing activation of defilements (*kilesas*), their latent tendencies or character traits of egocentricity (*anusayas*), and larger organizing sangsaric fetters (*samyojana*) for bondage—must be eliminated to liberate the mind. These classifications of the dark side of the mind contain overlapping concepts but summarize the strengths between ignorance, desire-thirst, and hatred at different levels of willed activity. They are all, to a distinct degree, the basis of conditioning suffering (*sankhara-dukkhata*)—always for the actor but often for others as well—and reveal a profound understanding of the human psyche and its obstacles to mental happiness.

The Buddha's realistic and psychological perspective on karma invites us to shift our focus from the potentially overwhelming complexity of its branching effects to a more grounded understanding of the specific causes behind our ignorance and desire-thirst. By identifying these root issues, we empower ourselves to address them directly. Addressing them not only demystifies the concept of karma but also provides practical tools for overcoming the obstacles that hinder our inner growth.

The Elimination of the Fetters

In insight meditation, we develop a comprehensive understanding of sankhara-dukkha in the accumulated life-historical actions and their biographical supporting conditions. This refers to episodic raw material from childhood up to the present that emerges with great clarity in deep states of meditation. For perspective here, it is only necessary to dwell on the list of ten fetters (*samyojana*)[9] that bind the mind to the repetition of existential disorientation, suffering, and dissatisfaction in the cycle of rebirths and misperceived ego-becoming.

The elimination of fetters is used as a parameter for the progressive liberation of the mind, which, as we shall see later, in many cases doesn't involve the elimination of all fetters at one and the same time, as was the case in the Buddha's enlightenment. The more common approach is for the meditator to eliminate a few fetters at each of the four stages of liberation of the mind, thereby gradually minimizing the unwholesome root conditions and their polluting influxes before their complete overcoming in full enlightenment.

At the time of the first stage of enlightenment, which is attainment of the fruit of stream entry (*sotapatti-phala*), three fetters are eliminated:

1. The wrong view of self (*sakkaya-ditthi*)—the illusory conceptual structure of the narrative of a core self
2. *Skeptical doubt* with the usefulness of the development of the noble eightfold path as the way to overcome ignorance and anguish, and more generally, the overall nihilistic doubt that it is possible to liberate the mind of existential disorientation and suffering
3. The belief in clinging to mere rules and rituals as a means of purifying the mind

This is the cultish archetype of the conventional religions. In the oldest Buddhism, it is considered to block the initiative of people for the liberation of mind through their own persistent effort and personal understanding. The remaining seven fetters that are only diminished at the time of stream entry consist of ignorance, "I am" conceit, restlessness, subtle sensual craving, subtle desires of refined states of consciousness, and ill will. Because these fetters are reduced, they also cease in activating several of the unwholesome mental states already mentioned. For example, the propensities for issa and macchariya are eliminated by the fruit of stream entry because desire and hatred are weakened.

The Hub of the Wheel

The fetter of wrong view is the foundational belief that holds the other fetters together in the psychological sphere of the illusorily separated individual (*puthujjhana-bhumi*). The misperceived construction of a core self in the narrative is like the hub of a wheel. When the hub is knocked out because of the transcendental experience of nibbana, the wheel no longer works and the spokes scatter in all directions. This corresponds to the remaining fetters. For example, "I am" conceit (*asmimana*) in the stream-enterer's partially liberated mind is latent but without giving rise to the view that the conceit is one's identity or core self. Although the stream-enterer is still capable of greedily grasping at objects (*This is for me*) or condemning objects (*This is not for me*), and thereby also experiencing the notion of "I am" conceit (*I am this*), the stream-enterer's mind doesn't any longer develop the "This is my self" narrative. And so for all other unwholesome states that remain potentially in the mind of the stream-enterer, their intensity is weakened.

An analogy that Munindra-ji used about the remaining fetters of the stream-enterer is the image of a tree that, after being cut down, continues to sprout until the sap in the tree is completely dried up. It means that the three unwholesome root conditions are weakened to such an extent by the removal of sakkaya-ditthi that the stream-enterer, with relative ease, can meditate on the stream of the noble eightfold path toward full enlightenment. The structural establishment of the path in the mind of the stream-enterer is the primary psychological transformation of stream entry. Whether the stream-enterer lives in withdrawal from the world or not, their meditative path is predominantly effortless. Their partially liberated and unhindered consciousness, therefore, does not fail to flow toward the full liberation of the luminous mind.[10]

I will return in later chapters to the teachings of stream entry, which is the portal to full enlightenment. The minor stream-enterer develops all the qualifying insights that lead up to it.

6 | The Noble Mindfulness with Clear Comprehension

Just after my arrival at the Burmese Vihara in Bodh Gaya, I spent an hour in breathing meditation—or, more correctly, on the development of mindfulness of in-and-out breathing (*anapana-sati bhavana*)—in the cool, whitewashed hall on the first floor of the monastery. After sitting, I had my first experience of walking meditation in the shade of the papaya trees along the walls of the garden. My kindred spirits were a handful of Western travelers who, like me, had traveled farther and farther east into Asia, farther and farther from home, before drastically changing direction to spiritual goals deep in our minds. On the first day in the Burmese Vihara, I naïvely asked Munindra-ji at what time meditation began in the morning. "The moment you open your eyes," he replied. It would be a help, he added, if, with the inner voice of my mind, I repeated the mental note, *Opening the eyes, opening the eyes.* That was what I had only begun to learn at the end of a long journey—at least that was how I experienced it in the time that followed.

Even for the villagers in Bodh Gaya, the vihara was like another world. They would often gather inside the garden, squatting silently by the little fountain in front of the main entrance to the monastery, and inhale deeply the condensed atmosphere of the garden's tranquility. The atmosphere in the garden was so intense when we moved slowly, absorbed in the shadows of the papaya trees, as if we were looking for something lost deep within ourselves. From the outset of practicing vipassana, every waking moment becomes an opportunity for meditation. And walking meditation serves as an ideal practice for cultivating deep mindfulness in every aspect of daily life.

This approach is especially impactful when applied to eating. The meals at the vihara were simple and consistent: rice, dahl, chapatti, and occasionally potato curry. Initially this modest fare did not seem particularly appealing twice a day. However, eating with heightened awareness—fully experiencing the unique sensations of seeing, smelling, touching, hearing, and tasting each bite—transformed the act of eating into an extraordinary experience. It's not only a very realistic way of eating but also very enjoyable.

Munindra-ji often emphasized that as long as consciousness exists, one should cultivate insight into the arising, changing, and passing away of each moment. The impermanence of each moment is a fundamental condition of life and forms the basis for insight in the vipassana practice. It is the accumulation of these transient moments that ultimately defines the nature of life and death. Yet within each fleeting moment lies an opportunity—a doorway to liberation from the existential suffering tied to change and loss. By approaching this doorway with a focused and mindful presence, we can explore the profound implications of impermanence for our understanding of ourselves. Through directly experiencing the transience of each moment—more fleeting than dew on grass—we can access a transformative liberation from the suffering that often accompanies our awareness of impermanence. This deeply transformative potential lies at the heart of vipassana practice.

The Parable of the Bowl

The Buddha has a striking parable about the ideal of mindfulness of the body in motion (*kayagati-sati*),[1] which illustrates in a practical and easily understandable way the very concept of right mindfulness (*samma sati*), the seventh link of the noble eightfold path. Imagine a marketplace in India where an extraordinarily lovely woman dances and sings on a platform in front of a gathering of men from the village. This is how the Buddha begins his parable. The men are cheering and shouting excitedly, "The most beautiful girl of the land is dancing! The most beautiful girl of the land is singing!"[2] As the crowd grows, a man is given the task of walking through this excitable crowd carrying a bowl filled to the brim with oil. Imagine that the good man's life depends on him walking so slowly and with such focused presence that he doesn't spill *a single drop of oil*, because if he spills *just one* drop, one of the king's guards, who are walking behind the poor man with a raised sword, will immediately cut off his head. Then imagine how this good man will walk with the bowl through this crowd if he values his life. Obviously the man will significantly slow down his body's tempo to preserve his life. The slower he moves, the more mastery he gains over his balancing act with the bowl and the more degrees of freedom he gains on his way through the undulating crowd—or in relation to any other matter in a pressure situation where an immersed presence is urgently required. The sutta continues:

> "What do you think, meditators? Would that man stop attending to that bowl of oil and out of negligence turn his attention outward?"—"No, venerable sir."—"I've made up this simile, meditators, in order to convey a meaning. This here is the meaning: 'The bowl of oil filled to the brim': this is a designation for mindfulness directed to the body. Therefore,

> meditators, you should train yourselves thus: 'We will develop and cultivate mindfulness directed to the body, make it our vehicle, make it our basis, stabilize it, exercise ourselves in it, and fully perfect it.'"[3]

Of course, there are different ways to walk. Here the Buddha is describing walking on the path with utmost dedication to the development of mindfulness and insight. In walking meditation, the lower limit of mindfulness is walking without being somewhere else in your thoughts—but that really is the goal to aim for in daily life outside of a retreat. The ideal way of mindful *retreat* walking is the higher limit: Our bowl is filled *to the brim*, and there is not *one aspect* of our movements that we are not fully aware of—the arising, the changing, and the cessation of each phase. Or we waste a drop of oil and senselessly lose our spiritual life in the sense of the parable.

The parable about walking with a *brimming* bowl isn't just an illustration of the walking meditation between sittings in vipassana. It illustrates the very concept of right mindfulness that is developed from the four foundations of mindfulness that embrace insights into "the All"—intuitively, personally, and directly, moment by moment. What is "the All" the Buddha asks the disciples? It is indeed all visual, auditory, olfactory, gustatory, tactile, and cognitive perception processes. It is the entire flow of diverse objects of senses, thoughts, feelings, and states of mind that arise in these contexts, whether pleasant, unpleasant, or neutral.[4] Walking with the "bowl" with deep presence into all the mind's outer and inner contexts without "spilling a drop" requires samadhi of a uniform strength on one focal point at a time, combined with a very flexible awareness of the immediate change of what you are present with. There is no object of the flow of everyday consciousness that is not suitable for developing insight into the changeability of the present moment. Thus in vipassana we enter the practice of the four foundations of mindfulness in a sustained awareness, as if it were a matter of life or death, whether we are sitting, walking, standing, or lying down.

The formal theorem of the four foundations comprises (1) the body, (2) the feelings, (3) the thoughts and mental states, and (4) all these objects as dhammas of the four noble truths (see chapter 8).

Mindfulness and Concentration

Sati has the connotation in Pali of "remembering," and what sati remembers is to be present. To be present is not something we need to learn. It's something we can be whenever we want. Or rather when we remember to be, because a nonmeditative mind often lacks the concentration (*samadhi*) to anchor our presence for extended periods of time, at least to the extent necessary to descend the noble eightfold path to deep transformative insights into the mind. As the development of meditation deepens, the absorbed presence in walking meditation is enforced with the mental one-pointedness that is developed in sitting meditation. Therefore, a focused presence with the body in motion as if walking with a bowl filled to the brim is the easiest way for the beginner to have an eye-opening experience of what meditative awareness is all about. It is not surprising that the Buddha declares meditation on the body in motion to be a matrix for the development of vipassana:

> Meditators, even as one who encompasses with his mind the great ocean includes thereby all the streams that run into the ocean, just so, whoever develops and cultivates mindfulness directed to the body includes all wholesome qualities that pertain to true knowledge.[5]

It is important to understand that as a path link, *samma sati* (right mindfulness) always arises together with *samma samadhi* (right concentration), which is the eighth link of the path, creating the special sustained observational immersion that characterizes meditative states in Buddhism. Walking with a bowl filled to the brim is a lucid metaphor for this practice. You can do light walking meditation right on the spot with a cup of tea or coffee in your hand. Fill your cup to the brim and walk from the kitchen to the chair in your living room. Your attention should be very flexibly aware as you walk deeply absorbed to avoid spilling. Even if it's only a few feet, in those brief moments, you will learn a great deal about the seventh link on the path, samma sati. Often in your life you are probably so present—but how often, really? Perhaps you might argue that it's not strictly necessary, and that is probably true. But it is indeed necessary if you want to develop insight into your mind *as it really is*, according to Buddha's instructions in vipassana. During a retreat, developing walking meditation at this very present pace will lead to a gradual deepening in all other bodily activities.

> A bhikkhu is one who acts with clear comprehension when going forward and returning; who acts with clear comprehension when looking ahead and looking away; who acts with clear comprehension when flexing and extending his limbs; who acts with full comprehension when wearing his robes and carrying his outer robe and bowl; who acts with clear comprehension when eating, drinking, consuming food, and tasting; who acts with clear comprehension when defecating and urinating; who acts with clear comprehension when waking, standing, sitting, falling asleep, waking up, talking, and keeping silent.[6]

Meta-Awareness

One way of understanding the state of mindfulness is the mind's ability to observe awareness itself. In modern psychology, the seed of this reflexivity is called meta-awareness or meta-cognitive awareness. This is simply an awareness of being aware. When you are mindful, you don't need to reflect intellectually on whether you are mindful. You know intuitively from direct experience, no matter *what* you are aware of. It is in stark contrast to the mental state of being distracted and preoccupied, when your awareness drifts away and you are lost in your thoughts about the past and the future. You are not aware of your awareness when you are absent-minded. You are, of course, aware to a certain degree, but certainly not of your awareness. Strictly speaking, in this shallow state of absence, you don't even know you're absent-minded. When you snap out of this state and realize you are absent-minded, *that* indicates you're back on track to being *aware of your awareness*—you will once again have the willpower of your attention. You can pull it back to where it drifted away from. In other words, you can avoid reacting blindly and automatically to inner and outer experiences that the nonmeditative attention is otherwise easily caught up in. You can avoid thoughts wandering with your attention and instead relate with degrees of freedom to these thoughts—and the feelings that the thoughts arouse.

The nonmeditative mind, even when practicing secular mindfulness, often lacks the concentration needed to anchor presence for extended periods of time. In a Buddhist context, it therefore can be more informative to translate the path factor of sati as "absorbed presence," and the like, as it makes sense to talk about very prominent degrees of mental one-pointedness in mindfulness because of the anchoring of samadhi.

The Guardian of the Mind

According to the fifth-century commentator Buddhaghosa, mindfulness as a path factor has the

> characteristic of not wobbling. Its function is not to forget. It is manifested as guarding, or it is manifested as the state of

> confronting an objective field. Its proximate cause is strong perception, or its proximate cause is the foundations of mindfulness concerned with the body, and so on.[7] It should be regarded, however, as like a pillar because it is firmly founded, or as like a door-keeper because it guards the eye-door, and so on.[8]

Like a vigilant watchman, the mindfully concentrated mind is not passively observing but actively investigating an object being observed, just as the present body awareness of the man in the parable will necessarily be very flexibly focused on the shifting micro-movements of his body. The purpose of walking meditation on a retreat is to exert the body between sittings but also to maintain the level of concentration, presence, and insight from the previous sitting. You're thus walking, with your symbolic bowl filled to the brim, into your next sitting in the meditation hall—and you are taking your bowl with this quality of one-pointed immersion into the way of observing each object in the stream of your inner mind in your sitting.

Meditation, Contemplation, and Intuitive Wisdom

Citta-bhavana is Buddhism's broad concept for meditation, which directly translated means "more becoming of the mind," or in modern words, mental development. *Vipassana-bhavana* translates into Western languages as "insight meditation" but literally means "more becoming of clear observation." The term *vipassana* is closely related to *anupassana*, which occurs frequently in the Buddha's utterances on applied sati, where *passana* means "observation" and *anu* adds the quality of "close repetition."[9] The concept of *anupassana* is often translated into Western languages as "contemplation." In the *Satipatthana Sutta*, according to most translations, the meditator is thus instructed in "contemplating the body as the body,"[10] which is the first foundation for mindfulness. But it's worth noting that *meditation* and *contemplation* are Western terms rooted in European philosophy and Christian mysticism, both terms referring to the observation of lofty conceptual consideration or reflection. This is misleading in the Buddhist context of mindful observation because in vipassana we meditate on the changeability of all kinds of sensations, whether pleasant or unpleasant; all kinds of states of mind and their associated thoughts, including anger, sensory desires, sadness, anxiety, sex fantasies, and catastrophic imaginings—*you name it*—which are far removed from the objects of the Western concept of contemplation.

The concept of meditation has changed meaning in everyday language since the 1960s, partly due to the spread of Buddhist meditation in the West, and the concept is therefore integrated into Western parlance today largely in the Eastern sense. The case is different for "contemplation," which to most people has connotations of thinking. More appropriate as a guide in vipassana, the concept of anupassana, as Ven. Bhikkhu Bodhi suggests, should be translated closer to etymology as "continuous observation." I would also suggest adding the word *immersed*, because the development of concentration (the eighth link on the Buddhist path), especially through meditation on the breath, creates the unique form of *sustained* immersed presence that is the key of Eastern meditation practices. Everywhere in what follows, I therefore translate *anupassana* as either "continuous absorbed observation" or, for the sake of convenience, simply as "meditation," where the modern usage of the word is understood.[11]

The immersive presence in observation over time holds the seed of a form of direct experiential knowledge (*abhinna*). *Intuition* is a fitting term for this insight-meditative way of understanding that directly experiences and comprehends what attention "sees into" during deep states of samadhi. Buddhaghosa highlights that insight knowledge is distinct from perception and thought.

Its defining feature is the mind's direct penetration of its object without relying on thought as an intermediary. The most fundamental form of knowledge in this sense is the understanding of the arising, changing, and cessation of what is observed. This is an existential experience that becomes spiritual when insight reveals the dukkha and anatta aspects of what is fleeting and impermanent—particularly in the meditator's self-perception. It's the thusness of dhammas.

A key element of this kind of experiential understanding is *sampajanna*, often translated as "clear comprehension." This refers to an awareness of the purpose of sati in a specific context. A common misunderstanding about meditation is the belief that the meditator becomes a passive observer of their life. This is entirely incorrect because vipassana is practiced in all aspects of daily life. When sati is practiced with clear understanding, you engage with deep presence: You eat with deep presence, you wash dishes with deep presence, and so on. Any activity can be done with deep presence. Sati is always connected to a clear understanding of why you are doing what you are doing, which aligns with the second link, right intention, on the noble eightfold path.

The knowledge that arises from right mindfulness that is anchored by right concentration is called right knowledge (*panna*), knowledge based on seeing into (*nana-dassana*), or experiential knowledge (*paccakha-nana*). In English, these and other synonyms are often translated as "intuitive knowledge" or "intuitive wisdom." Later in this chapter, we will explore the unique nature of Buddhist intuition in greater depth.

The Bamboo Acrobats

The Buddha offers another striking parable to illustrate the range of mindfulness. This parable highlights the interconnection of mindfulness with the section on morality of the noble eightfold path. It is the story about two "bamboo acrobats," an older one and a younger one, performing a dangerous trick on top of a bamboo pole. The younger one is apparently standing on the shoulders of the older one, who is standing on top of a pole. One day before their show, the older acrobat tells the younger one, "You protect me, dear Medakathalika, and I'll protect you. In this way, guarded by each other, protected by each other, we'll display our skills, collect our fee, and get down safely from the bamboo pole."

The younger one wisely replied, "That's not the way to do it, teacher. You protect yourself, teacher, and I'll protect myself. Thus, each self-guarded and self-protected, we'll display our skill, collect our fee, and get down safely from the bamboo pole."[12]

I'll look after you, and you'll look after me. What does this intention mean? In the spiritual sense of the parable, how does one take proper care of another person who depends upon you if you don't prioritize taking care of yourself? The older acrobat standing on top of the pole doesn't unconditionally exercise control over the balance of the younger one, who is standing on his shoulders. He cannot practice mindfulness vicariously for the young one. However, if the older one focuses all his awareness on his *own* balance, he can indeed exercise decisive indirect influence on the younger acrobat. The difference is the clear comprehension (*sampajanna*) of mindfulness in interaction with others. This means that the ethical ideal of interpersonal presence is equivalent to having the person you're interacting with balancing on your shoulders, so to speak.

"'I shall protect myself,' meditators: thus, should the foundations of mindfulness be practiced. 'I shall protect others,' meditators: thus, should the foundations of mindfulness be practiced. Protecting oneself, meditators, one protects others; protecting others, one protects oneself,"[13] the Buddha concludes this parable.

By carrying "the bowl" into the relationship with yourself and with others in all contexts of the mind, the foundations of mindfulness are developed "both internally and externally."[14] This means that the foundations are developed in deep introspection, when you are isolated as "an island" in sitting meditation "internally," but also "externally" in your empathic interaction with others and with the experience of the objects of the senses in general. The two parables complement each other in vipassana as an all-encompassing practice. The young acrobat's insightful reminder to the elder acrobat is urging us to be aware of our surroundings and the impact we have on those around us. By embracing vipassana fully, we cultivate a protective shield not just for ourselves but also for others who share our space. This highlights the broad implications by taking great care of our own well-being in a spiritual sense: We simultaneously uplift and safeguard those in our community. Developing a mindful presence is never merely an individual endeavor. It is a collective journey toward greater understanding and connection that enriches us all—and the concentrated exploration of the mind in sitting meditation is the spiritual source of this journey.

The Spiritual Faculties

Vipassana evolves from a base of sustained internalization of attention through breath meditation, although other specifically concentration-developing meditations can be used as a starting point for the transition to vipassana. But the way Munindra-ji taught vipassana branched from single-pointed focusing on the sensation of breath at the abdomen to a flexibly immersive awareness of the many objects of everyday consciousness that naturally pass by when sitting still in a meditative posture for extended periods of time. Practice is initiated by quieting the karma phase of perception to make mental space for the karma activities of the five spiritual faculties (*indriya*)[15] that exercise the psychological functions of the noble eightfold path. As the Buddha says,

> In the seen there will be merely the seen; in the heard there will be merely the heard; in the sensed there will be merely the sensed; in the cognized there will be merely sensed.[16]

This is an instruction in investigating the receptive phase of perception. Insight-meditative attention can be compared to the clarity of a stream's flow, where the muddy whirlpools settle, allowing one to see through the water's surface. As the objects glide by, the insight attention does not glide along but observes that the objects arise, change, and cease in the flow of one perception process at a time. By refraining from automatically and blindly (ignorantly) reacting to the objects as the nonmeditative mind is in the habit of doing, an inner mental space is created for presence to merely observe the flow of dhammas where the reactivity of clinging, condemning, and negligence is suspended. Meditative action should be only a continuous, intense observation of objects enabling the observer to perceive reality without the distortions of any obscuration.

The five spiritual faculties are most pragmatically understood as the manifestation of all eight links of the path in a single flowing state from the very beginning of vipassana. They include mindfulness (*sati*), concentration (*samadhi*), intuitive wisdom (*panna*), energetic effort (*viriya*), and confidence (*saddha*). At various stages of development toward full enlightenment, the faculties are transformed into irreversible "powers" (*bala*), which collectively define the normal state of the fully enlightened. However, from the first insight into an object's momentary changeability, the spiritual faculties manifest their qualities as factors of enlightenment.[17] In vipassana, it is practical to apply the theorem of the five spiritual faculties in connection with instruction, as it provides a simple model for reflecting on the necessity of an ongoing adjustment of the balancing of the path factors.

The Faculty of Confidence

Buddhism places great emphasis on developing an attitude of "spiritual urgency" (*samvega*) through wise reflection on the life conditions of aging, illness, and death, which are the large existential imprints of momentary changeability in our lives. It was samvega that got the twenty-nine-year-old Siddhattha to leave his wife when she had given birth to their son, and he once more was reminded of the brevity of life. It was samvega that got Siddhattha to sit under the Bodhi tree in Bodh Gaya with the awe-inspiring decision not to get up until he had gained the realization of the deathless. The Buddha also has a tongue-in-cheek version of spiritual urgency: "Consider what you would do if there was a fire in your turban?" he asks a congregation. Yes, the audience would, of course, do everything in their power to extinguish the fire right away. It is therefore clear that a sense of spiritual urgency is the closest cause for activation of confidence (*saddha*) that the liberative teachings of Buddhism can be verified by experience, which the motivated meditator engages in without delay.

The Faculty of Effort

The mind is filled with determination when the faculty of confidence—which corresponds to right intention, the second link of the path—is activated with a sense of urgency. In this way, saddha becomes the proximate cause of the four right efforts (*sammapadhana*), which are identical to the sixth link of the path, the right effort.

According to the stock phrase for the four efforts, the meditator strives for (1) the nonarising of unskilled states of mind that have not yet arisen; (2) getting rid of unskilled states of mind that have arisen; (3) the arising of skilled states of mind that have not yet arisen; and (4) the maintenance, development, and completion of skilled states of mind that have already arisen.[18]

The four efforts highlight the Buddha's unequivocal view that dhamma-faring presupposes many choices on the path into the mind and the freedom to act on them purposefully. When the four efforts gain momentum, they have the character of the four bases of accomplishment (*iddhipada*), which further emphasize the expansive impact of the will and earnestness in concentrated states of mind.

> Here a meditator develops the basis of accomplishment consisting in concentration due to zeal and determined striving. She develops the basis of accomplishment consisting in concentration due to energy and determined striving. She develops the basis of accomplishment consisting in concentration due to purity of mind and determined striving. She develops the basis of accomplishment consisting in concentration due to investigation and determined striving.[19]

This steadfast commitment lays a solid foundation for developing the five spiritual faculties. The dhamma-faring is marked by a profound transformation of existential orientation driven by unwavering zeal and determination.

The Faculty of Concentration

It requires a determined effort to develop concentration as a spiritual faculty corresponding to the eighth link of the path, right concentration, which internalizes mindfulness and protects introspection from distractions. The exploration of samadhi reveals its vital role as an enabler of profound presence. As we delve deeper into our practice, we discover that meditative states are developed in a balance between physical relaxation and energetically aroused attention, which are saturated by the four right efforts. In vipassana it is very important to be constantly aware of the balance between the one-pointedness of concentration and the receptivity of a flexible presence to the flow of impressions. We can develop moments of concentrated immersion that come to overshadow the insight into the stream of consciousness if the focus is anchored at too extreme a degree at the expense of the mind's flexibility. On the other hand, overactive and insufficiently anchored attention can also overshadow the insight because of the overlaps of superficial perceptions that obscure permanency.

If the energetic effort is forced, the result is likewise often a restless state of mind with superficial attention, sometimes with tension in the cranial muscles. But the right balance between relaxation and energy can also be upset due to excessive enjoyment of the relaxation that occurs because of *successful* concentration. When we lean back in the relaxed state too enjoyably, the energy begins to seep and the attention sinks drowsily into the object as when falling asleep. This happens to meditators who have initially been stressed and therefore overrelax when the samadhi gains momentum. At the beginning of a retreat, this problem is experienced by quite a few meditators.

It's through persistent practice that we cultivate insight meditative states by skillfully balancing physical relaxation with heightened energetic attention. This delicate equilibrium not only deepens concentration but also fosters an acute awareness of our receptivity to impressions, allowing for the continuity of subtle insights.

The Faculty of Mindfulness

Right concentration structures presence, deepens it, and protects it from intrusive distractions. But it is, of course, the seventh link of the path, right mindfulness, the vigilant guardian of the mind—and the entire meta-process of our awareness of being aware—that overall monitors the regulation of equilibrium between the states of the five faculties. Especially the balance between samadhi and the right efforts, which avoids both tension and drowsiness in immersion. At the same time, mindfulness monitors its own flexibility in relation to the anchoring of concentration. Just like walking with a bowl filled to the brim, you must be flexibly present with every micro-impression of the body to avoid spilling. It is with this subtle degree of flexibility in immersion that right mindfulness develops the depths of all four foundations of mindfulness allowing for very penetrative and transformative insights into momentary changeability.

One further important task of mindfulness is monitoring the balance between confidence and wisdom to ensure that saddha doesn't turn into blind belief and give rise to misperceptions of one's meditative achievement or lack thereof. This balance is crucial as it helps meditators discern genuine insights from mere assumptions, without falling into the traps of overconfidence or doubting. In this situation, being with a *kalyana mitta* is a great resource.

The Faculty of Intuitive Wisdom

The deep transformative level of the first link of the path, right view, is activated when anchoring samadhi is balanced with the flexibility of sati. Right view is identical to the faculty of intuitive wisdom (*panna*) when this balance is obtained, and the faculty of intuitive wisdom is to be found in the sense of *seeing into* (*dassana*).[20] Buddhism distinguishes between conceptual knowledge, which is based on one's own or others' thinking, and meditative knowledge, which is based on one's personal direct understanding in meditation. Meditative knowledge is a form of knowledge about the immediate perception of the object of knowledge. In principle, it is like how visual perception is a direct experience of a visual object. In this sense, it is very illustrative that the meaning of the Latin *intueri* (to see into) is the same as the Pali *dassana.*

Basically, intuition is understood in Western culture as a summarizing and holistically oriented seeing into of a certain condition without using the step-by-step and rationally progressive process of analytical thinking. In Western culture, intuition is also often perceived as being of a short-lived nature, although often of far-reaching consequences. It is believed that many forms of understanding—whether scientific, artistic, or otherwise—spring from or culminate in a sudden clarifying understanding of the deeper truth of a phenomenon's nature. Either way, in your intuitive perception of the object, you understand what you are seeing in an extraordinarily penetrative and conclusive way.

The intuitive understanding in vipassana, however, operates differently. Here, intuition is systematically cultivated through a grounded and continuous practice of presence, achieved by persistently observing phenomena within the flow of the universal law. The Thai vipassana master Bhikkhu Buddhadasa summarizes the course of all the profound aspects of insight in vipassana as follows:

> A complete realization of impermanence must include unsatisfactoriness, not-self, voidness, thusness, and the law of causality. When we see all of this, we have seen impermanence completely and in the most profound way.[21]

In the journey of dhamma into the depths of the mind, insights develop in the context of our biographical self-perceptions and the life-historical episodes in the stream of objects that are brought to consciousness in the mind's natural flow. The stream of insight is increasingly maintained for hours during intensive practice, becoming a predominant mental state of the meditator. A wealth of insights, both at the general psychological and personal level, is experienced in connection with the insights into the universal characteristics of phenomena (anicca, dukkha, anatta). The synergy among all eight factors on the path thus culminates in the deeply transformative action of intuition (*vijja*), which Buddhaghosa describes as having

> the characteristic of penetrating things according to their individual essences, or it has the characteristic of sure penetration, like the penetration of an arrow shot by a skillful archer. Its function is to illuminate the objective field, like a lamp. It is manifested as non-bewilderment, like a guide in a forest.[22]

There are many synonyms in Pali for this kind of illuminating and clarifying knowledge: direct personal understanding (*abhinna*), seeing into (*nana-dassana*), intuitive knowledge (*vijja*), non-ignorance (*amoha*), experiential understanding (*paccakha-nana*), intuitive investigation of dhammas, and so forth. Some terms—for example, *bodhi*—are applied only to the transcendent intuition of nibbana, which is the final reach of the intuition in vipassana. Implicit in several of the terms of intuition is a sub-aspect of conceptual knowledge, which includes partly intellectual orientation about the path, partly the meditator's conceptual reflections on their already-gained intuitive insights. Thus, immediately after his enlightenment, the Buddha developed several of the important theorems about the path found in the suttas.

The specific paranormal ranges of samatha intuition in highly developed states of samadhi will be elucidated separately in chapter 14. Other samatha meditations—for example, on loving-kindness and other positive emotions, where emotional intuition dominates—will be reviewed in chapter 13.

The Kutis

You could see rows of *kutis*, or meditation huts, between banana and papaya palms in the tropical garden of the Burmese monastery. Bougainvillea bloomed with heavy clusters of red, yellow, and blue flowers almost throughout the year, and sweetly scented bushes of jasmine crept over the tall, white walls surrounding the monastery. After the rains that came suddenly and ended just as abruptly, leaving everything fresh and wondrous, waves of perfume from these sweet flowers converged heavily and suddenly upon the meditator's olfactory senses. That would be the moment to switch awareness to a deep perception of intervals of the rise and fall of this sweetness. The tactile sensation of one's breathing would then instantly glide completely into the background. Then if some thought arose, perhaps about the popular local belief that the scent is from deva angels in the tall trees along the road, in that moment one would neither be aware of the breath nor of the olfactory experience but only the rise and fall of each passing moment of thinking. In your kuti, you would go on meditating with deeply absorbed mindfulness like that. Then a thought suddenly arose about my mother and next about the music of Beethoven and, as out of the blue, about a dog who died when I was ten. The more I concentrated, the finer the micro-moments of the dhamma stream I perceived. When no other objects naturally attracted attention, it returned spontaneously to observation of the rise and fall of the movement of my abdomen as the most domineering sensation until another object arose, and the focus shifted.

There would be nothing you would not know directly and instantly in this expansive and exceedingly peaceful perception of momentariness. Focus by focus. Moment by moment. Samma sati flexibly remembers the present in the present. Samma samadhi structures the presence, making it steady like a lamp's flame when there is no draught. But *samma-ditthi*, right view, is the insight. You "see intuitively into the rise and fall" (*udayabbaya*) *nana-dassana* of each moment *as it really is*—no matter what the content of the object. It is the first stage of insight into vipassana.

7 | The Development of Meditative Concentration

From the earliest times, the Buddha's teaching (*dhamma*) was a teaching about a specific practice in India's unique meditative spiritual tradition, which doesn't presuppose any other belief (*saddha*) than the necessary confidence that the meditative practice, the dhamma-faring, can be verified by experience.

> The dhamma is well proclaimed by the Blessed One, visible here and now, immediately effective, inviting inspection, onward leading, to be experienced by the wise for themselves.[1]

Thus, the Buddha's teachings were recommended by followers. Confidence in testing through meditative experience was the original meaning of *saddha* in Buddhism, which is without a belief in a creator god and therefore lacks the structures of the cultic religions. Buddhism is instead what we might tentatively call empirically, phenomenologically grounded. When the Buddha's disciples, whether laymen or members of the monastic order, are urged to follow in his footsteps, it specifically refers to the development of the same meditative techniques he himself had practiced. Followers are encouraged by the Buddha not to blindly believe what he says but instead to make an investigation of their mind themselves. This spiritual pragmatism is the hallmark of Buddhism and is most directly embodied in the sutta given to the Kalamas.

> It is fitting for you to be perplexed, Kalamas, fitting for you to be in doubt. Doubt has arisen in you about a perplexing matter. Come, Kalamas, do not go by oral tradition, by lineage of teaching, by hearsay, by a collection of scriptures, by logical reasoning, by inferential reasoning, by reasoned cogitation, by the acceptance of a view after pondering it, by the seeming competence (of a speaker), or because you think, "The ascetic is our guru." But when, Kalamas, you know for yourselves, "These things are unwholesome; these things are blameworthy; these things are censured by the wise; these things, if accepted and undertaken, lead to harm and suffering, then should you abandon them. . . . But when you know for yourselves, "These things are wholesome; these things are blameless; these things are praised by the wise; these things, if accepted and undertaken, lead to welfare and happiness," then you should live in accordance with them.[2]

Initially an investigation of the mind applies to the practice of concentration, internalization, and anchoring of attention to test whether this exercise really leads to a transformative direct understanding of the nature of the mind.

Many of the Buddha's early disciples were, like himself, accomplished yogis according to *samatha bhavana* (development of calm), the common Indian meditation teachings. Those teachings basically consisted of breathing meditation and similar meditations with a simple structure suitable for the development of samadhi (concentration), ultimately leading to the highly absorptive states of samadhi called the *jhanas*.

Breathing Meditation

Breathing meditation is undoubtedly the oldest and simplest of all meditation and is extremely effective for developing concentration and focused attention.

> Meditators, this concentration by mindfulness of breathing, when developed and cultivated, is peaceful and sublime, an ambrosial pleasant dwelling, and it disperses and quells right on the spot evil unwholesome states whenever they arise.
>
> Just as, meditators, in the last month of the hot season, when the mass of dust and dirt has swirled up, a great rain cloud out of season disperses and quells it on the spot, so too concentration by mindfulness of breathing, when developed and cultivated, is peaceful and sublime, an ambrosial pleasant dwelling, and it disperses and quells on the spot evil unwholesome states whenever they arise.[3]

We don't know the exact notions associated with this "sitting ritual" in pre-Buddhist times, but the purpose must have been to explore the mystery of the life-giving breath. The mystery of breath has interested many sages in ancient cultures, not only in India but also in China, ancient Greece, Persia, and Egypt. According to the thinking of ancient cultural societies, there was a close connection between the breath and the nature of the mind and the entire cosmos. It is evident that the spirit departs from the body when the breath does, and the seers of the Upanishadic teachings—for whom the term *atman* meant both "breath" and "cosmic soul"—made this astute discovery. The word for soul in ancient Greek was *psyche*, which was also the word for "air." This linguistic connection between spirit and respiration also exists in English, which is an Indo-European language.

Breathing is still quite an existential mystery, apart from modern physiological and medical understandings. Apart from this, the timeless philosophical question arises: Why exactly and for what does a person breathe? This is something for which we can pose many very different answers, but none of the ancient cultures approached their exploration of the question with such far-reaching consequences as the Indian yogis. Buddhism as a concrete practice for highly concentrated and immersed presence with intuitive insights into the realities of the mind is due to the Buddha's exploration of the mystery of the breath and what it brought with it. The Buddha must historically be seen as the exponent par excellence of the yogic meditative culture, which is India's great gift to humanity. The Buddhist scriptures also contain the most detailed account of the meditative life cycle in India's history. The Buddha's teachings have included the whole of the common Indian meditation teachings about sangsara, atman, karma, and samadhi as they were in the Buddha's time, although not their metaphysical implications, which he distanced himself from on the grounds of the insights of vipassana that explore the coreless stream of consciousness.

With some adaptations of the balancing of the five spiritual faculties to the practice of the specific Buddhist meditation *vipassana-bhavana* (development of insight), breathing meditation is the ideal frame of mind for the undisturbed development of intuitively seeing into (*dassana*) the four noble truths.

In the time of the Buddha, breathing meditation was already mapped out as a journey in well-defined stages into the mind. Siddhattha Gotama practiced mindfulness of breathing (*anapana-sati*) for the development of concentration in preparation for his enlightenment. Disciples were often instructed in samatha as a starting point for the development of vipassana, which branches out from samatha and leads to insights into the four noble truths. It was in this way that the jhanas found their way into Buddhism, where they are formally classified as the eighth link of the path, right concentration. Although the level of samadhi in vipassana doesn't require jhanic depth, there is always an element of samatha in vipassana, especially developed on the breath.

The Blissful Non-Distraction of the Mind

Although right concentration is the last link on the path, it is the mind's one-pointedness and immersion in samadhi that activates the path as a meditation practice. It is the concentration that anchors the presence that makes it deep and stable and gives it the character of a path link.

> Bhikkhus, develop concentration. A bhikkhu who is concentrated understands the dhammas, as they really are.[4]

According to Abhidhamma, the function of samadhi is to unify consciousness.

> It [*samadhi*] puts consciousness evenly on the object, or it puts it rightly on it, or it is just the mere collecting of the mind, thus it is concentration (*samadhi*). Its characteristic is non-wandering, or its characteristic is non-distraction. Its function is to conglomerate conascent states as water does bath powder. It is manifested as peace. Usually its proximate cause is bliss. It should be regarded as steadiness of the mind, like the steadiness of a lamp's flame when there is no draught.[5]

In the suttas, the development of samadhi is referred to with a mnemonic template of five links of absorption (*jhan'anga*).[6] The links are the fundamental structure of concentration in many levels of meditation in both samatha and vipassana and comprise: (1) initial focusing (*vitakka*), (2) sustained focusing (*vicara*), (3) energetic interest (*piti*), (4) bliss (*sukha*), and (5) mental one-pointedness (*ekagatta*).[7] According to the Abhidhamma's analyses of consciousness, the absorption links are rudimentarily present in even nonmeditative wholesome states of mind, such as patience, generosity, kindness, or just a general mindful presence (not yet anchored by the path link of samadhi). Even if the links of absorption in these contexts aren't significant enough to qualify as meditation, their development points to the fact that meditative states are naturally anchored expansions of everyday consciousness.

The five links of absorption always occur together with mindfulness (*sati*) and equanimity (*upekkha*), which are characteristics of all wholesome attention. But the mutual balancing of the spiritual faculties is, of course, different in samatha and vipassana. In samatha, concentration will be very prominent, and the intuitive way of knowing the three universal characteristics (anicca, dukkha, anatta) will be less prominent or completely absent because of the overshadowing of powerful concentration that tends to fixate on and get absorbed into the object. A certain flexible balance with mindfulness is always needed in vipassana.

However, with the development of samadhi arises a clarity and agility that are easily able to suppress or reduce the five hindrances to meditative introspection: (1) disturbing preoccupation with sensuous impressions—that is, clinging to the objects of the senses; (2) involvement with anger, impatience, and self-condemnation; (3) lethargy and drowsiness; (4) restlessness and worry; and (5) paralyzing doubt and skepticism with the aim of exploring the mind. By suppressing the five hindrances, it is possible to achieve the relaxing and uniform concentration that is necessary in samatha meditation.

The Focus in Breathing Meditation

The links of absorption always arise together in a single pre-jhanic state of mind. But in the process of development, they individually come to dominance in the order described below, where the first four links are the reinforcers of the fifth link, the one-pointedness of attention. In particular, the mental state of patience (*khanti*) is illustrative of this expansion of everyday awareness because meditation makes great demands on precisely this mental quality. Try sitting with your back straight, your legs crossed, your ankles crossed, and the flat, upturned soles of your feet resting on each opposite thigh. This is *the full lotus*, the sitting posture of the iconic Buddha figure and the pan-Indian meditation posture par excellence.[8] When the full lotus is practiced effortlessly, it locks the body into immobility. It has an almost immediate relaxing effect on the entire psycho-physiological state. The respiratory rate slows down to a deep, slow level. The vigilance of the sitter is supported by the immobility of the straight spine, and attention spontaneously focuses on how breathing causes the abdominal muscles to rise and fall, making this the body's most eye-catching movement in the locked position. Sitting for extended periods of time in the full lotus posture makes you acutely aware of the movement brought on by the diaphragm, which pulls the lungs downward during inhalation and raises the abdomen horizontally. When exhaling, the diaphragm contracts, and the abdomen drops accordingly. If you put your hand over the area around the navel for a moment, you will get an impression of the movement. If you remove your hand again, the movement in an area approximately the size of the palm of your hand will become clear. The tactile sensation in this focus is our object for the development of samadhi. As soon as the breath settles down, the focus will naturally narrow either to the sensation of the abdomen rising and falling around the navel or, for some meditators, to the sensation at the nostrils, where the breath brushes the sensitivity of the skin between the nostrils and the upper lip. There is no preference for one or the other of these two foci in the suttas. If breath meditation was developed by people sitting in the full lotus position, however, it is most likely that the abdominal breath was the original focus, because that is where the movement is most marked in the motionless lotus position. In addition, meditation on the sensation of the abdomen is associated with a strong focus on what is colloquially called the gut feeling, as a barometer that finely senses your emotional state—there is no corresponding sensitivity in the nostrils. Meditation on the abdomen thus brings your attention deep into your body and increases your susceptibility to the subtlety of feelings' nuances. The deep, slow breathing at the peritoneum is the relaxing and stress-relieving way of breathing, which most easily facilitates the four right efforts in meditation.

The Recipe for Samadhi

The recipe for the development of concentration emphasizes the constant repetition of the act of attention on a single object over a long period of time. In this way, the attention gradually becomes one-pointed. Regardless of where you choose your point of focus, the development of concentration consists in the continuous, intense observation of the attention on this one focus for a long time. Your breath is the perfect object for sharpening your attention. The breath is always with you; it is the life-giving movement. The full lotus position is the perfect posture for focusing attention on just the breath itself. Initially the attention is often derailed by wandering thoughts. It can therefore be helpful to repeat a so-called mental note with the inner voice of the mind to support the focus. Without lip articulation, you repeat *Rising* for the abdomen, if that is your focus, which rises on the inhalation; and *Falling* for the abdomen's movement, which falls on the exhalation. The note is used as a crosshair on the phase of the breath being noted. A synthesis arises between the attention, note-taking, and phase that is noted. In this way, it is easier to avoid thoughts invading the attention. You can use mental notes pointwise or all the time, as needed, until concentration gains momentum.[9] Although full lotus is considered the classic position, in early Buddhism no emphasis was placed on the formal requirements of the sitting position. You can sit in an ordinary way on an ordinary chair, for instance—the way the future buddha Metteyya is always depicted in sculpture as simply sitting on a chair with both his feet on the ground. What is important is the immobility of the body's position in a relatively comfortable way. You ignore the pain caused by the sitting after some time and suppress the pain up to a certain point, then make it the object of relaxed observation to avoid condemnation that will block the meditation. Try with the slow breath to enter into the pain and accept the pain instead of condemning and trying to push the pain away. Acceptance is the mental side of bodily relaxation. The deep, slow way of breathing is key to both modes. Sitting pains come on like ebbing tidal waves. Depending on how intensive your practice, the body eventually adapts to the motionless meditation pose, no matter what the preferred sitting position.

The Allegory of Striking the Bell

The first two links of absorption activate the phase, which Buddhaghosa compares to (1) the striking of a bell (*vitakka*, or *initial focus*), and (2) the reverberation or resonance (*vicara*, or *sustained focus*)[10] that orbits around the strike—like the sound of the bell—and guards against the invasion of distractions. These will typically be the meditator's impulses toward mental displacement activities that get the mind wandering away from the focus. In the beginning, however, you often must repeat the "hit" on the bell almost immediately—that is, intentionally refocusing attention on the breath to prevent distraction from invading the focus. But the better you become at focusing and refocusing, the longer the effortless "reverberation" of the extended phase will be.

Breathing meditation is very relaxing because the frequency of the breath is rapidly lowered, which sharpens the focus and increases the development of one-pointedness of the mind. Thus one enters a self-reinforcing positive circle that increases concentration, which increases relaxation, which deepens concentration. And so on. As previously said, if at the outset of the meditation you felt stressed out, your nervous system goes to the opposite extreme when you get concentrated—you'll overrelax and most likely doze when you enter deep concentration. But as your spiritual faculties get more balanced, you experience subtle, almost imperceptible breaths in a highly concentrated and relaxed state of alertness in which the discrete movements of the abdomen are nevertheless clearly perceived.

Energetic Interest

Everyday awareness usually requires that an experience, objectively speaking, must be interesting for attention to engage with it. However, in meditation, it is experienced that the true cause of interest in an object is not its content but the intensity of the attention directed toward it. Brain scans of trained meditators in the initial stages of samadhi show a strong activation of gamma brain waves, which function to harmonize the two hemispheres of the brain.[11] Psychologically, this harmonization is experienced as unity, centering, and one-pointedness of attention, leading to a high degree of intentional control over the direction of attention. When attention is refocused on the object, again and again, a very strong interest in the object arises. This energetic interest is the third factor of absorption (*piti*). In a very special way, the life-giving movement of the breath is increasingly experienced as intuitively meaningful. If one immerses oneself in this interesting focus for a long time, piti takes on the character of strong enthusiasm, tending toward euphoric upliftment, which has a very energizing quality. If one has never tried to meditate, breath meditation may theoretically sound boring. But the skilled meditator becomes absorbed in their focus in a way that causes tingling at the scalp and goose bumps all over the body from intense well-being. Sometimes uncontrollable tears of joy stream down the cheeks. During this process, piti can only initially be defined as strong interest. Subsequently a very prominent rapture can be experienced, as if it lifts the body up from the seating surface to float freely in the air. Added to this are perceptions of an inner light, which can be so dazzling that one often opens one's eyes to be convinced that the light source is not outside. These phenomena may sound like states of uncontrollable excitement but are rather a kind of as-if euphoria and monitored by the expansive state of equanimity due to samadhi. They are expressions of intense piti, which naturally greatly reinforces the one-pointed interest in the object.

Unfinished Business

However, memories that are rarely accessed by ordinary consciousness become easily conscious when intensely focused attention is internalized. When it comes to happy recollections, which can be very attractive due to their sharpness and detail, the beginner is quickly sidetracked from meditation's main objective. One might suddenly see a vividly sharp yet trivial memory from, for example, the age of seven. Or one may recall baffling details of a meal a long time ago. Refocusing on the breath and letting go of these curious thoughts, though, is not too difficult. The more concentrated you are, the easier it is. But it can also involve uncomfortable content of consciousness that the mind has so far kept suppressed. It may be memories of the bitter regret of something you once did or did not do, or something you said, or everything you perhaps did not say on the same occasion but should have. It may now suddenly emerge in starkly clear contexts, and it can provoke self-condemning reactions that derail the meditation. However, there are many examples in the annals of Buddhism of persons who, despite the accumulation of very bad karma, were nevertheless able to free the mind. But the rule is that the greater the accumulation of meritorious actions in the mind, the easier the development of samadhi becomes.

Unpleasant—perhaps painful or traumatic—memories that the mind has intentionally repressed can cling to the waking consciousness long after sitting meditation. These memories are invested with a strong sense of identity and charged with deep emotions such as sadness, anger, and anxiety. Such memories may express situations and life periods that the meditator has seemingly managed to push out of consciousness—so-called unfinished business—until then and perhaps has never fully understood the reasons for. The way of dealing with "unfinished business" is one of the crossroads for samatha and vipassana. If the meditator has many negative memories that keep coming up, there may be a solution to turning to vipassana at this point, which is described in later chapters. In vipassana, you develop the deconditioning insights of anicca, dukkha, and anatta in the very flow of your painful mental conditioning and thus develop *the karma that leads to the elimination of karma*. Very rarely does a meditator become psychotically productive in meditation—and it is never due simply to meditation. But it does happen to people who are predisposed to, for example, schizophrenia and who therefore should not meditate intensively, at least not without very close supervision.

Bliss

Conversely, for the meditator who effortlessly experiences deep samadhi, without too many sidetracking memories, a highly developed state of samadhi or even jhanic absorptions are achievable. In samatha, one constantly strives to suppress the ordinary content of consciousness to maintain the focus of meditation on the breath and increasingly succeeds in staying with the focus. As a result of samadhi's bulwark against distractions, the meditator achieves a profound sense of tranquilly serene bliss (*sukha*), which is the fourth link of absorption. This refined pleasure can suddenly rise to the fore while the *piti rapture* drifts into the background. To an even greater extent, this subtle pleasure reinforces the one-pointedness on the object. At this point, the meditator sits effortlessly for long sittings with deep intervals of unbroken one-pointedness with a shifting of intensity between piti and sukha.

The Parable of the Man in the Desert

Buddhaghosa compares piti and sukha to the state of mind of an exhausted man who is wandering through the desert and suddenly sees an oasis in the distance. This man will understandably experience a very energetic interest (*piti*) in what he sees. In step with the cooling shadows of the oasis, the sound of running water, and the smell of delicious food coming within reach of his senses, his interest increases to rapturous and physically perceptible elation, tending to extremely jubilant and energizing joy. You can imagine this good man running wild with enthusiasm on the last bit into the oasis. But this elation is only a little compared to the calm satisfaction that flows through him when, after eating and quenching his thirst, he lies deeply relaxed in a cool pool of water in the shade of the palm trees. Then the good man experiences a quiet state of bliss, which is comparable to the sukha absorption link. The serene refinement of sukha is the state of mind of one who has had all their needs met and no longer desires or craves anything, who is just happy about everything as it is now. To further illustrate the two states, sukha can be compared to the happiness people experience silently watching the sunset over the ocean after a long hot summer day at the beach, where everything has been just perfect. Piti, on the other hand, is more reminiscent of the energetic joy that people associate with the experience of rhythmic music that gets them moving in time. As the meditator's concentration gains momentum, the sukha will dominate over the piti and reinforce the fifth link, which is precisely the culminating anchoring of the continuous one-pointing (*ekagatta*) of attention that is constitutional for powerful samadhi.

Linear Development of Samadhi

Even though the development is experienced linearly, as described here, all the links are constantly present in the meditative process up to and including the first jhana. In the beginning, the repetition of the first two links will overshadow the other links. When the two links are activated in one significant flow, the energetic interest and its physical side effects will dominate, thus overshadowing the quiet joyousness. But when the expansion of sukha comes to the fore, the piti recedes. Meditative concentration (samadhi), as described here, is developed through a continuous, intensive practice of sittings, ideally all day long on a retreat, apart from periods of exercising the body. Some meditators skip the mentioned sequence and, after a short time, slip directly into the state of sukha but experience disappointment when they are subsequently unable to repeat the condition. The stability of the links develops only in the order of succession. Concentration develops most quickly in deeply relaxed states of mind that are energetically alert. You cannot force this process. But purposeful striving is necessary, as is evident from the theorem on the four bases for accomplishment (*iddhipada*), which emphasizes the freedom of volitional action to develop and master these meditative states. At a certain point, the focus on the breath will radiate into a so-called counterimage. Whether you start by meditating on the focus at the nostrils or the abdomen, the counterimage is perceived as a penetrating blue, orange, or white light of various shapes. This is the indication of a degree of samadhi called neighborhood concentration (*upacara samadhi*) because the concentration is somewhere in the "neighborhood" of the jhanic absorption. In English, this samadhi is often translated into "access concentration." It's the indication of a stable degree of samadhi in one-to-three-hour sittings with deep intervals of ten to twenty minutes of unbroken focus on the object.

The Jhanic Absorption

At the right time, the meditator can decide to enter the first jhana through the radiance of the counterimage or the physical uplift of the piti link—and at times in combination. The meditator aims for a focus where the rapture is most pronounced in the body and intentionally narrows the focus, which attention intuitively investigates in.[12] A strong piti that activates jhana can be experienced with a strength and suddenness, like "a rock cavern invaded by a huge inundation."[13] This vivid metaphor illustrates the overwhelming and transformative nature of the experience. It is perceived as being lifted by a violent wave and, with a jolt, washed into the jhanic absorption that causes the whole body to tremble. Whispering background thoughts arise in the jhana, excitedly interpreting the unique absorption and vivacious joy of the experience. But aside from this, thinking's regular operation is suspended. A jhana is too intensely experienced to contemplate discursively while you're in it. The sensation of the body and time also vanishes. The five links of absorption culminate in "the complete contact with the object that the surface of a box's lid has with the surface of its base."[14] The duration of absorption can range from minutes to extended hours, but the meditator can step out of the jhana whenever they want to. Eventually the experience of the jhana fades away, leaving behind an imprint that enriches and deepens the meditator's understanding of an experience of pure consciousness that transcends conventional boundaries of body and time. Since the experience was the result of a conscious learning process, the meditator is fully aware of how the absorption is later reactivated. With the bases of accomplishment, they next achieve jhanic mastery, which is the supreme impact of the meditative volitional action in states of samadhi.

> He adverts to the first jhana where, when, and for as long as he wishes, he has no difficulty in adverting, thus it is mastery in adverting. He attains the first jhana where, when, and for as long as, he wishes, he has no difficulty in attaining, thus it is mastery in attaining.[15]

Four Jhanas with Form

And so also for each of the other jhanas. Through the absorption in each jhana, the meditator eliminates some of the links of the jhana, resulting in even greater absorption. The meditator identifies the first two links of the first jhana and, with the aid of the bases of accomplishment, decisively withdraws the focus from the links. Thereby arises the second jhana, which is more peaceful than the first, since both piti and sukha are very prominent, but with a clear tendency toward the dominance of sukha's peaceful joyousness. Similarly, the meditator eliminates the grossness of piti, after which the even deeper absorption in the third jhana arises. In this way, sukha comes to shine through the consciousness with the refinement of quiet, serene pleasure. Finally, sukha ends in the fourth jhana, and "there remains only equanimity, purified and bright, malleable, wieldy, and radiant."[16] This jhana is firmly rooted. Thus the first three jhanas were fluctuations of the truly absorbed samadhi in mental imperturbability (*ananjam*), which is firmly rooted in jhanic equanimity. The fourth jhana with form isn't yet the end of samatha yoga. The last jhana's mental immobility can be intensified and enlarged into four formless jhanas (*arupa-jhana*), which include four spheres inside the fourth jhana but eliminate the sense of the consciousness's limitation in absorption. The highest jhanas are of such an intense nature that the meditator, without the help of a guide, can be misled into attaching to them unrealistic spiritual meanings foreign to Buddhism and which block insight into the thusness of consciousness.

The Mundaneness of the Jhanas

In the jhanas, the soul (*atta*) has attained the highest nibbana, according to the various sects in northern India, who had divergent conceptions of the nature of the soul according to which jhana their perspective was based upon.[17] According to Buddhism, the jhanas are neither eternal nor transcendental but rather absorptions in the most expansive layers of the impermanent and conditioned stream of consciousness.[18] Because of the overwhelming dominance of samadhi, there are no marked vipassana insights into anicca, dukkha, and anatta in the jhanas. Nevertheless, there are sustained, powerful insights into the wonderfully expansive nature of consciousness. The jhanas are in fact a third of the "inconceivable matters" that are impossible to understand analytically, though there are many technical analyses in both the suttas and the Abhidhamma.

But none of the jhanas is an irreversible spiritual gain. If the meditator doesn't live relatively withdrawn about her practice and maintain neighborhood concentration at a high level, then she gradually loses both parts in the slipstream of the karma accumulations of everyday consciousness. The jhanas also don't decondition the mind's accumulations of unwholesome karma nor eliminate the influxes (*asava*) of ignorance and craving, which is the aim of Buddhism's project of liberation, but suppress them temporarily. The jhanas, therefore, don't lead to comprehensive psychological and transformative insights as vipassana does. Siddhattha sensed these limitations due to the purity of his highly developed mind, after which he left his samatha teachers.

The Transition from Samatha to Vipassana

After the period of unsuccessful asceticism, the Buddha took up experimenting with breath meditation and found that by establishing concentration in the proper balance with the other spiritual faculties, he could engage in developing insights leading to a greater understanding of the mind.

In many suttas, the Buddha first guides his disciples in the development of jhanas and then transitions them to the practice of insight meditation as the Buddha himself did. The development of jhanas as a starting point for vipassana is one of the prominent approaches to enlightenment in the suttas. The meditator emerges from the jhana at the highest level of neighborhood concentration and then introspects the universal characteristics of anicca, dukkha, and anatta in the objects that naturally flow out for her flexible awareness after the emergence.[19] Vipassana thus branches out from the one-pointing of the mind on the breath to a broadening investigation of the mind in its normally flowing contexts. On other occasions, the Buddha instructed in vipassana based on many levels of pre-jhanic samadhi as a starting point for transition.[20] In post-Buddha times, this approach was called pure vipassana (*suddha vipassana*).[21]

As a rule of thumb, we relatively quickly develop samadhi on one primary object in samatha, but less insight, because we close off to the natural flow of other objects. The reverse is the case in pure vipassana. We open for meditation on the natural flow of objects of everyday consciousness relatively early in practice, combined with meditation on the breath when no other domineering object attracts attention. In this case, the development of samadhi occurs more slowly than in samatha because concentration is primarily developed through the insights of anicca, dukkha, and anatta in a multiplicity of objects in the stream of consciousness.

For most people, it is easiest to develop an undistracted state of mind in breathing meditation, and then apply it to focusing open awareness on each of the various objects in the stream of everyday consciousness.

For me, the first eye-opening experience of pure vipassana was the anchoring of my mind in "momentary concentration" (*khanika samadhi*). Momentary concentration is called "access concentration" (*upacara samadhi*) when developed solely in samatha meditation, because it accesses a deep state of absorption to the exclusion of all other objects, whereas in pure vipassana, the momentary samadhi focuses on just the rise and fall of every object to the exclusion of none. But because momentary samadhi develops in an increasing, stable flow of insight, the same degree of concentration is gradually achieved as at the highest level of access concentration just before entering the first jhana. In vipassana, however, the meditator doesn't enter jhana, because the development of insight into continuous cessation of phenomena doesn't culminate in fixation of the stream of consciousness but in its transcendence.[22] This is the realization of nibbana and the attainment of the fruit of stream entry. Instead of holding on to and fixating on the object as in samatha, the attention in vipassana constantly lets go of any object because of the insight into the object's immediate changeability. When these two approaches to exploring the mind—which for the beginner may be difficult to distinguish from each other—are developed very methodically, as on a retreat, they clearly lead to very different end goals: Samatha leads to the mind's jhanic absorption in expanded "mental immobility"; vipassana leads to stream entry and nibbana-dhamma, which is the fruit of stream entry.

Often the Buddha would guide the meditator in vipassana after the attainment of four jhanas, but the non-jhanic approach also has a very prominent place in the suttas. There are numerous examples of monks, nuns, and laypeople asking for brief instruction so that they can subsequently practice on their own. The Buddha then instructs them in the general practice of the four foundations of mindfulness as the direct approach, which always includes mindfulness of breathing in the balance of all five spiritual faculties, which is necessary for insight into the mind as a coreless stream.

8 | The Four Foundations of Mindfulness

We may call the objects in vipassana the flow of everyday consciousness as foundations for the development of insight into consciousness as a coreless stream.

> Come, friends, dwell in continuous absorbed observation of the body in the body, ardent, clearly comprehending, unified, with limpid mind, concentrated, with one-pointed mind. . . . Dwell in continuous absorbed observation of feelings in feelings. . . . mental states in mental states. . . . and phenomena (*dhammas*) in phenomena . . . in order to know [them] as they really are.[1]

In the last century, this comprehensive mindfulness practice had an extensive renaissance with the Burmese vipassana master Mahasi Sayadaw (1904-1982). Pure vipassana became known in the West as the Burmese *satipatthana* method, even though the meditation is based on the oldest canonical tradition in the Buddha's sermons—that is, the *Satipatthana Sutta*; and richly elaborated in the earliest postcanonical literature—that is, Buddhaghosa's meditation manual from the fifth century C.E. As such, there is really nothing particularly Burmese in the pure vipassana except that Mahasi Sayadaw recommended the use of mental notes during the learning of vipassana.

> Meditators, just as the river Ganges slants, slopes, and inclines towards the east, so too a meditator who develops and cultivates the four foundations of mindfulness slants, slopes, and inclines towards nibbana.[2]

The development of the four foundations is designated *ekayana* by the Buddha, meaning both the direct path and the only way. A good translation could be "the only direct path."

First Satipatthana: Meditation on the Body as the Body

The parables of the bowl and the bamboo acrobats point to the impracticality of dividing sati into four foundations. But apart from theoretical and mnemonic purposes, there is nevertheless a didactic progression in the splitting. The first foundation, mindfulness "of the body as the body,"[3] refers to the direct knowing of the senses—this is an instruction in vipassana. It is not contemplative thinking *about* the senses but the experiential *direct knowing* of the arising, changing, and cessation of sensual experiences in one focus at a time as the most basic experience of sensation, moment by moment.

> In this way, the meditator abides continuously absorbed in observation of the body as a body internally, or she abides continuously absorbed in observation of the body as a body externally, or she abides continuously absorbed in observation of the body as a body both internally and externally. Or else she abides in the body continuously absorbed in observation of its nature of arising, or she abides in the body continuously

> absorbed in observation of its nature of vanishing, or she abides in the body continuously absorbed in observation of its nature of both arising and vanishing. Or else mindfulness that "there is a body" is simply established in her to the extent necessary for bare knowledge and mindfulness. And she remains independent, not clinging to anything in the world. That is how a meditator abides continuously absorbed in observation of the body.[4]

It makes sense to categorize the observation of the sensory objects as one foundation to emphasize, on the dhamma journey into the mind, how important it is to be consciously anchored in the body. Breathing meditation, walking meditation, and meditation on other experiences of sensation and of the body in motion—for example, eating meditation—formally belong to this foundation.

The Mnemonic Template in Satipatthana

In the review of each of the other foundations, the sutta on the four satipatthanas repeats verbatim the entire mnemonic formula of observation of "the body as the body," only substituting the appropriate foundation—that is, "feelings as feelings," "states of mind as states of mind," and "dhammas as dhammas"—into the template. Each meditation implies the continuous, absorbed observation (*anupassana*) of the momentary changeability of the objects of the foundation in question. This is the basic learning process in vipassana. Sometimes either the arising or cessation phase of the object is perceived, but sometimes both arising and cessation are perceived in one flow of insight. This is the mature stage of *udayabbaya nana-dassana* (intuitive seeing into rise and fall). It is the first of nine insight stages in vipassana, which initially leads to the "minor stream entry" and later to the "fruit of stream entry"—which is the transcendental insight into nibbana-dhamma. At each foundation, the independence of the meditator is highlighted. She lives as "an island" to herself because she has the four foundations of mindfulness as her sole refuge, which the Buddha on his deathbed recommended to his followers.[5]

Although the *Satipatthana Sutta* is a manual in pure vipassana, the first foundation also mentions a series of samatha meditations that have the purpose of subduing preoccupation with mundane sensuality. Through awareness of the inevitability of death, these meditations furthermore have the purpose of activating the attitude of spiritual urgency (*samvega*). The meditations are discussed in chapter 14.

Meditation on the breath will take the meditator's concentrated focus deep into her body and, in balance with the other satipatthanas, sensitize the introspective awareness of her inner world of perceptions, feelings, emotions, and cognitions.

Meditative Postures

Buddhaghosa recommends that a meditator first try meditating standing, walking, sitting, and lying down for three days in each position before she decides on her meditation position.[6] This is not a general rule, but the absorbed presence in any of the body positions is considered suitable for gaining even very deep insights and emphasizes the important point that vipassana can be practiced in all body positions. In the Buddha's day, the monk Sona Kolivisa became enlightened while doing walking meditation. The Buddha's main disciple, Ananda, who memorized most of the Buddha's discourses, gained enlightenment midway between a standing and lying posture, while he was intensely present in the act of lying down on his sleeping mat. The nun Kisa Gotami was enlightened as she stood watching the wind blow out a row of oil lamps in the twilight. And the monk Channa gained enlightenment while meditating on the tactile sensation of the razor that shaved the hairs on the crown of his head during the ceremony of his ordination. Practice of all four foundations of deep presence is necessary in each bodily position.

Second Satipatthana: Meditation on Feelings as Feelings

The second foundation of sati emphasizes the importance of observing feelings as feelings while they occur in their flowing moments of arising, changing, and ceasing. The Pali word *vedana* (etym. "to experience") is translated into English as "feeling," "feeling tone," and "bodily sensation." There are three types of vedana: pleasant, unpleasant, and neither. They arise in both wholesome and unwholesome states of mind. We feel what we experience and experience what we feel. If we did not have feelings, we would experience nothing.

"Feeling tone" is a good translation, and it is not difficult to distinguish between the three tones. Coarse feeling tones are directly activated by body posture. For example, if one sits in a way that causes discomfort in the body, one changes the sitting position so that the feeling tone becomes pleasant. Other feeling tones arise because of the state of mind. For instance, joy is embedded in a light, warm bodily sensation. Conversely, irritation is experienced as tense discomfort in the body. Neutral feeling tones of boredom and indifference often lead to drowsiness and neglect of the object. Vedana can also be divided into worldly and spiritual tones. The displeasure associated with anger, for example, is a worldly feeling, while the pleasure associated with loving-kindness is spiritual. Spirituality can be expressed by neutral feeling tones, such as the state of equanimity attained through realizing how fleeting pleasure and pain are and then learning to be equally equanimous of them. The worldly neutral feeling that is without this insight can be based on merely insensitive and flat indifference toward the object. Neutral tones of boredom and indifference in unwholesome states often lead to drowsiness, boredom, and neglect of the object.

The Taste of the Object

According to the Abhidhamma, object stimulus (*phasso*) in the receptive phase of the perception process has the function of *squeezing the juice* out of the object, while the feeling tone has the function of *tasting the juice* with a view to the proactive response to the object. Vedana orients attention to an immediate desirability of experience, or lack thereof, and conditions, one way or another, the mind's subsequent response to the experience. But the choice between the wholesome and unwholesome root conditions is ethically free in the responsive phase, as outlined in a previous chapter. While the feeling tone, so to speak, *serves* the object for the active karma phase of perception and is therefore dominant in the receptive phase, the volitional impulse is dominant in the karma phase, which actively *does* something with the "taste." Volition, for example, in the unwholesome case, clings to, condemns, or ignores—or alternatively uses the ethical freedom of will to activate a wholesome response to an unwholesome object—for example, by seeing into the universal characteristics of the object and disidentifying the mind from it.

The meditator mentally carries her "bowl" filled to the brim with absorbed presence into a sustained observation of the arising, changing, and cessation (anicca) of the feeling tones, their potential for suffering (dukkha), and the character of the non-core self (anatta), because any feeling is a fleeting, composite, dependently arising phenomenon and not the core of the self. Disillusionment and disenchantment with feelings such as "mine, myself, my self" leads to equanimity of mind based on the understanding that there is nothing to cling to in feelings, nothing to condemn, and nothing to ignore.

> In this way, she abides continuously absorbed in observation of feelings as feelings internally, or she abides continuously absorbed in observation of feelings as feelings externally.[7]

Absorbed presence in the karma phase with the object in the receptive phase is clearly very important because insight is developed in this phase in response to the object. And the highlighting of this focus is the rationale for this satipatthana.

Third Satipatthana: Meditation on States of Mind as States of Mind

Immersed presence with feeling tones slides seamlessly into the foundation of immersed presence with states of mind (*citta*) as states of mind. Sadness and joy are emotional states embedded in sensations of feeling tones in the body. Feeling has the function of the immediate evaluation of the experience or object, while the third foundation directs attention to the ethical quality of the state of mind that activates the feeling.

According to the exposition of the foundation, the meditator intuitively understands the states of mind that are root-conditioned by desire-thirst, hatred, and ignorance and the states of mind free from desire-thirst, hatred, and ignorance.[8] The concept of *citta* is one of the Pali terms for consciousness, and here refers to the content of consciousness—that is, states of mind and thoughts that have the six roots as motifs.

Chapter 5 highlighted examples of mental defilements (*kilesas*), underlying tendencies (*anusayas*), polluting inflows (*asavas*), and fetters (*samyojanas*) that led to bondage and suffering. And previous chapters have reviewed the five spiritual faculties and a list of wholesome karma activities that led to liberation and happiness. The rationale for the third foundation is this distinction between wholesome and unwholesome states of mind, which is the basis of the karma teachings as a moral doctrine that supports the path to enlightenment. After meditating predominantly on the breath, we begin with the third foundation to open awareness to the deep presence with the whole stream of consciousness in the full-scale practice of vipassana.

Meditation on Thoughts

At the beginning of my meditation, I had many distracting thoughts that continuously diverted my attention. I then realized the usefulness of mental notes on thoughts. Munindra-ji recommended that I repeat the note *Thinking, thinking,* with the inner voice of the mind as a focus point for concentrating on the reality that a thought is just a thought, regardless of its content. But I changed the note to *It's just a thought, it's just a thought*, which sounded more everyday-like to me. The impermanence of thoughts is the reality that must be acknowledged when we carry the "bowl" of presence into the sustained observation of inner psychological processes.

Mental notes are especially helpful in taking a distancing step back from uncomfortable thought content and the emotional state that can be activated and instead keeping the focus on the thought as just a thought that arises, changes, and ceases. We become more aware of what is happening when we occasionally "spill a drop" and get sucked into the specific content of the thought, especially the time of the thought that then wanders with the attention. In that moment, we react to thoughts about the past or future as if the thought *is* the past or the future. But the reality is that thoughts about the past or the future are *just* thoughts that arise and cease *in the present*. I told Munindra-ji about my reformulation of the note, and it amused him. It's precisely about formulating the notes to fit your mentality, he said, adding that some meditators use many nuanced notes, such as *Planning* for thoughts about the future or *Ruminating* for brooding thoughts. In Burmese meditation manuals, there are indeed long lists of one-syllable notes for inspiration. But in my experience, the fewer the notes, the more effective they are experienced. The notes serve as focus points for sustained concentration on a difficult object. Both planning and rumination, like many other types of thought content, are fundamentally just thoughts. In any case, mental notes are very effective in preventing the mind from wandering.

Meditation on Feelings and Emotions

If a negative feeling is more prominent in perception than the thought that initially activated it, we focus on where and how the feeling is felt in the body, and we can use the mental note *Feeling, feeling* or *It's just a feeling*. If a difficult thought has first activated an unpleasant emotion, such as irritation or jealousy, you shift focus to where and how you sense irritation or jealousy in the body. With the inner voice of the mind, you can use identification of the emotion as a mental note, such as *Irritation, irritation*, *It's just irritation*, or *Just jealousy* to sharpen the distance-maintaining attention on the tension and unease that the difficult mental state triggers. Be aware that the tone in the repetition of the note is not "colored" by the unpleasant emotion, otherwise you are entangled in the reaction. Also, be aware that an emotional negative reaction changes the breath, making it quicker and shorter. Therefore, always bring the breath down to the deep, slow, and relaxing pace that facilitates the mindful way of calm observation.

Sometimes we need to switch many times between the respective notes concerning the focus on thoughts and sensations in the body where the emotion is embedded, until the difficult mental state has passed. Be aware that the notes are not used to block the object that the note is about. The idea is simply to sharpen the distance-maintaining attention on the object instead of reacting unhelpfully to it. *It does not belong to me; I am not this; this is not my self.* This is the recurring instruction in vipassana, whether the thought or feeling is the most dominant object.

Meditating on Mental Notes

The application of mental notes is a characteristic of the Burmese Mahasi Sayadaw tradition in the learning phase of pure vipassana. The use of notes probably stems from the mnemonic repetitions of meditation instructions in the canon. A mental note is a brief, active thought about what our awareness is focused on at the very moment. The note, repeated with the inner voice of the mind, makes it easier for us to turn the autopilot off and be attentively present with what the note is pointing at. The correct application of notes creates space for undisturbed observation, opening insight into both the causal conditioning and the impermanence of the difficult object, be it a thought, an emotion, or a sensation. Notes can be used in all activities, and you can make your own notes. The notes must be concise and easy to repeat and concentrate on. You apply notes just to the extent they are helpful to sustain your focus. It may sound banal, but in practice, it's a great help for many meditators in the learning phase.

Fourth Satipatthana: Meditation on Dhammas as Dhammas

As discussed earlier, *dhamma* is a phenomenological term in Buddhism for a thought, feeling, sensation, or emotional state that is intuitively understood as momentarily changeable (anicca), potentially or actually unsatisfactory (dukkha) and non-core self (anatta). We can therefore define the dhammas as the objects of the four noble truths, which summarize the entirety of the Buddha's teaching. When this dhamma foundation is the last in the series of four, it clearly indicates that we don't begin practice by directly understanding the objects in relation to the four noble truths. In the beginning, we focus on their content in the conventional sense and only gradually begin to understand the life-historical objects as dhammas of the four noble truths.

The last foundation repeats the entire vipassana practice. The meditator is first instructed to meditate on "dhammas as dhammas" in the five hindrances to meditation; then on "dhammas as dhammas" in the five aggregates of clinging; next, on the six spheres of object stimulus (i.e., the processes of perception); then on the seven factors of enlightenment; and finally on the dhammas in the understanding of the four noble truths.[9] For all practical purposes, the factors of enlightenment are synonyms of the spiritual faculties.[10] The many overlaps between these categories are a characteristic of the mnemonic structure in the canon. Nor does the order of the categories reflect a structure of progressive advancement in meditation, as is the case with the seven purifications (*visuddhi*), which I explain in chapter 11.

The Five Hindrances as Dhammas

The balance between five spiritual faculties can be invaded by the five hindrances (*nivarana*). They are conditioned by the unwholesome roots and include, as previously mentioned: (1) reactive involvement with sensory pleasures, especially sexual impulses, but also all forms of rapturous desire that eliminate the equanimity of mindfulness toward the object; (2) anger and condemnation; (3) sloth and torpor; (4) restlessness and worry; (5) and doubt and skepticism. In samatha, the development of strong concentration is a resource to suppress the hindrances when they arise. In vipassana, however, the hindrances are more often dealt with by understanding them as dhammas—that is, as momentarily changing, potentially painful, and identity-less states. Since this is the crux of insight meditation practice, it makes sense to start the explanation with a summary of the hindrances, which are merely thoughts, emotional states, and feelings that *become* hindrances when they are not understood as dhammas. The use of mental notes is particularly effective in managing the hindrances, which can activate strong emotions.

The hindrances are to be understood both as character traits that can prevent a person from even taking the initiative to examine the mind and as impulsively invading states within someone who is already meditating. It is in the latter context that their handling is reviewed here. If we are present with our personal obstacles from the moment they invade meditation, it is possible to become absorbed in them as objects of an intuitive investigation of the mind. We gain experience of how the specific hindrance derails meditation. We may also gain insight into the causal conditions in our biographical context that activate the hindrance so that we can prevent the hindrance from arising in the future, and if it has arisen, it will be easier to dismantle it with an appropriate measure. In this way, meditation on recurring hindrances leads to deep insights and cultivates a more profound and resilient meditation practice.

Without Clinging to Anything in the World

The full mnemonic formula for the foundation of mindfulness with "the body as the body" is the recurring instruction in vipassana in the *Satipatthana Sutta* with the necessary changes that adapt the formula to each of the other foundations. Again, the essence of the instruction is repeated at the end of the review of the five aggregates, the six spheres of object stimulus, the seven factors of enlightenment, and the four noble truths. Each time the insight into the rise and fall of dhammas is repeated both regarding the meditator's introspection and interaction, the necessity to dwell in independence as "an island" is emphasized. The many repetitions of course serve the mnemonic purpose, but certainly also to bring the main point home with as much clarity as possible—and as the matter stands, across more than two millennia.

> Again, meditators, a meditator abides continuously absorbed in observation of dhammas as dhammas in terms of the four noble truths. And how does a meditator abide continuously absorbed in observation of dhammas in terms of the four noble truths? Here a meditator understands as it actually is: "This is suffering"; she understands as it actually is: "This is the origin of suffering"; she understands as it actually is: "This is the cessation of suffering"; she understands as it actually is: "This is the way leading to the cessation of suffering."
>
> In this way she abides continuously absorbed in observation of dhammas as dhammas internally, or she abides continuously absorbed in observation of dhammas as dhammas externally, or she abides continuously absorbed in observation of dhammas as dhammas both internally and externally. Or else she abides continuously absorbed in observation of dhammas in their nature of arising, or she abides continuously absorbed in observation of dhammas in their nature of vanishing, or she abides continuously absorbed in observation of dhammas in their nature of both arising and vanishing. Or else mindfulness that "there are dhammas" is simply established in her to the extent necessary for bare knowledge and mindfulness. And she abides independent, not clinging to anything in the world. That is how a meditator abides continuously absorbed in observation of dhammas as dhammas in terms of the four noble truths.[11]

Munindra-ji often quoted Buddhaghosa's dictum that the four foundations of mindfulness are, in reality, pieces of the same reed. One part of the reed could therefore define the whole practice of insight meditation. In that case, it would certainly have to be the *foundation of mindfulness with dhammas as dhammas of the four noble truths*, as elaborated by the review in the next chapter.

9 | The Four Noble Truths

> Soon after his awakening, the Buddha was staying at Uruvela (present-day Bodh Gaya) on the bank of the river Neranjara at the foot of the Bodhi tree. There the Buddha sat cross-legged for seven days without moving, experiencing the bliss of freedom.
>
> —from the Vinaya, the *Theravada Collection on Monastic Law*

This fragment is from the account in the Vinaya Pitaka, which follows the events of the Buddha's life narrative but is now told by someone other than himself. According to the account, the Buddha spent the first four weeks under different trees, in each place delighting in the joy of liberation, and in between reflecting conceptually on the incomparable boon of enlightenment. Several theorems in the psychology of meditation are attributed to an origin in the Buddha's meditation under these trees. The guidance in the four foundations of mindfulness and the theorem of the five spiritual faculties were, according to the account, hatched under the goatherds' banyan tree near the Bodhi tree. But toward the end of the fourth week, the Buddha began to doubt whether it was worth the effort to spread the teachings to others. Nevertheless, he eventually felt compassion for "living beings with little dust in their eyes."[1] He therefore wandered from Bodh Gaya to Sarnath, to Isipatthana, the "Resort of the Seers," which was one of the most famous hermitages for samanas in the days of the Buddha.

Buddha's First Sermon

The Buddha gave his first sermon, "Setting in Motion the Wheel of the Dhamma Sutta," here. It was two months after his enlightenment and on the full-moon night *asalha* (July-August), which is the night before the monsoon begins in North India, according to the lunar calendar. The Buddha began the speech as the flickering sun of the drought sank below the horizon. The glowing, very red full moon, heralding the delivery of the rainy season in northern India, rose heavy and magnificent in the tropical night sky. At precisely this propitious moment, the Tathagata set the dhamma wheel (*dhamma-cakkha*) in motion with the exposition of the four noble truths and of the middle way, "which gives rise to vision, which gives rise to knowledge, which leads to peace, to direct knowledge, to enlightenment, to nibbana."[2] This is the first time he refers to himself as Tathagata. The audience is made up of five seasoned ascetic kinsmen who had earlier accompanied him in the mountains outside Bodh Gaya, and who had meanwhile arrived at the Resort of the Seers. After some hesitation, the ascetics themselves achieve enlightenment, partly after the first sermon and partly after the Buddha's second sermon, which goes into detail about the three universal characteristics of the phenomenal world: anicca, dukkha, and anatta. Despite the special character of perfect buddhahood, there was, as already mentioned, no difference in the degree of liberation which Buddha Gotama and his disciples attained. The exposition of the four noble truths is identical throughout the canon, whether the Buddha is speaking of his own enlightenment or instructing others on the path to liberation. To aid memory, the truths are formulated as a diagnostic model from ancient Indian medicine, a model that was known to all educated people in the Buddhist era. The first noble truth about suffering, dukkha, is the diagnosis. The second noble truth about the cause of suffering is the etiology of the disease. The third noble truth about the elimination of the cause of dukkha clarifies the prognosis for recovery. And the fourth noble truth states that the recipe for the necessary medicine is just the noble eightfold path. Motivated by this analogy, the Pali canon occasionally describes the Buddha as a great healer who heals humanity's affliction of existence.

The First Noble Truth

Basically, all impermanent existence is dukkha (etym., "bad hollowness"). It can best be explained as the absence of an unchanging substance core in the psyche and body and what this biological and psychological process condition entails of suffering and surrender to the vicissitudes and conditioning of the body and mind, over which the self (with a small *s*) is not the master. In this view, everything must be said to be dukkha, potential or actual.

> And this is the noble truth of suffering [dukkha]:
>
> birth is suffering, old age is suffering, sickness is suffering, death is suffering, association with what is disliked is suffering; separation from what is liked is suffering; not getting what you want is suffering. In brief, the five aggregates subject to clinging are suffering.[3]

In brief, it is a diagnosis of the dukkha of change and conditioning.

The Misperceiving Separated Individual

Who is the patient? It is a person who, in Western translations, is often referred to in vague terms as "an ordinary average person" (*puthujjana*). But the term *puthujjana* has a specific meditative psychological meaning, for which I propose the translation "an illusorily separated individual." The puthujjana is an ordinary person who misperceives their psychological separation from the stream of consciousness (*vinnana-sota*) because they perceive as permanent what is impermanent, because they perceive the potentially painful as a source of pleasure, and because they perceive the self in what is the non-core self. Because of their "distortions" (*vippallasa*) in perception, consciousness, and thinking, they live in an upside-down world. They try to create coherence in their separated world (*loko*) through the distorted narrative of being a static self (*sakkaya-ditthi*) that can and should exercise dominion over itself in all of life's circumstances. And this illusion becomes a source of much suffering.

> She regards consciousness as self, or self as possessed of consciousness, or consciousness as in self, or self as in consciousness. That consciousness of hers changes and becomes otherwise. With the change and becoming otherwise of that consciousness, her consciousness is preoccupied with the change of consciousness. Agitated states of mind born of preoccupation with the change of consciousness arise together and remain obsessing her mind.[4]

And it is the same as regards the change and becoming otherwise of the four other aggregates that are subject to clinging in the six processes of perception.

The Seed of Anguish

Any clinging to the misperception of a static core of the self results in a fetter that has the seed within it of change suffering (*viparinama-dukkhata*) that can be actualized in real suffering when the object ceases. *Dukkha* is often translated into Western languages as "suffering." But all aspects of the five aggregates are characterized by dukkha, including those pleasurable states that aren't, of course, painful at the same time. Because it is clear if the five aggregates that are subject to clinging were completely painful, dulled by pain, and untouched by pleasantness, then the mind wouldn't find delight in those five aggregates.[5] However, attention is often enraptured by pleasure. We must therefore distinguish between the *seed of suffering* in the changing objects, thoughts, emotions, and sensations, especially the pleasant ones when consciousness clings to them; and the suffering and dissatisfaction that is *actual* when the pleasure ceases, depending, of course, on the meaning of the pleasure to us. But one thing is for sure: It is impossible for the illusorily separated individual not to lose whatever they attach themselves to. They lose their youth, health, relationships, opportunities, love, abilities, money, prestige, hope, and so on. Finally, they lose themselves in the processes of aging, illness, and death. It is a form of suffering that most people have had a dim awareness of since the first nightmares of childhood.

The Suffering of Change

The puthujjana knows very well that they aren't the same person today as they were ten or five years ago, or maybe just last year, but they only recognize that in the flashback of their memory. They don't see intuitively into the momentary change of their life situation and self-perception, *while* the changes take place in their thoughts, states of mind, and sensations. They don't understand the non-core-self implications of what is changing continually in their lives. They don't understand, as a direct experience, the stream of the universal norm, which is the entrance to the dhamma-faring that could free them from the anguish of the distortion of their perceptions. On the contrary, an instinctual uncertainty of the impermanence of everything charges their desire-thirst to fasten consciousness, as it were, "like the dye of lampblack," tenaciously to almost any delightful object, even as this delusion repeatedly actualizes the inherent anguish in what is changeable.

The Suffering of Conditioning

When consciousness clings to pleasure, it is simultaneously reinforcing the tendency to condemn unpleasantness and to ignore neither-nor in the same obscured view of the process of perception. We often naïvely think that unpleasantness goes away when we condemn it. But the involvement of hate with unpleasantness prolongs it and reinforces the illusory notion of the core self. Condemnation is thus the negative clinging aspect of desire-thirst, often also associated with a paradoxical reassurance-seeking pleasure that is in the illusion of permanent identity—even when it is painful.

The experience of the condition of unpleasantness and the experience of the cessation of pleasure are overlapping aspects of dukkha and expressions of the same existential "hollowness." As long as the pleasure lasts, we do not care that pleasure is also conditional. But when pleasure is replaced by the condition of unpleasantness, our surrender to conditioning becomes apparent. And we understand better that instead of an unchanging and autonomous self that exercises sovereign dominion over itself, there are only the changing processes and their impersonal lawfulness and conditions.

All existential problems that we would rather not experience because we have no control over them are obvious examples of change and conditioning suffering (*sankhara-dukkha*). This applies to all experiences of loss, depression, anxiety, and the pain caused by illness, the decay of the body, and finally the surrender to death.

Seeing into Mental Conditioning

A banal orientation about potential suffering of conditioning is experienced when the mind wanders off with a random thought away from our intended focus. Being distracted isn't something we intend to be. But suddenly we experience the conflict between our intention and the surrendering to an impersonal process. We may condemn ourselves for not being in control of the wandering thought, thus identifying with being at the mercy of our conditioning, but there is only the conditioning and the changeability—and no core self to condemn. In meditation, a deeper insight into the suffering of conditioning arises when we begin to see into the karma accumulations of past desire-thirst for an unchanging core self in the life-historical contexts embedded in our long-term memory. We see into the past activity patterns of clinging, condemnation, and perhaps repression of various life-historical episodes, which become conscious with cutting clarity in deep meditation. We begin intuitively to understand the dark side of the mind: the contaminating influxes (*asava*) of ignorance, desire-thirst, and hatred; the activation of defilements (*kilesas*), their latent tendencies or negative character traits (*anusaya*); and larger organizing sangsaric templates (*samyojana*) for bondage at work in the mind. They are all the basis of the potential and actual suffering of mental conditioning.

The Painful Suffering

The actual aspects of suffering activate the entire repertoire of distressing feelings and emotions, which can be despairing and unbearable. It is a matter of sadness and depression over the losses that have occurred in the past and the fear and unease of being at the mercy of the losses that will occur in the future. It is furthermore about all the difficult ego-centered emotions, such as guilt, shame, anger, jealousy, envy, despair, regret, embarrassment, and so on, to which the state of misperception of a separate ego in the stream of consciousness is potentially subject. And, indeed, it is also about the hardships of old age, illness, and death. This plain suffering of painful emotions and feelings is called *dukkha-dukkhata*, which literally means "painful suffering."

The Buddha declares that all the general and personalized aspects of dukkha falling within the first noble truth must be fully, intuitively understood in insight meditation.[6]

The Second Noble Truth: On the Cause

Introspecting in vipassana the life-historical contents of the first noble truth, the illusorily separated individual gets to understand that it is because of clinging to the "distortions" of their mind that they are at the mercy of the three kinds of suffering that bind them to the despairing treadmill of loss and privation.

> And this, meditators, is the noble truth of the origin of suffering:
> the craving that leads to rebirth, that comes with delight and sensual desire, ever delighting in this and that,
> that is, craving for worldly pleasures, craving for existence, and craving for non-existence.[7]

In the Buddha's sermons, the detailed exposition of the second noble truth is often unfolded with an understanding of the causal relationships between desire-thirst and ignorance in the six processes of perception. This condition is shown by the theorem of dependent origination, while the third noble truth about the elimination of the cause of suffering is explained by the deconditioning of the process as it evolves in the practice of vipassana.

Dependent Origination

Both accounts of dependent origination belong to the first conceptual reflections of the Buddha immediately after his enlightenment. In the standard version, the theorem accounts for the relations between the unwholesome karma action and the fruition through any three periods of before, now, and later in the stream of perceptions in the present life. At the same time, the theorem shows the coherence of a biological rebirth series that cross-connects past life, present life, and potential future life. In the Abhidhamma, the two series are called karma-becoming (*kamma-bhava*) and re-becoming (*punabbhava*). The Pali term *punabbhava*, which translates into Western languages as "rebirth," literally means "re-becoming"—that is, of the stream of consciousness according to the conditions of karma. The series are intertwined, since karma-becoming in the process of perception—which is associated with ignorance—always contains the seed for rebirth in the big picture. Dependent origination is a cornerstone of the Buddha's teachings and is expressed in the visual arts as Buddhism's renowned "wheel of life."

Structural Ignorance

Whether one puts ignorance or desire-thirst as the primary cause of dukkha in the process of dependent origination amounts to the same thing: "Not to understand suffering, its origin, its cessation, and the path leading to its cessation: this is called ignorance."[8] In this broad sense, ignorance is simply the definition of a lack of enlightenment. It is the fetter that is deeply rooted in the illusorily separated individual. When they are dealing with the wholesome or unwholesome root conditions of the awake perception process, they do so with the structure of ignorance and desire-thirst as either the root condition (for unwholesome action) or the support condition (for wholesome actions).

The first two conditions of dependent origination, ignorance (*avijja*) and formative karma activities (*sankhara*), refer to this structural ignorance of the unenlightened consciousness. The conditions are the results of past ignorance and specific acts of karma from either an immediately previous process of perception of karma, a long time ago, or both. This implies, in the receptive phase of perception in the present, that:

> consciousness is the condition for mentality and the senses; mentality and the senses are the condition for the six sense spheres of object-stimulus; the six sense spheres of object-stimulus are the condition for object-stimulus; stimulus is the condition for feeling.[9]

All these passively formed activities are co-arising in the receptive phase of present perception. The object-stimulus is *not the objective content of an object*—for example, a burglary in one's home—but the passively formed quality of perception, which indicates that *what is seen* in a visual process in the present is *the way of seeing* as conditioned by past karma.

The Thief's Hand

Feeling is the culminating focus in the process because vedana carries out the function of "tasting" the quality of experience, as previously explained. Metaphorically speaking, it is at this point in the unwholesome karma phase that "the thief's hand" is reaching out for the object in the present:

> feeling is the condition for craving; craving is the condition for grasping; grasping is the condition for existence. . . . This is how there is the origin of this whole mass of suffering.[10]

The standard formulation of dependent origination highlights desire-thirst ("craving" in the below quote) as the root condition for the karma phase, as this formulation also refers to the final reaction in the death process that leads to rebirth for the unliberated. The absolute opposition to precisely these conditions is synonymous with full enlightenment.

> With the end of craving comes the end of grasping; with the end of grasping comes the end of existence; with the end of existence comes the end of birth; with the end of birth comes the end of old age and death, the end of sorrow, lamentation, pain, aversion, and distress. This is how there is the end of this whole mass of suffering.[11]

Thus the distorted ego-becoming (or "existence" in the above quote) in the karma-becoming series ceases, and at the end of life, the rebirth series also comes to an end. According to the tradition in the Vinaya Pitaka, the structure of the theorem, in forward and reverse order, was due to the first conceptual reflection by the Buddha right after his experience of enlightenment that broke the chains of sangsara with the complete elimination of ignorance and desire-thirst.

> Seeing the significance of this, the Buddha uttered a
> heartfelt exclamation:
> "When things become clear
> To the energetic brahmin who practices absorption,
> Then all his doubts are dispelled,
> Since he understands the natural order and its conditions."[12]

If sangsara is to be transcended, all that the second noble truth comprises of ignorance and "thirst" must be "eliminated."

The Third Noble Truth: About Cessation

> And this, meditators, is the noble truth of the end of suffering: it is the full fading away and ending of that very desire-thirst; giving it up, relinquishing it, releasing it, letting it go.[13]

For, despite the structural ignorance of the mind, the illusorily separated individual has the ethically free will to choose the wholesome root conditions of the waking perception process and begin to develop insight into the four noble truths. Just as the great ocean gradually deepens, so too does the development of insight gradually revert the order and consequence of dependent origination—and decondition and liberate the mind from structural ignorance. The term *cessation* (*nirodho*, "non-prison") is one of many synonyms in the suttas for the transcendental nibbana, which is precisely the absolute meaning of the third noble truth when ignorance and desire-thirst are fully eliminated. But like several other buddho-meditative synonyms for nibbana, *nirodho* also has a psychological and developmental meaning, referring to the insight meditative course of deconditioning ignorance and desire-thirst, which I detail in chapter 9, through the "seven purifications" (*visuddhi*).

Disillusionment, Fading Away of Clinging, and Liberation

It is sufficient for now to clarify that the effect of disillusionment with the structuring of life history with the illusory notion of a core self has a powerfully liberating impact on the puthujjana's mind. Sometimes in the suttas, the cause of disillusion (*nibbida*) is stated to be the insight into the three universal characteristics (anicca, dukkha, anatta). Other times, insight into the conditioning of the life story is mentioned, fully or partially described with "the turning-around" in dependent origination. Both descriptions are standard in the suttas. The impact of disillusion and disenchantment piles in the mind on a life-historical level, the "raw material" of which is made conscious in ever larger and intuitively more comprehensive contexts of the meditator's mental conditioning. *Simultaneously*, this conditioning is understood in the penetrating insights of anicca, dukkha, and anatta.

> Seeing thus, monks, the instructed noble disciple becomes disenchanted with form, disenchanted with feeling, disenchanted with perception, disenchanted with volitional formations, disenchanted with consciousness. Becoming disenchanted, he becomes dispassionate. Through dispassion [his mind] is liberated.[14]

Just as an awake person who sees a snake hanging down from overhanging leaves doesn't grasp at the snake believing it to be a branch, insight consciousness no longer grasps at the objects of misperceived self-identity but draws back from them and thus brings about a state of "fading away of clinging" (*viraga*), which sees the mind *as it really is*. Therefore insight consciousness no longer identifies with the objects, and the equanimity of liberation (*vimutti*) develops. The episodic raw material of the meditator's life story, which has been conditioned by the *wholesome* root conditions of karma, is also made conscious in the process, although these activities are without misperception of ego and are therefore only deconditioned for their relativized association with structural ignorance. According to this understanding, overcoming the past lives' fetter of ignorance does not presuppose an awareness of all the karma of past lives. Fortunately, it is possible to eliminate fetters of past lives through the deconditioning of present life accumulations that bind the present life to the fetter. And all the karmic patterns made conscious by meditation, which are root or support conditioned by ignorance, cease when they are fully understood intuitively. In fact, *viraga* also means "fading away of karma." In this process, the self-narrative changes drastically due to the meditator's de-identification with the episodes and the many psychological insights into the life story.

Gradually the karma conditions of the misperception of "separateness" run out into the sand, leaving nothing but the wisdom and remembrance of healing. This does not mean that the meditator gets amnesia for the life-historical episodes that are deconditioned but that nibbida, viraga, and vimutti are the beginning of *the tracklessness* in the meditator's self-understanding. According to the sutta, all that the third noble truth encompasses of nirodho must be fully intuitively penetrated.[15]

The Fourth Noble Truth

The last of the four noble truths explains the "medicine" that cures the patient.

> And this, meditators, is the noble truth of the way leading to the end of suffering: just this noble eightfold path; that is, right view, right intention, right speech, right action, right livelihood, right effort, right mindfulness, right concentration.[16]

Despite the lofty spiritual goal of the noble eightfold path, the path has its origins in everyday consciousness. According to the Abhidhamma, it is true for all wholesome states of mind, including the non-meditative ones, that they are states of mindfulness (*sati*) that relate with a degree of equanimity (*upekkha*) to the object. These wholesome states are without "distortions" because they are non-egocentric states without clinging, condemnation, or ignoring. However, despite the absence of ego-referring misperceptions, the non-meditative wholesome states are without any deep continuous observation (*anupassana*) of the objects and therefore without the power of liberating insights into the three universal characteristics. This is especially due to the lack of samadhi, which is the result of the methodical development of the five links of absorption—for example, in breathing meditation—and which, in balance with properly immersed mindfulness, activates the insight-qualifying intuitions.

But the non-meditative states, which are conditioned by all three wholesome roots, contain the seeds of all the thirty-seven dhammas pertaining to enlightenment (*bodhipakkhiya-dhamma*), which through the noble eightfold path are methodically developed from the non-meditative soil of equanimity and everyday mindful presence.[17]

The Buddha's Spiritual Testament

In the last sutta prior to the final nibbana at his death, the Buddha refers to the thirty-seven enlightenment dhammas as his spiritual legacy.

> And what are those dhammas I have taught from my direct knowledge? They are the four foundations of mindfulness, the four right efforts, the four bases to accomplishment, the five spiritual faculties, the five spiritual faculties as powers, the seven factors of enlightenment, and the noble eightfold path.[18]

As has been seen from the review of these theorems, all the theorems are "threads" that emanate from the noble eightfold path. The many synonyms are examples of the contextualization by the Buddha's instructions to different people around the Ganges Plain during his lifetime—and as an expression of so many ways of clarifying the path out of compassion. It isn't necessary here to summarize the investigation of each "thread." But, for example, "right view," the first link of the path, is identical with "the spiritual faculty of intuition." It has the character of the enlightenment factor "intuitive investigation of dhammas," which in every practical sense includes "concentration of intuitive investigation" as a base for accomplishment, the goal of which in vipassana is nibbana, and thus the transformation of the spiritual faculty of intuition into "a power."

When the Buddha so often in the suttas emphasizes that the dhamma is lovely in the beginning, lovely in the middle, and lovely in the end,[19] he points toward an uplifting understanding that every step on the noble eightfold path contains within it the seeds of all the psychological qualities, moral virtues, and spiritual conditions of the Buddha's teachings, the development of which leads to liberation. For this reason, the Buddha said that, just like the great ocean has but one taste of salt, his teaching is all about liberation. In other words, these thirty-seven dhammas are the great ocean that gradually deepens as a metaphor for the entirety of the Buddha's teachings during the insight meditation process.

The fourth noble truth—which is the noble eightfold path—must be "developed," and in Buddhism development (*bhavana*) means meditation.[20]

10 | Enlightenment and Liberation

When dukkha is understood with intuitive wisdom in any of its aspects, such as impermanence or conditioning, the cause of dukkha, which is craving, is abandoned. As such, the deconditioning of the cause, the disillusionment, and the letting go of clinging are intuitively penetrated while the path develops. The perceptions of the four noble truths increasingly occur at the same time as absorbed awareness in the process of deep insight meditation.

When the insight-meditative mind becomes disillusioned in the proactive phase of the perception process, intuition turns away from the misperception of objects. When disillusionment culminates, intuition turns toward the unconditioned and objectless nibbana. In the meditator's karma phase, this will initially mean "that his consciousness no longer enters into or settles down on or resolves upon any field of formations at all, or clings, cleaves or clutches on to it, but retreats, retracts and recoils as water does from a lotus leaf."[1]

In what will be the ultimate buddho-meditative polarization between the expansion of the spiritual faculties and the culminating disillusionment and disenchantment that causes insight consciousness to sink and yield from the six doors of perception—

where anicca, dukkha, and anatta are seen with overwhelming clarity—consciousness turns toward nibbana that transcends the very *sphere of consciousness*.[2]

Non-Manifestative Consciousness

In the moment before the breakthrough, the insights into anicca, dukkha, and anatta have the character of "three gateways to liberation,"[3] through which the flowing insight consciousness "enters into nonarising . . . enters into cessation, nibbana. . ."[4] through one of the insights in which expansive illumination culminates. This is the "entering into" that the Buddha describes as "non-manifestative consciousness,"[5] which is paradoxically "infinite" and "luminous," in which the mind's ingrained fetters, bonds, and inflows of ignorance are irreversibly eliminated, either totally or partly, with a force "like a tree struck by a thunderbolt."[6]

In their enlightenment, the meditator intuitively sees to the bottom of and through the stream of consciousness. The "thirst" for hallucinated immutability in the fleetingly changeable is forever quenched by the transcendental insight into the deathless (*amata*).[7] The fully enlightened one who eradicates all ten fetters at once will be an accomplished one, an arahant.

Transcendence of Dependent Origination

However, the transcendental direct experience cannot be explained or accommodated by a conceptual or symbolic expression, since all language and imagination are conditioned by the impermanent and conditional origination of becoming. The unconditional, causeless, and uncreated nibbana is completely beyond any process. The negation of all twelve relations in the theorem of dependent origination therefore belongs to the mnemonic formalities in the description of enlightenment.

This does not mean that the arahant's physiological processes cease in enlightenment, but that transcendence of the perception series is at the same time a guarantee for the attainment of the definitive cessation of the rebirth series at the end of the life span.

This also means that the causal processes in this life in the mind of the arahant are subsequently merely functional and not karmically productive anymore (see below). In the suttas, the surmounting of biological re-becoming is always declared to be the subject of the enlightened one's first reflection of the emergence of the stream of consciousness after the transcendence: "Destroyed is birth." This statement refers not only to future rebirth but also to the elimination of illusorily and hallucinatorily *ego-becoming* in the remaining life of the fully enlightened person.

Nibbana, the Deathless State

Although the whole of the Buddha's teaching is thematically about how to overcome ignorance and desire-thirst, the Buddha refrained from philosophizing about the transcendental absolute. However, there are meaningful expressions spread throughout the suttas.

> Nibbana is directly visible, immediate, inviting one to come and see, applicable, and to be personally experienced by the wise.[8]

And nibbana is characterized by the three characteristics of the unconditioned:

> No arising is seen, no vanishing is seen, no alteration while it persists is seen. These are the three characteristics that define the unconditioned.[9]

And

> This is peaceful, this is sublime, that is, the stilling of all activities, the relinquishing of all acquisitions, the destruction of craving, dispassion, cessation, nibbana.[10]

Furthermore,

> It is not something fixed, / it moves not on, / it is not based on anything.[11]

And

> Nibbana is happiness.[12]

And of course,

To the list of synonyms for nibbana can be added: *the subtle, the safe*, *the wonderful*, *the refuge*, and *the end goal*.

Blown Out

There are several etymological layers to the concept of nibbana. It is, in one interpretation, it is the cessation of desire. In another interpretation, the concept means "blown out," which refers to a blacksmith's bellows in the sense that the fire goes out when the bellows cease, and desire, hatred, and ignorance are this very fire. According to another interpretation, the concept of nibbana means the cessation of the weaving of the process activities (*sankhara*). Several similar interpretations are possible. Furthermore, viraga (fading away of clinging), in an absolute perspective, is another synonym for nibbana, just as cessation (*nirodho*) is.[13]

A Nirvanized Mind

In addition, the concept of nibbana is used in a secondary and ethical-psychological sense of the liberated person's stream of consciousness, which is "here now cooled and extinguished (*nibbuto*)"[14]—that is, sangsarically "blown out" because of the elimination of desire-thirst, hatred, and ignorance, although the liberated person still lives in the world with its valleys and mountains.

> The destruction of greed, the destruction of hatred, the destruction of delusion: this, friend, is called nibbana.[15]

The arahant is still living in the world, but when all ten fetters are eliminated in enlightenment, their stream of consciousness is no longer associated with the structure of the ignorance/desire-thirst cycle. This means that their perceptions and actions no longer flow within the law of karma, with its binding relation to the sangsaric cycle, and therefore are said to flow in a causal context that is purely functional (*kriya*).[16] Their consciousness flows "above the world" (*lokuttara*)[17] in the sense of insight consciousness that doesn't cling to and identify with the objects, whereby the "world" (*loko*) otherwise arose for the illusorily separated individual. It implies that the actions of the enlightened person are "pure doing" (as *kriya* can also be transcribed); or that the actions, sangsarically speaking, are "non-acts"—that is, they are karmically inoperative activities in accomplished insight-meditative emptiness (*sunnata*) or thusness (*tathata*). According to the Abhidhamma's overview of types of consciousness, the karmically inoperative types of consciousness of the arahant that flow "above the world" (*lokutarra*) are schematically identical to the wholesome types of consciousness of the unenlightened person.[18] The former are merely kriya, due to the complete elimination of structural ignorance, and greatly expanded as a result of the irreversible integration of the thirty-seven enlightenment dhammas as the normal state of the liberated mind.

The Immeasurable Deliverance of Mind

The mind of the arahant, in all its psychological purity and existential clarity, has "become the universal norm" (*dhamma-bhutam*). This means that the mind has been transformed into a continuously unhindered experience of what is general and universal about consciousness, freed from its "dark" side. That is why the Buddha says, "One who sees the universal norm [*Dhamma*] sees me. The one, who sees me, sees the universal norm."[19] The arahant lives in the wholeness of the freed stream of consciousness—unhindered by ignorance, hatred, or desire-thirst—and experiences emptiness and thusness without obstruction. For this reason, liberation is also known as "the immeasurable deliverance of mind."

Transformation of Spiritual Faculties

The five spiritual faculties are irreversibly transformed into faculties, like powers (*bala*), as the enlightened person's normal state of consciousness with its transcendental range. The enlightened one is able, whenever they wish, to transcend the stream of consciousness again and dwell in unconditional nibbana for up to a day at a time. This is the arahant's fruit-attainment (*phala-samapatti*),[20] which can be repeated as often as the enlightened person wishes. The enlightened person exerts mastery over the primordial paradox of the universal norm: Their experience encompasses the pure phenomenal stream and the transcendental non-location of consciousness. Their mind is paradoxically grounded in what is without foundation (or location) and has an all-radiating opening toward the infinite and unconditional.

Enlightenment and Memory

The functions of consciousness still operate in causal contexts, and perceptions are thus also accumulated in the enlightened one's memory, even though in Western Buddhist literature, one sometimes comes across the assumption that the mind of the enlightened person is beyond cause and effect. That is not so. Memory and perception are constituents of human consciousness and, in this sense, have nothing to do with the law of karma. Imagine the dilemma that would have faced the five hundred arahants who gathered and committed to memory the Buddha's sermons during the First Council following his passing, had the enlightened ones been unable to accumulate memories or recall "what they heard." On the contrary, the enlightened mind is endowed with a very expansive and plastic memory that can easily be developed to recollect the knowledge of past lives, as we shall see in chapter 15.

Enlightenment and Equanimity

The two elements of nibbana, which I have outlined, are called the element of nibbana with residue—that is, the five aggregates that are now freed of clinging—and the element of nibbana with the elimination of the five aggregates, which is the final nibbana (*parinibbana*) at death. But if the aggregates have not gone, the enlightened mind continues to experience the agreeable and disagreeable, to feel pleasure and pain.[21] Even though the process of becoming subjectively ceased in the transcendental experience, the stream of the five aggregates reemerges after enlightenment because of reproduction karma (see chapter 15) from the last biological process of rebecoming. This karma cannot necessarily be eliminated here and now since it is expressed in the form of a body and a lifetime of such and such a length of time. The ending of desire-thirst, hate, and delusion in the arahant is thus the element of nibbana with a residue.[22]

The mind of the enlightened one is unfathomable like the ocean,[23] at the same time as their perception processes are precisely "functioning" within the six spheres of object-stimulus, but without being influenced in a sangsaric way by desirable or undesirable objects. Thus, the liberation of the monk Sona Kolivisa, who had just been enlightened and explained to the Buddha how his mind had changed:

> It is as if, Lord, there were a rocky mountain slope without a cleft, without a hollow, of one mass, and as if wild wind and rain should come very strongly from the eastern quarter—it would neither tremble nor quake nor shake violently; and as if wild wind and rain should come very strongly from the western quarter . . . from the northern quarter . . . from the southern quarter—it would neither tremble nor quake nor shake violently. Even so, Lord, if shapes cognizable by the eye come very strongly into the field of vision of a monk whose mind is wholly freed . . . [if sounds, smells, tastes, touches come very strongly into the field of the respective perception] . . . if mental objects cognizable by the mind come very strongly into the field of thought of a monk whose mind is wholly freed, they do not obsess his mind, for his mind comes to be undefiled, firm, won to composure, and he notes its passing hence.[24]

This unshakable equanimity (*upekkha*) is Buddhism's ideal of happiness. It is like the rock that is not moved by the storms but is easily moved by compassion, love, and other pure acts as ethical expressions of the flow of the universal norm. The liberated mind is no longer able to respond with ignorance, craving, and hatred. It stays equanimous no matter what it is exposed to, and it's an equanimity that is not merely grounded in samadhi as in the jhanas but in the irrevocable eliminations of the fetters. The enlightened one is neither someone who causes harm to themselves nor to others but is here now soothed and *nirvanized*, or *cool-become*, and one who lives in pure delight with the process self *greatly developed*.[25] The life of the Buddha serves as a profound example of how a fully liberated mind can actively and meaningfully engage with the world. After attaining enlightenment, the Tathagata, or the "Thus-Gone One," devoted the final forty-five years of his life to traveling across northern India, sharing his teachings with anyone willing to listen. His message, delivered with deep compassion and unshakable clarity, has endured for over two millennia. This timeless wisdom teaches us how to free ourselves from the illusions of the ego—letting go of our attachment to temporary pleasures and our fears of loss and discomfort—so we can act with true freedom, guided by kindness and genuine care for ourselves and for others. The Buddha's clear and unaltered voice continues to illuminate the path to mental development, helping us see the world as it truly is.

The Untraceability of the Tathagata

After biological death, the enlightened person becomes completely nirvanized (*parinibbuto*). They advance from the phenomenological arena permanently and slip into nibbana without a residue,[26] also called the final nibbana (*parinibbana*)—that is, with the permanent cessation of the five aggregates. However, this has no effect on nibbana at all: "even if many meditators attain final nibbana by way of the nibbana element without residue remaining, neither a decrease nor a filling up can be seen in the nibbana element."[27]

This is the culmination of the dhamma-faring. It would be a misunderstanding to think of nibbana as the immortality of the soul, as absolute death in the Buddha's teaching is not anyone's death. Whether an enlightened person exists after death, or is nonexistent, or both exists and does not exist, or neither exists nor does not exist after death—all are mere speculations, empty fantasies.[28] The Tathagata himself is "untraceable" even in this life.[29] The tracklessness was precisely the accomplished arrival of the Tathagata.

The Four Stages of Enlightenment

However, it was only people "with a little dust in their eyes" and a great accumulation of merit from past lives who eliminated all ten fetters in the first insight into nibbana and thereby at once attained the limitless emancipation of the mind. If the fetters are deeply rooted, then five or seven of them will be reactivated by the power of "the reproduction karma" in the stream of consciousness after transcendence. In these cases, the liberation attained is limited, and it is necessary to further develop the path at a higher level of partial liberation. In most cases, the meditator must go through a total of four path processes, each time culminating in the transcendental realization with the weakening of the remaining fetters until their complete elimination is attained.

There are thus four stages of enlightenment, or arahantship.[30] Since the doctrine of liberation is woven into the notion of rebirth, the purity and extent of the first three stages of enlightenment are also weighted according to the number of remaining rebirths that the partially liberated person must go through, unless they purposefully strive to develop all path processes in their contemporary life and therefore won't be reborn if they attain them.

Any of the three partial liberations, however, entails a transformation of consciousness to such an extent that whether the partly liberated person strives in seclusion or lives normally in the world, sooner or later their consciousness will inevitably flow through the subsequent higher path processes. If the meditator has been predisposed to the first level of arahantship, then they will eliminate the first three fetters in the first insight into nibbana. Of these fetters, the conceptualized illusion about the core self (*sakkaya-ditthi*) is, as previously mentioned, the most important, since this fetter keeps all other fetters linked together in the psychological sphere of the illusorily separated individual and their sangsaric world. Meditators who eliminate the first three fetters have once and for all been disillusioned with their illusorily separated world and cannot be tied to it as before. "They have entered the stream of the dhamma"—that is, the stream of the universal norm[31]—and are therefore called stream-enterers (*sotapanna*). The winning of the dhamma stream refers to the accomplished insight into *aniccata*, "momentary impermanence," being from then on an insight that is irreversible and effortless. However, the stream-enterers have yet to accomplish the insight into dukkha and anatta at the level of an arahant. The stream-enterers haven't yet arrived but are ensured arrival.

11 | The Seven Purifications

In many of the Buddha's sermons, monastics are encouraged to settle under a tree to meditate. A tree is the ideal dwelling for one who goes "from home to homelessness" (*pabbajja*), which is the term for a layperson's transition to life as a monk or nun in the sangha. Even after the establishment of monastic communities in several places around the Ganges Plain, many members of the sangha continued to live under a tree in the forest or in small groups in hermitages far from the monasteries, as is still the practice in Buddhist countries. For when the student has received an instruction, typically for the beginner, precisely in meditation on the breath, "she resorts to a secluded resting place: the forest, the root of a tree, a mountain, a ravine, a hillside cave, a charnel ground, a jungle thicket, an open space, a heap of straw.

On returning from her almsround, after her meal she sits down, folding her legs crosswise, setting her body erect, and establishing mindfulness before her."[1]

Intensive meditation is practiced today under almost the same simple conditions in prolonged withdrawal from the world, where the meditator dwells "like an island unto herself" (or "like her own lamp") to spend time meditating from early morning until late at night for weeks or months at a time. Since the earliest time, the sangha has been a community of meditative individualists, intensely focused on developing insight into the mind. This was the purpose of the monastic order, which had no cultic functions. Many monastic communities today exist in a Spartan and almost timeless atmosphere because of the rules established by the Buddha for the regulation of the order.

Your Good Friend

To begin with, the most important advice for any meditator, both in the past and today, is to seek out a good spiritual friend, a *kalyana mitta*, as described in the Buddhist tradition. A spiritual friend is someone who understands where you are on your spiritual journey and where you aspire to go. With this understanding, they can guide you step-by-step through the terrain to the mind's Bodh Gaya.

> Meditators, this is the forerunner and precursor of the rising sun, that is, the dawn. So too, meditators, for a meditator this is the forerunner and precursor for the arising of the noble eightfold path, that is, good friendship. When a meditator who has a good friend, it is to be expected that he will develop and cultivate the noble eightfold path.[2]

I was so lucky that Munindra-ji became such a good friend to me. He was teaching at the Gandhi Ashram just across the Maha Bodhi Temple in Bodh Gaya but later moved to the Burmese Vihara at the outskirts of the village. It was a monastery with a rest house for Burmese pilgrims, but because of the political turmoil in Burma, no more pilgrims were coming. The *mahathera* (great elder) of the vihara—the loveable, cigar-smoking Venerable Buddha Baba, who always had exorbitantly good humor—generously opened the vihara for Munindra-ji and his students. Meditation huts in the large, lush garden and on one of the flat roofs of the monastery soon popped up. It was a makeshift meditation environment but centered around a highly qualified teacher.

Modern Masters

With his characteristic generosity, Munindra-ji invited the Indian expatriate teacher S. N. Goenka in 1970 to teach at the Burmese Vihara in Bodh Gaya, which Goenka-ji subsequently did several times. Goenka-ji's way of teaching was based on a recent Burmese vipassana tradition that emanated from Ledi Sayadaw,[3] who in Burma is known to be the one who popularized vipassana for the laity. In this simplified approach, the focus is primarily on the so-called body scan of tactile sensations. Munindra-ji, with an open mind, invited his students to "sit" on a retreat with Goenka, something I did at Sarnath in 1969. This was Goenka-ji's first retreat in English following his exile from Burma. Goenka-ji, who did not have the same Buddhist academic background as Munindra-ji, recommended his students seek out Munindra-ji for clarification of complex theoretical Abhidhamma questions. There was no rivalry between these two masters, and the influence of their presence in Bodh Gaya at that time can hardly be overestimated from the point of view of Western Buddhism. From the late sixties until the mid-seventies, Bodh Gaya was an important place for Westerners in search of Buddhist enlightenment when it was next to impossible for political reasons to travel to Burma, where vipassana teachings experienced a veritable renaissance because of several remarkable teachers. It is especially the line of teachers from Mahasi Sayadaw who have spread the classic vipassana, the pragmatic simplicity of which has been the catalyst for the mindfulness wave that has swept through the West in the last decades. It was in this line that Munindra-ji taught, and this approach forms the basis of my account, as it is rooted in the canon for the development of insight into "the All," as the Buddha says.[4] Thus, the meditation involves not only an awareness of sensations but also immersion in the inner psychological, life-historical flow of thoughts and mental states.

The Stations of Purification

The dhamma journey is very concretely mapped out with the description of seven purifications (*visuddhi*), which the Buddha illustrates with the parable of a traveler who changes horses at each of seven stations to cover the next stretch with a rested horse before reaching the journey's goal.[5] The purifications include (1) morality (*sila*), which entails at a minimum the observance of the five *sila* with the aspect of celibacy during the period of retreat. Next, (2) purification of insight-qualifying concentration as described in previous chapters. Purifications 3-6 encompass the specific vipassana process with insights into the four noble truths. The seventh visuddhi is the insight into nibbana with winning of the fruit of stream entry and the irrevocable elimination of the first three fetters. The seven purifications are the subject of comprehensive and often very nerdy scholastic reflections in extracanonical literature. I will only describe the main line of the meditative experience according to the nine *vipassana-nanas*, insight stages or intuitive knowledge that develop with purifications 3-6. These insight stages are described in a scripture attributed to one of the Buddha's chief disciples, Venerable Sariputta, also known as the Dhamma General.[6]

Beginning Vipassana

Vipassana is often developed from breathing meditation, which branches out in the sitting to focus flexibly on the flow of many different objects of the everyday mind. This gradually and naturally involves all four foundations of mindfulness in the development of the course of insight. At the outset, it is not easy to remain absorbed in introspection of the flow of spontaneously arising thoughts, feelings, and emotional states of mind for long periods of time. It is difficult because of the mind's disposition to cling to objects with a pleasant feeling tone, condemn those with an unpleasant tone, and often neglect objects with a neutral feeling tone, activating drowsiness and boredom. Because the life-historical stuff of these deeply ingrained reactive habit patterns is conditioned by past karma, the mind tends easily to stray from the present moment on extended excursions with diverting ideas and stories. This happens in all types of meditation but especially in vipassana because the objects of meditation are our everyday mind, the content of which is changing constantly. If mental notes are applied at least to some extent, the objects initially flow more easily into states of equanimity (*upekkha*), where any activity of clinging, condemnation, or drowsy neglect is more quickly disconnected. As previously mentioned, the use of mental notes is a characteristic of the learning phase of the Mahasi Sayadaw method.

The Arising Moment of Change

When I began insight meditation, Munindra-ji said that it was important to sharpen the focus on the moment of *arising of each object*. After several sitting sessions, I perceived this moment with increasing clarity, while the moment of cessation remained blurred by the arising of the next object in line, which now suddenly imprinted itself with surprisingly prominent clarity. For example, I clearly perceived the arising of auditory awareness the moment a distinct sound captured my attention. If a thought about the sound arose, the moment of the thought's arising was perceived as very prominent as well. If the thought aroused a significant feeling, such as irritation or unease, my attention was immediately sharpened on the arising of where and how the feeling of discomfort arose in my body. I could observe this process with complete mental equilibrium, without reacting, even when, for instance, outsiders came chatting loudly on a sightseeing tour in the vihara and seemed to believe there was something very interesting to see in the meditation hall where I sat with six to seven others. It was annoying but also eye-opening to meditate on.

I gradually became very aware that my experienced world consisted of only six separate perception processes, as awareness could only immerse itself in the clear insight of one perception process at a time. Buddha refers to this simple fact as our "whole world." I had of course understood this theoretically before, but I had never consciously experienced it from moment to moment with such clarity nor with the unaffected equilibrium resulting from this awareness. The mind cannot immerse itself mindfully in two focus points at the same time. It is the mindless short circuit that causes us to lose our lives in the sense of the parable of the bowl, and which had probably often caused me to "spill" when I had reacted blindly and inappropriately to experiences it was better for me to have focused on with unwavering equanimity—as I now was capable of.

The All

The objects' arisings imprinted themselves with great clarity on my mind, simply because I cultivated an intention to focus on this moment. I frequently incorporated standing meditation into my walking meditation practice. I observed the swaying wind in the treetops, the grass, and the bougainvillea bushes. I focused on even the slightest movements in my visual field, as well as the movements of other meditators as they walked. It was like watching clouds drift across the sky—no single impression stayed the same. As I stood, I also listened to distant voices, the sound of birds in the trees, or a song fading far away in the village. Each sound's arising, changing, and fading away, no matter how trifling, was so clear, harmonious, and intimate. By practicing presence in this way between sitting meditations, I quickly enhanced my development of insight, and gradually all three aspects of anicca perception became naturally prominent. I transitioned effortlessly into the flow of the next sitting meditation, and I was soon able to sit for two hours or more. Between sittings, I maintained the development of samadhi and insight, and consequently I experienced at one point that the meditation seemed almost effortless. Mahasi Sayadaw says of this wonderful state,

> As a result, mindfulness seems as if plunging into an object that arises. The object, too, seems as if it is alighting on mindfulness. One comprehends each object clearly and singly. Therefore, the meditator then believes, "Bodily and mental processes are very swift indeed. They are as fast as a machine or an engine. And yet, they can all be noticed and comprehended. Perhaps there is nothing more to know. What is to be known has been known." He believes so because he knows by direct experience what he has not even dreamt of before.[7]

This surprisingly deep activation of insight into the dhamma stream is the learning phase of the first stage of "intuitive knowledge of arising and cessation" (*udayabbaya-nana*). Going with "the bowl" into all contexts of the mind in long sittings took place within the third visuddhi, the purification of view. You don't understand anatta at this stage, but your general orientation in life begins to drastically change, especially in relation to your self-perception. At this stage, the view that is refined is primarily based on conceptual reflections.

When I stopped constantly shifting my body and chose to sit intentionally still for longer periods, I opened up to the bag of bodily pains and the experience of how fragile the body really is. However, if you adjust your position every time discomfort arises, it interrupts the process of building concentration. A key step in learning meditation is at one point deciding to sit still, even when it's challenging. The way to deal with these raw sensations of pain is to first check whether the pain has altered the deep, slow breathing at the abdomen, and if so, to get the breath back down in the relaxed way of breathing. As the next step, concentrate on focusing and intentionally relaxing into the pain area where the body is tensing up. The pain may not go away completely, but insofar as we observe the pain for a while in a state of relaxed, mental acceptance, it often gets easier to ignore the pain—just parking it, as it were. Up to a certain point, the body adapts to sitting motionless, and gradually sitting pain does not occur at all for considerable periods of time.

The Insight into Life History

I spent seven months on my first retreat with Munindra-ji. I began to have many life-historical insights as deeper layers of my accumulated karma patterns became conscious with the development of samadhi and the clarity of the insight. In the beginning, these patterns arose in compositions of very different layers of my life history. But increasingly I dwelt on the insight of the specific relation between this and that (*idappaccayata*) in the coherent flow of biographical episodes and the general existential conditions that I realized I had been at the mercy of in my life. Beginning with the stage of "intuitive insight into arising and cessation," anicca, dukkha, and anatta constituted a deepening cycle of insights with spontaneously changing insight angles from momentary change to the suffering of change, conditioning, and non-core self. Munindra-ji instructed me to focus strictly on the general characteristics of the mental content, not on the content itself. Like "a skilled man drilling a gem with a tool watches and keeps in mind only the hole he is drilling, not the gem's color, etc., so too the meditator wisely keeps in mind only the ceaseless dissolution of process activities, not (the content of) the process activities."[8] Because I was very concentrated, I couldn't avoid being even more aware of the content than the nonmeditative mind that focuses only on the content. But the priority of my focusing was increasingly on the spiritual insights into anicca, dukkha, and anatta. I still found the intermittent application of mental notes very useful. It reminded me of the distancing from the content of the objects when I sometimes became too focused on the content. For now, in deep introspection, I began to see with astonishing clarity how my mind had been and was conditioned by past karma patterns, partly directly (as the fruit of karma) and partly indirectly (as an accumulated support condition for new karma patterns). I intuitively became aware of the interconnected entirety of a multitude of things that had happened to me biographically and existentially in these causal contexts. I began to understand the suffering of change and mental conditioning as both potential and actual aspects of the first noble truth. To the same extent, I understood the second noble truth about ignorance and desire-thirst that caused the hallucinations and illusions of immutability, source of joy, and core self. And because of my disillusion and disenchantment with the distortions of my life history and the consequent fading away of the clinging (*viraga*) to these perceptions, I penetrated the third noble truth about the abandonment of the cause of dukkha. In all of this, to the extent that I developed the five spiritual faculties, my mind dwelt "in continuous absorbed observation of dhammas as dhammas in terms of the four noble truths."[9]

I also learned that each time my mind was reactively involved with the pattern of objects, the attachment to the pattern was strengthened. But each time my attention de-identified itself from the objects, the pattern was weakened and the objects diminished in karma strength. This was a continuous process that I could not help but notice changed the perception of my life story both in the past and present.

> When, meditators, a carpenter or a carpenter's apprentice sees the impressions of his fingers and his thumb on the handle of his adze, he does not know: "I have worn away so much of the adze handle today, so much yesterday, so much earlier"; but when it has worn away, he knows that it has worn away. So too, when a meditator is intent on development, even though he does not know: "I have worn away so much of the influxes [*asava*] today, so much yesterday, so much earlier," yet when they are worn away, he knows that they are worn away.[10]

Gradually the karma accumulations were deconditioned. Gradually the spaciousness and mental balance of whatever I meditated on increased. Deeply conditioned karma patterns with branching dukkha content that had been woven into an ingrained belief of a wounded life-historical core identity led to many profound realizations. This spontaneously involved increasingly larger contexts in the insight cycle accompanied by deeper disillusionment and cessation of clinging. And all these created lucid insights and great enthusiasm in my mind.

We were usually six to seven meditators sitting together in the cool, windowless hall located in the center of the main building of the vihara. But by and by we followed our own schedules in the surrounding rooms or in the kutis in the garden and only met randomly during the walking meditations outside. In the beginning, the whole group gathered every day for an interview with Munindra-ji about the practice. But over time, the interview shifted to each of us talking with Munindra-ji whenever and wherever we encountered him—on the stairway, in the garden, on the roof, or even on the road to the village. It was very informal, very friendly, and immensely inspiring. We all felt that we had a very special relationship with him, which is precisely what defines the kalyana mitta—in the sense that the Buddha had talked about himself as being just his disciples' good friend.

Corruptions of the Insights

At this stage, I began to experience a strong emotional attachment to the Buddha's teachings—a feeling that I will call piety, a feeling of reverence—a feeling that had been completely foreign to me until then and that I had previously only referred to with irony. I also seriously began to consider entering the monastic order. Between sittings I found myself in a state of unshakable mental equanimity, completely free of thought and relieved of all existential heaviness. My insight into instantaneous changeability was profound and seemingly flawless. During the sittings I experienced a huge aura of orange light. Occasionally a white light burst forth as if coming from far away and struck my interior with a powerful radiance. Spontaneous tears of joy trickled down my cheeks while shivers of well-being ran zigzagging across my skin, all over my body and scalp. Sometimes I felt elation, as if I were physically floating freely in the air. These so-called *piti* states are well known from the samatha meditations, where they intensify the absorption in the object. But in vipassana, where the opposite is aimed for—namely distancing from the object through insight into the universal characteristics (anicca, dukkha, anatta)—these euphoric states easily become obstacles.

In vipassana, the phenomena are called "agitation about higher states of intuitive insight," and they distort the clarity of insight.

The inner light is referred to as pseudo-nibbana because it leads some meditators to imagine that they have experienced nibbana. Even my sense of reverence was categorized in a manual as an outcome of this "agitation." In fact, it was common at this stage to want to study Pali and to be ordained and talk about it (rather than just embarking on the next sitting). With Munindra-ji's help, I became very aware that I was identifying with the noble eightfold path. I had to let go of these euphoric spiritual states of mind, which are also anicca, dukkha, and anatta. All of this takes place in the fourth visuddhi, "the purification by overcoming doubt."

Knowledge of What Is Path and What Is Not

I began to sharpen my attention on the least perceptible moments of the arising of the phenomena of light, upliftment—and even the felt sense of equilibrium I tried to distance myself from—with the same meticulous care you walk with the bowl filled to the brim, moving slower and slower to be more present with the slightest flowing movement.

Working assiduously in this way with unperceived micro-moments of changeability of light and upliftment, the fourth visuddhi slipped into the fifth, where the light and euphoric side effects of insight ceased. Buddha Gotama defined the ideal of this absorbed, unbound, and buoyant awareness of insight for his son Rahula, who became enlightened at age twenty:

> Like unto space, Rahula, practice meditation. For Rahula, by practicing meditation space-wise, the contacts that have arisen—acceptable and disagreeable—will not continue to obsess your mind. Just as the vault of heaven, Rahula, is not attached to any place; even so yourself, Rahula, like the vault of heaven, practice meditation.[11]

This instruction illuminates the transformative power of recognizing subtle micro-moments of change, paving the way for a seamless transition to minor stream entry that occurs between the fourth visuddhi and the fifth, the purification of intuitive knowledge of what is path and what is not. The vault of heaven that doesn't cling to anything, that doesn't feel aversion to anything, or neglect any object—it is the path itself. Knowing this means "the overcoming of doubt." It signifies the mature stage of the first *nana* (of arising and cessation) with effortless sittings of several hours and completely flawless insight into all three moments of changeability. Although the three moments of aniccata of the object of insight are present to varying degrees from the beginning of the entire insight-meditative process, the moments are seen continuously and flawlessly only at this stage. It marks the end of the learning phase of vipassana and the beginning of the minor stream entry—and the purification by the course of practice, which is the sixth visuddhi.

Insight into Dissolution

Just as this wonderfully flowing process gained momentum, the second nana of insight, "intuitive insight into dissolution" (*bhanga-nana*), emerged with amazing suddenness from one moment to the next—and the first stage changed abruptly in one and the same sitting. The moment of cessation of the object appeared longer and longer, and suddenly the moment of the arising of the next object became imperceptible—everything was perceived in one flowing cessation. Until then the insight had been at the object level. Now the cessation of insight consciousness was intuited right after the cessation of perception of the object—by the proceeding moment of consciousness. The object dissolved into micro-moments of cessation from the same moment the object arose, and in the same flow the cessation of the knowing consciousness was intuited. This insight was now constantly evolving at all doors of perception. I tried to fixate the perception of the shape of the door in the cell, the window, a book lying in front of me on a table, but it was impossible—everything was formless—and at the time it was amazingly peaceful. Mahasi Sayadaw comments on the insight into the dissolution of dhammas:

> It is like seeing the continuous successive vanishing of a summer mirage moment by moment; or it is like the quick and continuous bursting of bubbles produced in a heavy shower by thick raindrops falling on a water surface; or it is like the quick successive extinction of oil lamps or candles, blown out by the wind, as these lights are being offered at a shrine by devotees.[12]

When it was a full moon in Bodh Gaya, large choirs from the villages broke out in *kirtan* singing to swirling tabla drums, which filled the air with vibrations until midnight. I stood one such evening on the flat roof of the monastery under the October full moon, marking the end of the rainy season, as Buddhist monks once again wandered among the hermitages in Buddha's days. That evening I felt a particular restlessness and depth in my psychological "homelessness," which I now referred to as my "project." Until then, I had a dim understanding of the core self of nothingness, without being completely convinced of the mind's inherent emptiness—in my particular case. This doubt now felt like an air image: "Only formations break up; their breakup is death; there is nothing else at all."[13] That was precisely how I saw and felt it. The five aggregates that are subject to clinging are really "like murderers with raised weapons."[14] That was exactly how I began to see, feel, and think about it. These thoughts appeared objectively depressive, but the insight at that time was clarifying and peaceful, even though it didn't evoke joy like the first stage of insight. However, the second nana of insight into dissolution now quickly slipped through three subsequent stages (*nanas*), which Buddha summed up as the third noble truth's deep disillusionment with the mind.

The Readjustment of the Mind by Disillusionment

The three stages are called "intuitive insight into fear," "intuitive insight into danger," and "intuitive insight into disillusionment" (*nibbida-nana*). These three knowledges, or stages, are aspects of the culminating process of disillusion and disenchantment that the Buddha so often refers to when the meditator sees the three universal characteristics. They are sometimes referred to in Western books on vipassana as "the long dark night of the soul." This is a term originating from the Catholic mystic Saint John of the Cross and has nothing to do with Buddhist insight meditation but refers to a state of hopelessness in the Christian mystic who, after a long period of solitude in prayer, suddenly feels abandoned by God. The Christian mystics were obviously not practicing vipassana, and these three insight knowledges are about something else. In bhikkhu parlance, the stages are called "the phase of rolling up the mat" because vipassana monastics in the East have traditionally tended to roll up the meditation mat at this point and quietly disappear from the monastery in the dead of night. This sense of existential panic stems from a continuously accumulated understanding of the painful and unsettling nature of change. The realization can feel overwhelming because it challenges the unconscious mind's basic assumptions about life. It's at this point that resistance emerges—a strong, almost instinctive reaction to an insight that threatens to upend one's previous understanding of self and existence. I experienced bewilderment during the sittings, which I constantly interrupted, only to immediately return, although without being able to find tranquility. It was as if the concentration suddenly became dysfunctional, as if the clarity had been lost, as if the insight had the character of suffocating negativity.

> Just as a line drawn with a stick on water will quickly vanish and will not last long, so too, meditators, human life is like a line drawn on water with a stick. It is limited and fleeting.[15]

In truth, very briefly. I saw it now—not just at once, but all the time. This knowledge remained the fundamental insight throughout the rest of the process, and it is still with me to this day. But back then, I was overwhelmed by what the Buddha had called "the six kinds of grief based on renunciation" (*nekkhamma*).[16] If the attitude of samvega were divided into steps, the "grief of renunciation" is the subtle stage, because one understands that *everything* in the past, present, and future is subject to the condition of immediate change, disappearance, and cessation. Then arises with each of the six processes of perception the grief of renunciation, conditioned by a longing for liberation. At that time I made the decision to spend the rest of my life in meditation.

It was not like the enthusiastic desire to become a monk that I had experienced during the euphoria of the first insight stage. Instead, my decision sprang from the necessity of liberation from *all* attachment to the impermanent, which seemed to me like a nightmare.

On the other hand, I knew how I could awaken. This was my symbolic pabbajja, my spiritual journey into "homelessness." This was the great existential tree I had sat under in India, and I had no doubt for a moment about how I could awaken from this nightmare.

One of the first Western Buddhist monks in the East, the German Bhikkhu Nyanatiloka—who founded a meditation monastery on a lagoon island in Sri Lanka at the beginning of the last century and where I later spent nine months—wrote about "homelessness," that it consists of the severing of all familial and social ties to live the pure meditative life in the realization of the ultimate goal of liberation, as pointed out by the Enlightened One.[17] It is one of those moments of the dhamma-faring when experiencing the spiritual intimacy of a kalyana mitta, is a strong resource. Munindra-ji's eyes sparkled with cheerfulness when I told him that the thought of sneaking away from the retreat in the dead of night had just crossed my mind. But where to? His warmth suddenly felt like the most inspiring validation of what was, realistically speaking, a significant progress on my path—right after the book by the Dhamma General himself, Venerable Sariputta. My mind was as restless as a heap of ashes in the wind; my body felt heavy like a stone, and I felt completely down in the dumps. Yet I managed to concentrate on observing my thoughts and decided to meditate all night.

In the days that followed, my mind worked through the next two stages of insight, carried by a powerful, almost electric flow of energy, as if meditation were borne onward by itself, knowing in depth each micro-moment. Once again, I walked with the "bowl" of presence late into the night, fully present in each step. I returned to long sitting meditations that lasted several hours, where I felt a deep sense of calm, trust, and clarity. I continued to see the line drawn on the water in everything I observed, but now my mind seemed to have taken an unwinding step back, allowing insight to effortlessly and peacefully flow. Everything was indeed one, even that which was not, without it making a difference. It was the eighth sublimely liberating stage, *intuitive knowledge of equanimity* about formative activities (*sankharupekkha-nana*), that I had arrived at.

Equanimity

Developing equanimity is a steadily progressing process from the very beginning of insight meditation, just like disillusionment and the fading away of clinging are closely related to the intensive development of the five spiritual faculties.

> When, by knowing the impermanence, change, fading away, and cessation, of forms of sounds, of odors, of flavors, of tangibles, and of mind-objects, one sees as it actually is with proper wisdom that both formerly and now are all impermanent, suffering, and subject to change, equanimity (*upekkha*) arises.[18]

But *sankharupekkha-nana* denotes the establishment of equanimity, grounded in the accumulated experience of insights into the universal characteristics of the unity and interconnectedness of all things—in immediate changeability—where everything is one without the one—and I experienced the immense arch of the noble eightfold path opening within me.

> It's as if the meditator doesn't need to make any additional effort. Previously, due to insights into the dissolution of formations, immediately one after another, the aspects of fear, danger, (dejection of) disillusionment, the desire for liberation, and dissatisfaction with the knowledge gained so far arose. But these states of mind "no longer arise even though, in the present state too, the breaking up of formations which are dissolving more rapidly is closely perceived."[19]

The retrospection patterns of karma and their summation into life-historical wholes of the four noble truths are of a particularly enriching nature at this stage because of the sublime tranquility that is in the mind. When Munindra-ji confirmed my attainment of the stage of *sankharupekkha*, he also told me, "You will see everything that has ever happened in your life." And it was true. In books on Buddhism, the importance of biographical insights in the dynamics of vipassana is often not given much attention, perhaps because they somehow are considered at odds with the teaching of non-self. But it is my experience that universal insights are the most transformative in life-historical insights. This kind of timeless, effortless, and serene meditation that goes on and on is experienced in jhana with no indication of a life-history context or insight other than into the expansive vastness of the phenomenon of consciousness. In contrast, in vipassana, one experiences extraordinarily rich layers of episodic memory with a wealth of details that are easily understood intuitively in the context of anicca, dukkha, and anatta.

> Even when the meditator thinks about something fearful or sad, no mental disturbance will arise, be it in the form of fear or sorrow. This, firstly, is "the abandoning of fear," at the stage of "Equanimity toward formative activities." At the earlier stage on attaining "Intuitive insight into arising and cessation," great joy had arisen on account of the clarity of insight. But now this kind of joy does not arise, even though there is present an exceedingly peaceful and sublime clarity of mind belonging to "equanimity about formative activities." Though he actually sees desirable objects conducive to joy, or though he thinks about various enjoyable things, no strong feeling of joy will arise. This is "abandoning of delight" at the stage of "equanimity about formative activities."[20]

Here the ground is measured for the rock of equanimity in Buddhism, the foundation of happiness that cannot be moved by the storms. This is the stage that at the right time culminates in the "fruit of stream entry."

The Course of the Practice in Retrospect

Although it is always difficult to say anything about how long it takes to develop a meditative state, which depends entirely on individual disposition and practice, the following can be outlined: Virtually all motivated individuals can develop incipient momentary samadhi in a relatively short time on a retreat. During the following intensive practice, most people attain the first nana of intuitive insight into arising and cessation. And though this stage is not flawless, it is at the stage where biographical karma accumulations begin to appear in continuous perspectives. The stage is long-lasting, and it isn't possible to say anything concrete about the length of time. It depends entirely on the baggage of the meditator, in which respect no two minds are alike. It is at the end of this stage that the learning of vipassana ends, culminating in the flawless stream of insight that characterizes "minor stream entry" either as a "confidence practitioner" or a "wisdom practitioner" (see below).

In comparison, the second nana of the inception of insight into dissolution (*bhanga-nana*) is short-lived, and the transition process of insight into *fear, danger, and disillusionment* is even shorter. Taken together, in intensive practice on a retreat, the meditator typically goes through these nanas over the course of a week. The two subsequent stages, "desire of deliverance" and "knowledge of reobservation," are correspondingly short-lived. On the other hand, the stabilizing and maturing stage, which denotes the nana of equanimity about formative activities (*sankharupekkha*), is the longest-lasting stage of the process leading up to the fruition of stream entry.

In terms of time, Munindra-ji said, if the meditator has originally been motivated by a personal pain to meditate intensively, then the motivation for intensive practice often decreases when the meditator achieves the stage of equanimity about formative activities. The meditator now experiences a clarification and mental equilibrium that does not depend on the vicissitudes of concentration but on the self-insight achieved. The meditator who has realized that "the All" is continuously and instantly changeable does not later fall back into disorientation about this existential reality. And what is deconditioned in insight meditation is not reactivated again. This transformation of the mind is due to the development of penetrating insights that are not based on intellectual analysis or belief.

12 | Stream Entry

I once asked Munindra-ji what happened when he experienced nibbana. At that time, I had been living with him for three years. We spent the hottest time in July that year in a monastery outside Kalimpong at the foot of the lower Himalayas. He was staying in a huge teak building along a winding road. I was staying in a stone cabin farther up the mountain with a view of the silvery misty wall of Kanchenjunga opposite. In the afternoon, I came down from the mountain and had lessons in Abhidhamma with Munindra-ji.

He looked at me with amusement and replied, "I died. Oh, how painful that was." He began laughing his contagious laugh, such that his body was trembling, and I had to laugh along with him, even though I didn't know what I was laughing at. I had asked because at that point in time we were going through the theory of stream entry according to Buddhaghosa's great fifth-century meditation manual.

Purification by Knowledge and Vision

The able meditator will, at the right time, bring the development of the sixth visuddhi, "purification by knowledge and vision of the course of practice," to completion with the ninth stage (*nana*) of insight, called "knowledge of adaptation to the truth." It happens in one all-pervading penetration of insight in which the culmination of the thirty-seven dhammas that lead to enlightenment converge in a single breakthrough (*abhisamaya*)[1] and, as mentioned in chapter 10, the angle of insight according to which one of the three insights in anicca, dukkha, or anatta the meditator has been disposed to deepen in the process. Here Mahasi Sayadaw, who had been Munindra-ji's teacher in Rangoon, comments:

> That act of noticing any one characteristic out of the three, which has a higher degree of lucidity and strength in its perfect understanding, becomes faster and manifests itself three or four times in rapid succession. Immediately after the last consciousness in this series of accelerated noticing has ceased, *magga-phala* (path and fruition) arises, realizing nibbana, the cessation of all formations.[2]

In this way, the dhamma-faring of the minor stream-enterer ends with the seventh visuddhi, the purification by intuitive knowledge and vision (*nana-dassana-visuddhi*), which in this context is a synonym for the transcendental nibbana insight and the attainment of fruition of stream entry.

Path and Fruition

According to the model of understanding in the Abhidhamma, which is used in connection with the Burmese vipassana method, the indescribable "non-manifestative," "infinite," and "all-radiating" entering nibbana of the stream-enterer is formulated with the technical terms "change of lineage" and "path and fruition."[3] All three terms mean nibbana. The first term refers to the elimination of the psychological sphere that takes place once and for all for the illusorily separated individual. When nibbana is intuited, the consciousness of the partly enlightened person flows after enlightenment in the sphere of the "noble" and "above the world" (*lokuttara*) of deluded separation from the flow of the stream of consciousness. The second term, *path*, is Abhidhamma speak for the transcendental elimination of fetters—namely the first three fetters out of a total of ten. The "path" in this sense arises only once, because the fetters eliminated by enlightenment do not need to be eliminated again. In contrast, the third term, *fruit*—which is also nibbana—means that nibbana can be reexperienced as often as the stream-enterer wishes, just as was the case with the arahant's fruit. These are all very technical terms, but as we become serious vipassana meditators, we want to know about this. In other spiritual traditions such terms typically would be classified as "esoteric" knowledge, but in Buddhism sharing these terms is an expression of "the open hand" of the Buddha.

The Fixed Course of Rightness

The accomplished stream-enterer, whom Munindra-ji cheerfully called *maha-sotapanna* (the great stream-enterer), has attained the first degree of arahantship and the first degree of "nibbana with the residue left" (*sa-upadesesa-nibbana*). They have attained the structural stream of the noble eightfold path with all that it entails in terms of psychological ease and freedom. They dwell "independent of others in the Teacher's dispensation."[4] The Buddha compares the amount of unwholesome karma that is deconditioned and "worn away"—partly in the process leading up to transcendence and partly in the transcendental "blown-out-ness" of the mind—to a mountain of waste that has been removed, while what remains is comparable to just seven grains of gravel the size of mustard seeds.[5]

The accomplished stream-enterer has not only eliminated the first three fetters: the illusion of the core self (*sakkaya-ditthi*), doubt and skepticism about the dhamma-faring, and the belief in the significance of rituals for the purification of the mind; in addition, the stream-enterer has also weakened the two fetters of sensual desire and hatred to such an extent that they are free from the underlying tendencies (*anusaya*) of jealousy/envy (*issa*) and stinginess (*macchariya*). If they are not a monastic, they dwell "at home with a mind devoid of the stain of stinginess, freely generous, and open-handed, delighting in relinquishment, one devoted to charity, delighting in giving and sharing."[6]

The stream-enterer has seen the ocean of the dhamma. Their spiritual faculty of confidence (*saddha*) is therefore transformed into a power (*bala*); and their confidence in the Three Jewels—Buddha, Dhamma, and Sangha—is unshakable and inalienable: "They possess the virtues dear to the noble ones—unbroken, untorn, unblemished, unmottled, freeing, praised by the wise, ungrasped, leading to concentration."[7] Because of the path's relatively effortless progress, the stream-enterer's future is "fixed in destiny, with enlightenment as their destination."[8] The perceptual psychological fruit of stream entry is the almost effortless insight into the flow of the noble eightfold path as the partially liberated mind's normal state. Whether the stream-enterer strives further in seclusion or lives the everyday life among common people, their consciousness will sooner or later pass through the subsequent higher courses, win their fetter-eliminating path, and finally be established in consummate arahantship.

The Dhamma Eye

Many bhikkhus and bhikkhunis, as well as laypeople of both sexes, in the spiritual milieu in the days of the Buddha were declared to have attained accomplished stream entry. On one occasion, when many lay followers died because of an epidemic in the market town of Natika in the Kosala country, five hundred of these good people were stream-enterers. Many other lay followers had won even higher paths, according to the Buddha's clairvoyant inspection of their death and rebirth processes.[9]

The stream-enterer has a comprehensive understanding of anicca, but to let go of all clinging, their insight into dukkha and anatta needs further deepening. The stream-enterer develops these insights at the level of the path, leading to the fruit of the next level of liberation, the so-called once-returning. Meanwhile the "once-returner" completes the path that leads to the fruit of "non-returning," and the "non-returner" completes the path that leads to the fruit of arahantship, full enlightenment.[10] Each of these courses is nevertheless identical to the nine stages, or nanas, that the minor stream-enterer traverses but now at the respective higher levels of an attained path. The fruit at each path—which is nibbana—can be reexperienced, while elimination of fetters needs to be worked through by the nine stages as described in the previous chapter. Many members of the order developed all four paths in one and the same life. For example, the Buddha's chief disciple, Venerable Ananda, attained full arahantship twenty-five years after his stream entry, while another chief disciple, the Dhamma General, Venerable Sariputta, became an arahant only a week after eliminating the first three fetters. Attaining stream entry is also described in the suttas as attaining "vision of the dhamma" (*dhamma-cakkhu*, what I call "the eye of the universal norm").[11] With the attainment of this vision, one is irrevocably opened to effortless insight into the stream of the dhamma. A fixed formula is used to describe this experience:

> Just as a clean cloth with all marks removed would take dye evenly, so too, while the householder Upali sat there, the spotless immaculate vision of the dhamma arose in him: "All that is subject to arising is subject to cessation." Then the householder Upali saw the dhamma, attained the dhamma, understood the dhamma, fathomed the dhamma; he crossed beyond doubt,

> did away with perplexity, gained intrepidity, and became independent of others in the Teacher's dispensation.[12]

The accomplished stream-enterer realizes this in absolute terms: "'Whatever has the nature of coming to be, has the nature of passing away'—thus, being convinced at the time of transcending, he is known to transcend at one stroke the five aggregates."[13] This happened to the layman Upali while he was still sitting in front of the Buddha, who had just instructed him in the four noble truths. It also happened to Kondanna, one of the early five *samanas*, at the end of the Buddha's first sermon in the Resort of the Seers. This sudden enlightenment is mentioned in many suttas. It was assumed to be a possibility when face-to-face with the Buddha, but it was always about people of an unusual spiritual disposition, and a summary of the preceding circumstances is hardly totally improbable. Others became enlightened after a long, strenuous pursuit—for example, Sona Kolivisa spent three months continuously sitting and walking without sleeping leading up to enlightenment.

The Major Versus the Minor Stream Entry

In comparison, the minor stream-enterer (*cula-sotapanna*)[14] finds themselves somewhere along the noble eightfold path as described in the previous chapters, but without having either developed a complete course or relieved the mind of the entire weight of the first three fetters and all the biographical karma accumulations of "waste." The minor stream entry is a *functional* stream entry that is the prerequisite for attaining the fruit of stream entry (nibbana) and the dhamma eye. However, only the "great" stream-enterer has irrevocably achieved the *structural* transformation to the effortless flow of the noble eightfold path, along with all that it entails in terms of psychological freedom.

The concept of the minor stream-enterer is postcanonical. There is no scriptural concept like "a great stream-enterer" to clarify the distinction from "the minor stream-enterer." But the Buddha declares that already at the level of a dawning understanding of anatta, the meditator who is not yet a stream-enterer has won a fixed determination to liberation and is "one who has entered the fixed course of rightness, entered the plane of superior persons, transcended the plane of the worldings [puthujjana] . . . incapable of passing away without having realized the fruit of stream entry."[15] This insightful meditator is referred to by the Buddha in several suttas as a "confidence practitioner" (*saddhanusari*) or a "wisdom practitioner" (*dhammanusari*). The first is motivated to practice predominantly by confidence (*saddha*) in the teachings, the second by wisdom. Both have won "the fixed course of rightness,"[16] which over time inevitably leads to the fruit of stream entry.

The perception of the gradual ending of the illusorily separated individual's "world" dovetails with the suttas' perception of the gradual development of the path, whereas the Abhidhamma's categorical view of the transition in just a moment from the puthujjana to the sotapanna emphasizes the irreversibility of stream entry. But the suttas don't mention *which* specific level of insight qualifies for "the fixed course of rightness." In contrast, Buddhaghosa applies the concept of minor stream entrance to the meditator at the end of the fourth visuddhi, the purification of overcoming doubt. By then the meditator has gained a disillusioning insight into their mental conditioning and the illusion of a core self, and the meditator is beginning to experience the impact of deconditioning of distressing life-historical objects. According to Buddhaghosa, this meditator "has found comfort in the Buddha's dispensation, he has found a foothold; he is certain of his destiny, he is called a lesser stream-enterer."[17] Although the notion of the minor stream-enterer is not canonical, its meaning appears to align with the two categories of insight meditators on the path to the fruit of stream entry that the Buddha discusses. It is not unlikely that it was about this first informative perception of the stream of the dhamma that the Buddha uttered the solemn verse in the *Dhammapada*:

> Better than one hundred years lived
> Without seeing the arising and passing of things
> Is one day lived
> Seeing their arising and passing.[18]

This is because the ability to dwell on the insight into momentary changeability for a whole day signifies a high level of development that is of crucial importance for a person's meditative course and orientation in life. It's a fine definition of a minor stream-enterer.

13 | Practicing Loving-Kindness

At a vipassana retreat, metta meditation is often practiced alongside vipassana. This was always the case when Anagarika Munindra taught. Just as a bird needs two wings to fly, enlightenment of the mind requires both wisdom and loving-kindness, according to a traditional metaphor—and Munindra-ji's way of teaching was the embodiment of this image. The practice of loving-kindness in speech, action, and the way of earning a livelihood is the ethical foundation of the Buddha's teachings.

The Four Brahmaviharas

What is unique about the Buddha's view of love is not the emotion itself, which is basically universal, but the way it is learned and developed methodically as a meditation. Loving-kindness (*metta*) is the first meditation of the so-called four divine abodes (*brahmaviharas*),[1] which, in addition to loving-kindness, include compassion (*karuna*), empathetic joy (*mudita*), and equanimity (*upekkha*). Meditation is developed according to the samatha structure as described for breathing meditation, but with the difference that the objects predominantly consist of visualizations of people from one's life history, in which relation the emotion in question is developed. The development of each of the meditations culminates with the intention of encompassing all living beings in the four corners of the world. For this reason, the four brahmaviharas are also called limitless or immeasurable meditations, and they can all be developed to the level of jhanas.

There is a very close connection between metta and vipassana—as Joseph Goldstein has pointed out. Both wisdom and loving-kindness are without self-reference. Loving-kindness, says he, "is developed and expressed on the relative level of separate individuals, one being to another. And yet its highest manifestation comes from the understanding of emptiness, that there is no one ultimately there to be separate."[2] Next to the breathing meditation, the most widespread samatha meditation in Buddhism has always been the meditation on loving-kindness.

Taking Yourself as an Example

We begin the meditation by reflecting on egoless self-love as a guide to loving others. True self-love implies being able to see ourselves in others and to see others in ourselves, which is the prerequisite for genuine empathic connectedness. The meditator takes herself "as an example,"[3] as Buddhaghosa says: "Just as I want to be happy and dread pain, as I want to live and not die, so do other beings, too."[4] Next you focus on the mental image of a person who has been important to you in learning about the meaning of the goodness of loving-kindness. You recall a situation in which you were the object of someone else's unreserved loving-kindness, and you start from this specific memory and focus on visualizing the portrait of this dear person. It can be a situation with a parent, a child, a sibling, a grandparent, a nice aunt or uncle, or just a good friend—anyone with whom you share a history of loving-kindness that is egoless, desireless, and unreserved.

The Benefactor

The lovable person who vividly activates the attitude of loving-kindness in you will be your primary loved one, or "the benefactor," as Buddhaghosa calls the person. The benefactor is the icon for your sense of ethically unconditional loving-kindness—someone you'll return to in your meditation whenever you feel you lose contact with the meaning of the intention of metta and need to restore it. The benefactor should not be a deceased person whom you are mourning, because true metta is without associations of sorrow, which is a subtle form of aversion. Metta should be developed with a living person as the object. The iconic person must also not be a person with whom one has a sexual relationship—metta is a lust-free state of mind that, for this purpose, must not easily be invaded by erotic sensations. If you have a photograph of the beloved one, studying the photograph can sharpen the learning of the visualization.

Next, focus on the afterimage with your eyes closed, and think about the lovable qualities of that person. During the learning process, you may substitute the iconic dear person if you think you haven't found the right one. But after a while, you should make up your mind and stay with just the same person to enter the depths of your relation to this very important image of someone who will be your true teacher of love.

Structuring Metta Meditation

When the afterimage is clear, with the inner voice of the mind, begin to repeat without lip articulation the intention of loving-kindness with a felt sense for the unreserved meaning of the words directed toward the visualization of the iconic loved one. A fixed formulation of the statements is an important structure for developing concentration. The standard version of the intention that I learned from Munindra-ji goes like this: *May you be happy. May you be free of suffering. May you attain nibbana.* If perhaps the last statement doesn't immediately mean anything to you, you can instead wish that the loved one may live in peace. Nibbana is the psychological freedom attained through the irrevocable elimination of the unwholesome root conditions, as described previously. According to the Buddha, the highest happiness is found in a mind that, like a rock, is never moved by the storms of life and is therefore always spontaneously capable of embracing all with understanding, goodwill, and compassion. This is the portrayal of happiness by the enlightened mind, and you must formulate the intention with the words that make the most sense to you. It isn't the words themselves that are important in your formulation but rather their meaning as an expression of your understanding of the unreserved goodness of love. Examples of alternatives could be: *May you be free. May you be in the best of health. May you be safe and protected from all evil.* You can have several statements of intention, but the formulations must be short, concise, and suitable for concentrating on—and make sense in wishing for the benefit of all living beings. Some people just *think* about the person who is the object without repeating their intentions. However, there is more structure, faster learning, and greater karma fruition when intentions are verbalized. For some people, visualization is easy; for others, it is more difficult. But gradually the visualization becomes anchored and clarified, and the repetition of the words slips into a rhythmic cycle with an ever deeper intuitive meaning. In metta meditation, the emotional aspect of intuition is very prominent, whereas the intuition aspect of wisdom predominates in vipassana. Also, the understanding in vipassana of the three universal characteristics (anicca, dukkha, anatta) of the other person's life and difficult circumstances can be the source of compassionate empathy—both wisdom and loving-kindness take the bird of enlightenment to its wings.

After intuitively seeing the meaning of your intention directed toward the iconic loved one, you should direct your intention toward yourself—just as when you grew up, you learned self-love because someone loved you selflessly. Now let go of the visualization of the loved one, and with the same deep sense of the meaning of the words, focus on the intention directed at yourself. Your intention could be as follows: *I want to be happy. I want to be free of suffering. I want to live in peace.* In your selfless self-love, you may be able to find the source of Buddha's wish to care for all living beings.

Meditation on Ordinary Dear People

In the same sitting, we can meditate for a few minutes at a time on the afterimages of several different dear people, one at a time. All dear people other than the benefactor are those we could call the category of ordinary dear people. In the learning sequence that I learned from Munindra-ji and which I often use when instructing in metta meditation, we meditate in the order of the iconic dear person, yourself, several ordinary dear persons, a neutral person, and a hostile person. But in your daily practice, there is no fixed procedure for the order of people you meditate on. If a parent isn't your primary dear person, the parent is included in the category of ordinary dear people, which includes family members, a partner, a spouse, friends, neighbors, working colleagues, acquaintances—anyone who doesn't stir a neutral or adverse feeling in you when calling their images to mind.[5] You should meditate long enough on each image to get into contact with the meaning of the goodness of your intention (for example, one to five minutes on each image). In the transition from one image to another, you can repeat a collective intention directed toward all beings. It serves the purpose of both generalizing the attitude of loving-kindness to *all* and avoiding perceptual overlapping of one image with another in the transition between various images. The collective intention is a reminder of the spiritual ideal of the whole practice, and it may sound like this: *May all beings be happy. May all beings be free of suffering. May all beings attain nibbana.* Usually I do the collective intention without an image three times for less than a minute in the transition to every new image.

Changing a Negative Mindset

Loving-kindness is developed through meditation on yourself and on many different dear people whose images gradually integrate into your daily practice. By and by, in your practice, just like the ocean deepens gradually, you should include images of people you have a different attitude toward, so you can try embracing these people too with the intention of unconditional goodness. We work on changing an indifferent or negative mindset in our relationship with another person by seeing our existential needs of happiness, freedom, and peace being reflected in that other person's existential needs—even though that person right now may be acting contrary to their true needs. In metta, you put yourself in the place of the other person, as if you were identifying yourself with them but without ego-reference or clinging—you don't lose the as-if condition in genuine empathy. As you develop, integrate images of dear, neutral, and even negative people into the meditation. Try to "break down the barriers"[6] between the categories of people so there will be no difference in your attitude of kindness to anyone, including yourself. As a default mode, use the repetition of the collective intention directed toward an unlimited number of beings. Meditation on loving-kindness is, as you may begin to realize, a spiritual *life* project that can change our relationships with others in the most rewarding way for them and for ourselves. Embracing this practice can lead to profound personal transformation, allowing us to connect more authentically with ourselves and others in an increasingly complex world.

The Reach of Metta

It is a psychological law that intention comes before action. Try repeating your intention silently in your mind, directing it toward people you like while you are with them. Then try repeating the intention toward people you usually feel neutral about while you are with them. Finally, experiment with directing the intention toward people who evoke negative feelings in you while you are with them. All meditation involves learning through practice, and this is especially true for metta meditation. Try to broaden the meaning of the collective intention by focusing on a specific group of people or beings. For example: *May all children in the world be happy. May all children in the world be free from suffering. May all children in the world be at peace.* Reflecting methodically on elevated topics like this from time to time can be very beneficial.

If you feel a lack of motivation, visualize your benefactor. A benefactor is someone who embodies genuine learning and inspiration for the meditator. While meditating on a dear person, a neutral person, a negative person, or even yourself, you may sometimes feel emotionally "cold." You might find yourself repeating the intention over and over without it resonating. In that situation, it is important to visualize the iconic loved one and meditate on this image to be recharged with the authenticity of the ethically unconditional intention. Then go back to the visualization where you went "cold" and embrace the person with the recharged meaning. You apply the same procedure when you "go cold" in the meditation on yourself.

At times, this process can make you feel happy, uplifted, and lighthearted. However, some people feel disappointed if they don't experience strong feelings of joy during meditation. It's important to remember that joy is not the only measure of success. Even if the feeling of love doesn't arise immediately, connecting with the meaning behind the intention of empathetic connection is already a significant achievement. The more people you include in your meditation, the more meaningful and heartfelt the intention becomes, and this expansion brings energy, emotional uplift, and spiritual refinement.

When I lived in the Burmese monastery in Bodh Gaya with Munindra-ji, I gradually realized how deeply the intention of loving-kindness was woven into his life and actions. For meditators fortunate enough to learn metta meditation from Munindra-ji, he often became the inspiring image of a benefactor in their practice. The aim is not to love the benefactor more than anyone else. Instead, one chooses an iconic beloved as a guiding star for the love you seek to extend to all living beings, including yourself. In Buddha's teachings, it is essential to continually remind oneself of the possibility of this universal goodness.

Metta as a Foundational Emotion

In early Buddhism, loving-kindness was perceived as the primary interpersonal emotion, while later Mahayana Buddhism emphasized compassion (*karuna*). The prioritization of metta was psychologically justified because metta, as shown here, is the developmental prerequisite for compassion. However, there is a close connection between these two emotions, and they should be seen as an ethical unity. But they develop in different psychological contexts. Loving-kindness spontaneously transforms into compassion when the person one embraces with love suffers, because compassion, unlike love at first glance, is characterized by the intention to actively do something to alleviate the other's suffering. When the meditation on karuna is practiced in a formal process, one begins with the visualization of a dear person who is suffering.

Then the series of dear, neutral, and difficult people is reviewed, with the meditation on oneself and all other living beings as occasionally interspersed objects. If none of these persons is in an acute state of physical or mental suffering, then one should intuit their existential abandonment to the suffering of change and conditioning in life. The help that the meditator is motivated to actively provide is thus precisely the knowledge of the four noble truths, which overcomes the attachment to sangsara and eradicates all dukkha.

Metta is the source of all positive interpersonal emotions. In another context, loving-kindness spontaneously transforms into empathetic joy (*mudita*) with a person's success, because it is easy to rejoice with and over a person to whom one has the attitude of loving-kindness. *Mudita* is defined as the genuine congratulatory attitude toward others' success and happiness. These are examples of how loving-kindness functions as the root condition (non-hatred) for various positive mental states, which include respect, tenderness, generosity, tolerance, devotion, gratitude, forgiveness, solidarity, and patience. It is evident that in a concrete situation, it is always easier to be, for example, patient with a person we embrace with loving-kindness than with a person we are not kindly disposed toward. In other words, metta's goodwill is necessary to have compassion (*karuna*) for others in their suffering and rejoice with and over them in their success. Therefore, metta meditation should be developed first.

Each state of the brahmaviharas has, psychologically speaking, "a direct and indirect enemy" that can invade and harm the state if the formative activities of mindfulness and equanimity toward the object aren't sufficiently consolidated by the five links of absorption. The "direct enemy" of loving-kindness includes all shades of hatred, anger, dislike, aversion, irritation, and impatience, while the "indirect enemy" is the intermingling of clinging and sexualization that derails true metta. Of course, loving-kindness can be included in condensates of erotic love (*raga*), but undiluted metta is without sexuality—like the parent's love for their child.

Meditation on Karuna and Mudita

Compassion's direct enemy is evil and, in its milder form, schadenfreude, which is a perverted joy in the adversity of others. The indirect enemy is passivating despondency, depression, and powerlessness in confrontation with the sufferings of others. These reactions may be humanly understandable in difficult situations, but spiritually they are not expressions of compassion. The intention of loving-kindness can be adapted to meditation on karuna with an introductory addition so that empathy for the person's suffering isn't distorted. The intention could be as follows: *You are suffering* (the unmixed recognition of the suffering). *I will help you* (the sublime intention of acting upon recognition). *I will show you care and understanding* (defining the action that relieves). *May you be happy. May you be free of suffering. May you be at peace.* The more one-pointed compassion is, the subtler the serene joy (*sukha*) of wanting to help, which is one of the five links of absorption. The perseverance and energy of true compassion are often based on the ability of samadhi to anchor and block the invasion, in this case, of a lurking indirect enemy called despondency. If the meditator feels a lack of ethical motivation to open herself to others' suffering and the intention to help, she returns to the visualization of the iconic dear person to get in touch with the loving-kindness that opens her mind in the distressing situation.

In the meditation on mudita, too, the loving intention is changed so that it reflects the characteristics of empathetic joy—for example, *It's wonderful to see you are happy. How you deserve it! You are so talented. And it makes me so glad! May you always be happy. May you always be free of suffering. May you always be at peace.* The direct enemy of empathetic joy is jealousy and envy of the other person's success, while the indirect enemy is the dissimulation of merriment. In the meditation on mudita, you begin with the visualization of "a boon companion," which is a person who finds it easy to radiate joy—the most joyful person you can possibly recall is suitable as an iconic image. The series of visualizations is then reviewed as in the other meditation, and it is important to focus precisely on the reason for each person's most joyful moments.

Equanimity of Mind

As previously mentioned, equanimity of mind (*upekkha*) is a structuring formative activity in relation to any object in all wholesome states. It is technically the development of the five links of absorption and the resulting state of equanimity that consolidates the states of pre-jhanic brahmaviharas and protects them from the intrusion of the "enemies." Ethically speaking, it is the function of equanimity of mind as the fourth brahmavihara to perceive all living beings as equal. The indirect enemy of interpersonal equanimity is partiality toward other people, while the direct enemy is cynical indifference toward them. However, these enemies are basically also the enemies of loving-kindness because metta neither discriminates against nor ignores any being but treats everyone as equal. It is therefore important to understand that metta, karuna, and mudita are indeed also states of equanimity. They are all mental states characterized by mindfulness without clinging, without aversion or neglect—and thus without ego distortion. When equanimity (*upekkha*) emerges as the fourth brahmavihara, even though it is also a prerequisite for each of the other virtues, it is likely due to the division of brahmaviharas as formally based on the mnemonic template for the four jhanas with form. The first three brahmaviharas can each be developed up to and including the third jhana. The absorption links of energetic interest and rapture (*piti*) and bliss (*sukha*) are very powerful in the first three brahmaviharas because of their sublime emotional content, whereas these absorption links are completely absent in the fourth jhana.

The Vision of Unbounded Metta

When the meditator no longer experiences a difference in the stability of loving-kindness, regardless of the dear, neutral, or difficult person she is meditating on, including herself, then the counterimage arises, radiating a firmly anchored aura of white or orange light at the level of neighborhood concentration where the absorption links of rapturous and energetic interest (*piti*) and bliss (*sukha*) are very strong. Then the counterimage can be expanded meaningfully to an intuitive vision of unlimited numbers of living beings in all directions of the universe—this is the very concentrated version of the collective intention.

> She abides pervading one-quarter with a mind imbued with loving-kindness, likewise the second, likewise the third, likewise the fourth; so above, below, around, and everywhere, and to all as to herself, she abides pervading the all-encompassing world with a mind imbued with loving-kindness, abundant, exalted, immeasurable, without hostility and without ill will.[7]

This is similar in principle for the other brahmaviharas. But a brahmavihara doesn't need to be developed to this level to bring about noticeable and extensive levels of emotional catharsis in the mind. In your daily life, the scope of your endeavor may be to meditate exclusively on a limited number of people. This is where the secularized variant in Western mindfulness psychology differs from the spiritual practice in Buddhism.[8] In spiritual practice, we begin working with the meaning of *trying* to love *all* other beings *as much* as we love our iconic dear one. Love is not a finite resource; rather, it flourishes when shared freely, unencumbered by the limitations we often impose on ourselves. In the Buddha's teaching, it is very important to remind oneself of this great truth. It may not be realizable in our lives to the extent it is in the lives of the enlightened, but it is important not to lose sight of the ideal.

The Moral Foundation of the Dhamma-Faring

The brahmaviharas belong to the category of samatha meditation, and the nature of the liberation gained through jhanas isn't of an irreversible character that eliminates the negative tendencies (*anusaya*), the samyojanas, the asavas, and the kilesas. If these dhammas are the dark sides of an ignorant mind, then the brahmaviharas certainly can be viewed as the inborn "enlightened" dhammas. When we wish to follow in the footsteps of Buddha, we must learn to practice these exalted states of mind as our ethical foundation. There will be right speech whenever our intentions are filled with loving-kindness. There will be right actions whenever our intentions are filled with loving-kindness. There will be the right livelihood of harmlessness in all respects whenever our intentions are filled with loving-kindness. The three links of the moral section of the noble eightfold path have karmic consequences that imply the bliss of non-remorse and the absence of self-blame in the future. This causal connection is the supportive cause of the growth of undistracted focusing (samadhi). The cultivation of intuitive knowledge (*panna*), which through the practice of vipassana liberates and awakens the mind, requires such an undistracted mind. As virtues, the four brahmaviharas are integral to the path of dhamma and form the cornerstone of moral and meditative growth that leads to the ultimate liberation from suffering.

14 | Other Samatha Meditations

The structure of samatha meditation is found within all meditative teachings of the East, which, according to the nature of the matter, have been free to formulate their own objects of meditation with special meanings for religion. Later schools of Mahayana Buddhism developed some highly complex meditations based on mantras and visualizations of symbolic diagrams (Skt. *mandalas*), saturated with Buddhist cultic and metaphysical symbolic content. But in early Buddhism, the samatha meditations were distinctly simple, without metaphysical superstructures. They were mainly aimed partly at one-pointing the mind with a view to coupling with vipassana meditation, and partly at toning down or maturing a certain basic psychological attitude within the meditator.

The Charnel Ground Meditations

Apart from metta meditation, a very good example of Buddhist meditation as a kind of spiritual therapy is the "ten charnel ground meditations" (*sivathika*), which involve visualizing a skeleton and a corpse in various stages of decomposition. The meditations undeniably belong to a different psychic atmosphere than the brahmaviharas and are a testimony to the semi-ascetic samana environment in which early Buddhism grew up.

By chance, I learned about these meditations while staying at a forest monastery in southern Sri Lanka.[1] Upon my arrival, I was immediately assigned the kuti where Ven. Bhikkhu Nanamoli had lived in his last years while translating the *Visuddhimagga*. It was a Spartan stone hut located on the edge of a saltwater lagoon, where the water shimmered in the sunlight just below the window. Close to the equator, the sun sinks as if in a burning grave, and moments later, it is pitch-dark in the forest. In the kuti, there was a bed, a table with a petroleum lamp, a chair, and a mahogany cabinet. I investigated the cabinet—at the bottom lay a bag containing a human skeleton and a skull. Astonished, I assembled the bones on the stone floor and sat down, gazing at it. Then I opened Venerable Nanamoli's translation of the *Visuddhimagga* and read about the meditations. Although charnel ground meditations are rarely practiced by laypeople, they have traditionally been popular among monastics because they promote a settled attitude regarding death's inevitable conclusion—and the toning down of sexual drives. Meditation thus leads to an attitude of spiritual urgency (*samvega*) to overcome any attachment to impermanent existence. They are often mentioned in suttas because samvega is a facilitating motivation for intensive meditation.

Meditation on a skeleton serves all purposes in this respect, but various states of decomposition of a corpse are suitable for meditators in various situations. Buddhaghosa states that a bloated corpse is suitable to meditate on for a meditator who is disturbed by a lustful disposition toward the beauty of bodily forms, whereas a discolored corpse is better for a person with a disposition for the beauty of shiny skin. But for a meditator with special sensibilities for perfumes and arousing body odors, a stinking corpse is even better.

> Again, meditators, as though he were to see a corpse thrown aside in a charnel ground, one, two, or three days dead, bloated,

> livid, and oozing matter, a meditator compares this same body with it, thus: "This body too is of the same nature, it will be like that, it is not exempt from that fate." As he abides thus diligent, ardent, and resolute, his memories and intentions based on the household life are abandoned; with their abandonment, his mind becomes steadied internally, quieted, brought to singleness, and concentrated. That too is how a bhikkhu develops mindfulness of the body.[2]

As monstrous as this may seem, it is nevertheless an effective methodology for those interested. An amazing therapeutic effect is that the meditation exchanges disgust for the bliss of samadhi. Because of concentration on the corpse's afterimage, the meditative counterimage arises, radiating a powerful aura that is associated with energetic interest, rapture, and bliss. Due to the object's particular nature, corpse meditations can, however, only be developed up to and including the first jhana. However, a meditator who is hindered by a quick-tempered and irritable mind to an extent that has hindered the development of even breathing meditation should not alternatively attempt charnel ground meditation because the initial repulsive content of the object will activate their propensity for aversion. Instead, it is better for them to one-point their mind through the meditation on loving-kindness, which, as a side benefit, effectively tones down aversion and anger. On the other hand, a meditator who is overly preoccupied with sexual imaginations and longings shouldn't immediately attempt the meditation on loving-kindness, since this is easily invaded by sexual impulses. Instead, it would be better for them to develop samadhi through a charnel ground meditation that precisely assuages sexual impulses. In both cases, the samadhi attained can then form the basis for other developments—for instance, vipassana. It's all very pedagogical.

Other Meditations on the Body

Similar benefits are attained through mindfulness practice on the thirty-two parts of the body, according to ancient Indian anatomy.[3] As far as the psychological purpose is concerned, this meditation is a version of charnel ground meditations. The same applies to the meditative "analysis of the four material elements," which is especially intended for an intellectual temperament.[4] The meditation includes an abstract analysis of the body parts according to the symbolic elements of earth, water, fire, and air.[5] This type of meditation also includes perception of the loathsomeness of food, which involves the visualization of, for example, the details of the digestive process, which will lead to a disillusioning toning down of the urge to overeat, but at the same time rewarding the meditator with the joy and equanimity associated with the development of the five links of absorption.[6] Because of the complexity of the visualizations, the latter two meditations lead only to the gathering of the mind in neighborhood concentration. On the other hand, the visualization of the thirty-two parts of the body leads to the first jhana when the absorption is provided through the counterimage of one visualized body part at a time—for example, the heart or the lungs. Munindra-ji told me that in Burma he had at one point instructed lung cancer patients to achieve jhanic absorption through this meditation, which enabled them to be pain-free while in the jhana.

The Spheres of the Formless Absorptions

The fourth jhana with form, referred to as the highest meditative stage in *samatha bhavana*, can be further expanded into four formless spheres of consciousness. Just as the meditator earlier during the ascent through the fourfold jhanic hierarchy of form eliminated the grosser absorption links of a preceding jhana to enter the deeper grounding of a subsequent one, so the intuition of the first formless jhana, which is "the sphere of the boundlessness of space," is developed by eliminating the fourth jhana with form.[7] The perception of the formless spheres is a deepening of the fourth jhana but is often classified as separate *arupa-jhanas* (formless jhanas), and the meditator isn't absorbed in the boundlessness of physical space but in the pure intuition of spatial perception unbounded by form. Similarly, the capable meditator next expands the fourth jhana into "the sphere of the boundlessness of consciousness," then "the sphere of the boundlessness of nothingness," and finally consciousness radiates into the "sphere of neither perception nor not perception."[8] The subtlety of jhanic awareness culminates in this absorption, which Siddhattha's last yoga teacher mistook for consummated enlightenment but which, according to the Buddha, still isn't transcendental in relation to the conditioned stream of consciousness. This jhana, too, is an expanded immersion in the stream of consciousness, which is impermanent, causally conditioned, and structured by the perception of an object.

Paranormal Causality

Even though the jhanic absorptions did not lead to enlightenment, they were known to lead to paranormal abilities within the common Indian spiritual tradition. Early Buddhism had to deal with the paranormal sidetrack too. Paranormal abilities are not the primary objective of samatha meditation but are considered as potential by-products of profound states of samadhi. In these deep meditative states, consciousness is perceived as distinct from the body and physical matter, creating the impression that it might exert influence on the material world in ways that transcend conventional cause-and-effect relationships. But what does this truly imply?

Imagine a scenario where your consciousness impacts the world not only through deliberate actions but also via mechanisms we have yet to fully comprehend. While this idea might sound like the realm of science fiction, modern scientific discoveries suggest that the universe does not always conform to our expectations.

In classical physics, the universe operates under well-defined principles of cause and effect. Every action produces a predictable reaction, linked in both time and space. For instance, if you push a ball, it rolls—straightforward and reliable. However, quantum physics, which governs the behavior of nature's smallest components, reveals a far more intricate reality. Phenomena like quantum entanglement demonstrate that two particles can become so deeply interconnected that measuring one instantly provides information about the other, regardless of vast distances separating them. This leads to a fascinating and unresolved philosophical question: Could consciousness itself be linked to the world through similar, yet undiscovered, mechanisms? A solution to this intriguing question is deeply connected with what scientists refer to as the hard problem of consciousness—the profound enigma within science of how subjective experience arises from physical brain processes.[9]

In Western science, the dominant perspective posits that the brain generates consciousness. This approach is supported by many observations from neuroscience and is considered a strong model. However, it is not a definitive explanation but rather a hypothesis that has gained broad acceptance, and it has not solved the hard problem of consciousness. But that is not what is to be discussed here; I only wish to emphasize that the materialistic view is fundamentally—that is to say, scientifically speaking—a belief system, which in turn is today a common mindset in Western culture. And for our context here, it is only necessary to highlight that in Buddhism, consciousness is regarded as fundamental. Accordingly, consciousness is not regarded as a product of the brain but the very backdrop against which both the brain and the world unfold. This reversed relationship makes it easier to understand certain perceptions in Buddhism that would otherwise be difficult to grasp. This includes, among other things, Buddhism's view on death and what lies beyond.

Dipa Ma

One of Munindra-ji's earliest students was a Bengali woman named Dipa Ma who lived in Calcutta. She was enlightened and even possessed all the paranormal knowledges mentioned in Buddhist scriptures. She had these abilities from past lives, according to Munindra-ji, who had been her vipassana teacher in Rangoon, when paranormal abilities spontaneously appeared in her insight meditation until Munindra-ji taught her to control them.

Dipa Ma came from modest circumstances in an Indian immigrant family in Rangoon. Her late husband, who worked for the railway, left her with a meager pension. She had lost two children shortly after her husband's death and then suffered a severe depression that left her bedridden for several years. In Calcutta, Dipa Ma lived with her daughter Dipa, who was a stream-enterer because of her mother's instructions. Many of Dipa Ma's friends and acquaintances, most of them housewives from the same street where she lived in Calcutta, had also attained stream entry under her guidance. Dipa Ma was a small woman with marked features who shone with a persistently loving, almost blissfully tender glow with very powerful eyes behind large horn-rimmed glasses. She came occasionally to the vihara in Bodh Gaya. I visited her once in her small apartment on the fourth floor of one of the humble residential quarters of Calcutta, where there was a blacksmith on the ground floor in the building. I don't remember what I talked to Dipa Ma about on this occasion, probably because my Hindi was as bad as her command of English—and Dipa, who would translate, wasn't at home that day. But I left with a deeply serene feeling, as after a very meaningful conversation that had shed light on many things. Such was the effect this unusual person had on people. Dipa Ma means "Dipa's mother," and it is the name by which she has become known as one of the teachers who contributed to the spread of vipassana in the West, which she visited a few times, although she didn't speak English and only rarely taught other than small groups. Dipa Ma is mentioned with loving respect in books by the American vipassana teachers Joseph Goldstein, Jack Kornfield, and Sharon Salzberg, who all met her and came to perceive her as a teacher for them. Dipa Ma, by her extraordinary example, was an incredible inspiration to others and was a true teacher of teachers.[10]

During the summer when I was studying Abhidhamma with Munindra-ji in Kalimpong, I came to understand some of the paranormal abilities Dipa Ma had mastered. We went through Buddhaghosa's great meditation manual from the fifth century, which I will use to draw an outline of these abilities in the following. Based on the many stories that abounded about Dipa Ma in the vihara in Bodh Gaya, I often asked Munindra-ji questions about how she had learned to master this or that ability, and the conversation then turned to be about Munindra-ji's teaching of her.

The Kasinas

In the samatha system, the *kasinas* (total symbols) occupy a special place. The fourth jhana mastered with kasinas as objects is the foundation jhana for the development of several paranormal abilities that Dipa Ma had learned to master. The primitive design of the kasinas testifies to high antiquity in the common Indian spiritual tradition, and kasinas have undeniably been prototypes for the complex mandalas of later Mahayana Buddhism, which also potentially lead to various paranormal purposes. The ten meditation objects of the kasina series include the symbolic elements of matter, earth, water, fire, and air;[11] the colors blue, yellow, red (the primary colors of the color spectrum), and white; the perception of light; and the perception of limited space. Each kasina develops in a specific sphere within which a certain form of paranormal mastery is possible.

For now, we will follow the process Dipa Ma went through to gain effortless mastery of the samatha meditative skills she possessed. As a starting point, she had to master all ten kasinas. To develop jhana in the earth kasina, Dipa Ma sat down in front of a circular disk of earth with a diameter of about one and a half feet and focused on the kasina with open eyes. The kasina is both an object of one-pointing of the mind and a universal symbol whose resonance is intuitively awakened and deepened in the mind. By alternately focusing on the kasina with her eyes open and on the afterimage with her eyes closed, after a while Dipa Ma could meditate continuously on the intuitively meaningful afterimage, which was then the object of her meditation. This is "the learning sign," which is fixed and developed up to the level of neighborhood concentration. But the counterimage "appears as if breaking out from the learning sign, and a hundred times, a thousand times more purified . . . like the moon's disk coming from behind a cloud."[12]

She then developed all four jhanas following the guidelines, as described in connection with breathing meditation. The preparation of the subsequent kasinas basically follows the earth kasina.[13] According to the instructions in Buddhaghosa's meditation manual, focusing on the full moon under an open sky is ideal for the yellow kasina, although all the colored kasinas can be produced using objects in which the desired color appears with clarity. The meditator can, for example, fill a tray with blue lotus flowers or sprinkle blue-colored powder on the earth kasina. When Dipa Ma first developed jhanic mastery in one kasina in all four jhanas, she quickly developed competence in the other kasinas. She also quickly mastered the kasinas because she had already mastered the four jhanas through breathing meditation.

Mastery of Kasinas

As the basis for accomplishment (*iddhipada*) Dipa Ma then sought optimal mastery of her spiritual faculties in samatha. The five spiritual faculties are constellated in a different strength relationship in samatha because the one-pointedness of the concentration is very dominant. The four bases for accomplishment include a persistent, significant effort of will, supported by a significant concentration of intention, energy, awareness, and intuitive investigation (see p. 83). The exercise of the spiritual faculties as bases of accomplishment for the achievement of paranormal abilities need only be outlined here. First and foremost, it was necessary that Dipa Ma attained all ten kasinas in an unobstructed introspection within each jhana. This means that she initially entered the first jhana in the earth kasina, emerged and next entered the same jhana in the water kasina, and so on—the entire range in the order. Thereafter, she successively entered through the order of the kasinas in the second jhana; then she entered from the beginning of the order through the third and fourth jhanas.[14] Finally, as quickly as possible, she introspected the jhanas in the reverse order in an unbroken succession of absorptions and ascents, from kasina to kasina, through jhana after jhana, as if the absorptions were mere thoughts she was thinking in her extremely anchored and expansive state of samadhi. After a while, Dipa Ma could be absorbed in both the arbitrary and nonarbitrary sequence of the jhanas and kasinas—that is, she could easily step directly into, for example, the fourth jhana's mental immobility in the blue kasina, emerge, and then effortlessly step into the grosser mental uplift of the first jhana in the fire kasina, and so on, exactly as she wanted to.

Psychic Powers

In other words, Dipa Ma achieved jhanic mastery of "the total symbols" of the universe. She became able, at the jhanic level, to dwell in visualizations of the physical world's symbol-elements (earth, water, fire, and air), spatial dimensions, colors, and light. In rapid succession she could intuitively proportion these cognitions at will. With the four bases of accomplishment, Dipa Ma then took control of the counterimage's expansion and precise delineation of each kasina in the approach to the jhana. For it was within the notion of the exact extent and character of the counterimage that she exercised the ability to mentally manipulate physical processes within each of the spheres of earth, water, fire, and air—for instance, psychokinesis, materialization, paratransport, levitation, and so forth. All these psychic powers (*iddhis*) are of an intended, predetermined length of time, after which Dipa Ma again conformed to the limitations of normal shared reality. There were many anecdotes about Dipa Ma's experiments with these abilities, which also aroused the curiosity of Westerners during her visits to the West.[15] Psychic powers and meditative methods for their mastery are also found in Hinduism and other teachings that deal with meditation, but the methods are described in great detail in Buddhism, even though they have nothing to do with the specific teachings of the Buddha.

Munindra-ji rarely spoke unprompted about these powers. When he did so, it was in the context of Buddhism's traditional warning about the danger of abusing iddhis. On the one hand, there is the fuss they can cause with ordinary people who interpret them wrongly—namely, as an expression of the practitioner's superhumanity or divinity. On the other hand, and especially, there is the temptation for the unenlightened meditator to use iddhis for ego-inflating purposes, about which there are quite a few anecdotes in the annals of both Buddhism and Hinduism. There is a rule in the Vinaya Pitaka that forbids the members of the

Buddhist monastic order to put paraphenomena on public display, probably also because the Buddha didn't want his teachings to be infamous (i.e., in India, more like famous) as thaumaturgy. But Dipa Ma had never been a monastic. And there nevertheless are many examples of paranormal mastery in the canon.

The Buddha Eye

The Buddha used to scan the surroundings with his so-called Buddha eye,[16] which was the term for his special ability within the celestial eye, the designation for clairvoyance that is developed through the light kasina in the fourth jhana. Dipa Ma had this ability, which is referred to often by the Buddha. In this way, the bhikkhu Anuruddha and other bhikkhus received guidance in developing the celestial eye after the Buddha, by the same path, got wind of their problems of fixing the clairvoyant light after emerging from the jhana.[17] Anuruddha developed over time to become the one among the bhikkhus who particularly mastered this ability. But Maha Moggallana was also very skilled. On one occasion, when he was in Bamboo Grove in Rajagaha, he conversed clairaudiently and clairvoyantly with the Buddha, who was over 150 kilometers away in the Jeta grove in Savatthi. The two great samanas saw and heard each other as they spoke (just like on Zoom but without the electronic device).[18]

The Celestial Eye

The celestial eye includes several variants of clairvoyance that Dipa Ma mastered—for instance, mind reading or telepathy—and the ability to intuit contemporary distant or near physical objects independent of the eye's normal range and resolution. This applies to all the clairvoyant ranges; they can be activated independently of the physical distance to the object. The celestial eye is often referred to in the suttas as the ability to retrospect the death and re-becoming processes of other persons. On several occasions, the Buddha recounted the spiritual levels of highly developed monastics and laypeople at the moment of their deaths, with the aim of inspiring listeners to strive for these auspicious partial liberations themselves. Consider:

> Just as though there were two houses with doors and a man with good sight standing there between them saw people entering the houses and coming out and passing to and fro, so too, with the celestial eye, which is purified and surpasses the human, a meditator sees beings passing away and reappearing, inferior and superior, fair and ugly, fortunate and unfortunate, and she understands how beings pass on according to their actions [karma].[19]

This ability is called "knowledge of faring according to deeds," which Buddhists considered very useful.

The Celestial Ear

Clairaudience, known by Buddhists as *the celestial ear*,[20] is the ability to hear sounds far away, independent of great distances, and sounds close by that aren't normally perceived by the human ear. The meditator who wishes to master this ability must first gather the mind through absorption in the fourth jhana of the air kasina. Thereafter, they prepare and sharpen the ability by focusing on rough sounds within the normal hearing range; then on finer sounds such as "the sound of birds, the sound of the wind, the sound of footsteps, the fizzing sound of boiling water, the sound of palm leaves drying in the sun, the sound of ants, and so on."[21] At a certain point, they spontaneously enter the fourth jhana but fixate on the wave vibration of a barely audible sound as an absorption object. Immediately thereafter, emerging from the jhana, the clairaudient faculty is activated in expanded union with their normal hearing, initially directed toward the sound source, which was the object of the absorption. But the fully developed celestial ear can be directed to any distant auditory object beyond normal hearing range.

Like all the samatha-developed states, paranormal abilities are not inviolable gains. They are even easier to lose than jhanas due to misuse and thus the accumulation of distracting unwholesome karma, which destroys the ability to immerse oneself in high uniform levels of samadhi. Spiritually speaking, the development of paranormal abilities is a sidetrack. Paranormal abilities neither presuppose nor lead to the liberation of the mind from ignorance, desire, and hatred. But in the early period of Buddhism, a rich meditative environment flourished, experimenting with the entire spectrum of meditative developments, where these abilities naturally had their place.

Paranormal Memory

In the Buddha's teachings, the four noble truths are formulated in context with the understanding of the cycle of rebirths that expresses the Buddhist view of death, although the meditative direct experience of dukkha, and thus disillusionment and the liberation of the mind in present life, does not depend on the understanding of past and future lives. But the existence of potential rebirth-creating relationships between all sentient beings is a significant implicit aspect of the concepts of karma and sangsara. In this context, we get the obvious causal explanation for the all-embracing vision of love in the Buddha's teaching, which levels everything that conventionally separates sentient beings, even though they are without a permanently fixed identity—or rather, perhaps precisely because of that. We also gain a spiritual understanding of the reason why there exists a specific body with all that it entails of pain, illness, and ultimately physiological death—although the original first cause of sangsara cannot be known—and we are offered an understanding of how and why these conditions may cease in the future, and the spiritual significance it entails. Among Westerners interested in Buddhism, the main resistance to the rebirth view of death is probably the classical materialistic science's entrenched belief that consciousness cannot exist independently of the brain—if the premise of matter as primary in relation to consciousness is true. There are many different notions of consciousness within modern sciences, ranging from the negation of consciousness as a nonmaterial phenomenon to the view that consciousness is at best only related to the brain as an epiphenomenon—just as the appendix is purposelessly related to the gastrointestinal system. However, all these theories stand and fall with the fact that materialistic science has never been able to explain the relationship between the brain and the experience of being conscious—that is, how the relationship between consciousness and the brain scientifically should be understood. For Munindra-ji, these notions of consciousness—which many Westerners believe to be scientific, and which they are not—were odd in an amusing way that could make him break out in his hearty laughter. All the Buddha's essential teachings are indeed expressions of consciousness's inherent sovereignty over the body—and Munindra-ji's teaching of the Buddha's dhamma was permeated by this understanding. But he never tried to convince skeptical Westerners. When questioned, however, he claimed that in Buddhism there is a verifiable method of paranormal memory of past lives.

15 | Knowledge of Recollection of Past Lives

The theorem of the four noble truths can only be understood in its original Indian context, together with the knowledge of the recollection of past lives unfolding the full implications of the cause and the cessation of suffering—that is, the second and the third noble truths. The recollection of past existences is the only paranormal ability that isn't obtained through a kasina but through breathing meditation, and it is the samatha-based knowledge to which the Buddhists ascribed the most importance. In combination with the celestial eye developed through the light kasina, the meditator who develops their paranormal memory function can also retrospect another person's past life. Dipa Ma had these abilities, and Munindra-ji helped her to achieve mastery of them. But for the time being, we follow the meditator, who only develops a memory of their own past lives.

Concentration of Memory

The meditator intent on "knowledge of recollection of past lives"[1] must enter the fourth jhana through breathing meditation, emerge, and prepare for meditation at the highest level of neighborhood concentration. In this concentrated state, she must retrospect in reverse chronological order all the events that preceded her sitting down and entering the jhana. She thus recalls the series of situations, from the moment she entered the meditation cell, went to the meditation cell—ate breakfast just before—got dressed before breakfast, bathed before she got dressed, got up from bed, and back to the moment when she woke up and opened her eyes. Next, she recalls in reverse chronological order all the situations that took place the day before, down to the smallest detail and in the same way—she then proceeds to retrospect the week that preceded. The preparation for paranormal recall thus consists in the training the normal memory in the pre-jhanic state, where the recall function is already very plastic and controllable because of the samadhi.

The Recall of the Moment of Rebirth

The guideline for retrospection is the strictly reversed chronology of the episodes of memory. The more expansive the memory, the more summarized the memories will be.

> But if anything is not evident, he should again attain the basic jhana, emerge, and advert. By so doing, it becomes as evident as when a lamp is lit. And so, in reverse order too, he should advert . . . to ten years, twenty years, and so on as far back as his own rebirth-linking[2] in this existence, he should advert to the mentality-materiality occurring at the moment of death in the preceding existence; for a wise meditator is able at the first attempt to remove the rebirth-linking and make the mentality-materiality at the death moment his object.[3]

"Mentality-materiality" is a synonym for a moment of the five aggregates that sum up the psychophysiological constitution.

In this context, *rupa* also means "materiality," but in the above context, it is more like just the perception of the body. After having perceived the "relinking object," the meditator intuitively tries to penetrate the cause of it, which is the moment of death of the previous life. If this moment in the stream of consciousness initially appears impenetrable to the recall, "he should again and again attain that same basic jhana, and each time he emerges, he should advert to that instance. . . . and at length he removes the rebirth-linking and makes the mentality-materiality that occurred at the death moment his object."[4] At the same moment the meditator penetrates the moment of "relinking," he spontaneously slips into the fourth jhana, but with the memory of the moment of death of the previous life as the object of absorption. Then he once more emerges from the jhana and begins the methodical retrospection of the past life in the same way that she just reviewed the present life.

> It is with the mindfulness (memory) associated with that knowledge that he "recollects his manifold past lives," that is to say, one birth, two births, three births, four births, five births, ten births, twenty births, thirty births, forty births, fifty births, a hundred births, a thousand births, a hundred thousand births, many eons of world contraction, many eons of world expansion: many eons of world contraction and expansion: "There I was so named, of such a race, with such an appearance, such was my food, such my experience of pleasure and pain, such the end of my life span; and passing away from there, I reappeared elsewhere; and there too I was so named, of such a race, with such an appearance, such was my food, such my experience of pleasure and pain, such the end of my life span; and passing away from there, I reappeared here." Thus, with details and particulars, he recollects her manifold past lives.[5]

The Cane and Bridge Method

When Dipa Ma practiced vipassana in Rangoon, intense and amazing memories from her past lives occasionally appeared in her meditation. But when she learned to control the paranormal memory, based on her jhanic mastery, she could unfold the retrospection in the paranormal dimension in the same methodical stepwise way as "a blind person walks by tapping in front of herself with a cane." Once Dipa Ma had penetrated the veil between the present life's relinking and the previous life's moment of death, she was able, after some practice, to focus successively on pairs of reconnection links and moments of death without having to unravel all the intervening events of each life. In this way, she went back into her mental continuum as if on a bridge. But the cane and bridge methods can be combined, and thus she was able to go back to an existence in the lifetime of the Buddha where, on one occasion, she heard a sermon by the Enlightened One. And once she exercised this kind of sovereignty over her paranormal memory, it no longer invaded her vipassana meditations. There is a great deal of anecdotal literature about people who have been able to remember episodes from previous lives, sporadically and without intention. Spontaneous recall is recognized by both Hinduism and Buddhism, and the phenomenon is, of course, primarily registered in the East.[6]

Paranormal memory involves a methodical expansion of the normal function of memory, which can probably give the person who is remembering a certain disillusioning perspective on the changeability of life. But paranormal recollection doesn't imply insight into non-core self, anatta, which is developed in vipassana within a different constellation of the five spiritual faculties. According to the Pali scriptures, many non-Buddhist samanas had the ability of paranormal recollection in the days of the Buddha, about which meditators he said, "Thus, he remembers various past lives, their conditions, and details. And he says: 'The self and the world are eternal, barren, steadfast as a mountain peak, standing firm like a pillar. And though these beings roam and wander (through the round of existence), pass away and re-arise, yet the self and the world remain the same just like eternity itself.'"[7] The meditator is thus reinforced in his belief in the immutability of a core self.

And in the biological process of death, it is precisely the desire-thirst for the hallucinated core self that prompts the unliberated person to crave the conditions of rebecoming in a future life—to which all the accumulated karma patterns of the deceased, all of which are potentially *forming* karma activities, are transferred. Buddhaghosa mentions that the transfer, symbolically speaking, takes place as a mirror image or an echo in the universal network of relationships that exists between all conscious beings.

Types of Karma in the Death Process

In the consciousness of the unenlightened person, the last course of the death process will invariably bring to fruition one of four categories of karma, accumulated from a recent or distant past and thus made conscious as fruit in the last receptive phases of perception. The dying person's final reaction to this will be *reproduction karma* (*janaka-kamma*),[8] which will come to fruition where the supportive conditions are present in a subsequent existence.

As previously explained, the volition to act implies the scope of a choice, ethically independent of what is being responded to. But this very possibility is put out of play in reaction to the first category of coming to fruition—namely, the so-called *weighty karma* (*garuka-kamma*). This type of karma will overshadow all other accumulations because of its strongly conditioning content, which entails a predetermined reaction in the death process. Weighty, unwholesome karma includes extremely evil acts, such as killing a father or mother, or killing or attempted killing of a person who, by virtue of her liberation, has become the universal norm. Conversely, weighty, wholesome karma includes magnificent acts of great love, generosity, self-sacrifice, and highly developed meditative states—for example, achieving a jhana.

If, however, the dying person hasn't accumulated a particularly weighty karma, she may bring to fruition *habitual karma* (*acinnaka-kamma*). This is the type of karma that she has repeated most often throughout her life upon the activity plan of the body, speech, or mind, and which has therefore left deep traces in the mental continuum. For the wholesome aspect, this kind of karma may stem, for example, from a meditative practice that hasn't reached a high stage of development but has nevertheless been developed persistently as a dominant habit. This would be *bhavana acinna karma* in the case of a minor stream-enterer. Unwholesome karma—such as stinginess—also leaves deep traces. If this type of karma isn't found in the continuum with sufficient significance, the dying person could bring a *death-proximity karma* (*marana-sanna-kamma*) to fruition—that is, one of the karma activities performed on the deathbed itself. If for one reason or another these three types of karma aren't current, then the dying person will inevitably become aware of the fruit of a *reservoir karma* (*kattata-kamma*), which is any other karma pattern from the lifetime, if the pattern is sufficiently significant to form the final course of the death process.

Meditative Assistance with Dying

The fruition of these last three types of karma doesn't predetermine the reaction on them but implies scope for modification of the free will, although within the margins of the support-conditional accumulation—which is to say, a previous development of the pattern that is enacted. It is with a view to this promising possibility that Buddhists rarely surround those who are dying with a tragic atmosphere, which could influence the death process in an unwholesome way. Buddhists have a tradition dating back to the days of the Buddha of reciting meditative instructions to those who are dying. It is well known in the West that the twelfth-century *Tibetan Book of the Dead* (*Bardo Thödol*) is a manual used by Tibetan Tantric Buddhists for this purpose.[9] It is less well known that a similar practice has existed in the countries of Theravada Buddhism. In the Pali canon, there are several examples of spiritual help being given to both dying monastics and laypeople. A monastic, or a dhamma-knowledgeable layperson who is close to the dying person, should make the dying person reflect on their previous wholesome actions. Recalling this can bring bliss (*sukha*), which is the proximate cause of samadhi. Having been made serene in this way, the dying person must be faced with the fact that they are dying. They must be helped to realize the futility of any longing for relatives, friends, and sensual pleasures they once enjoyed. Instead, they must focus all their energy and attention on the momentary change, dukkha, and non-core self of the objects present. These insights will establish their mind in a meditative equilibrium (*upekkha*) of distancing and disenchanted presence, which is the best imaginable state in which to face death.

There is an obvious suggestive element of the death process in the practice of vipassana in that the meditator constantly refrains from clinging to and identifying with the object and therefore, from a spiritual perspective, dies to it. But for this last phase to be successful at the end of life, it is a prerequisite that the dying person has previous experience with insight meditation. If this has been the case, the ultimate consequence of methodical introspection into the intensity of the death process may be a direct experience of transcendental nibbana immediately before the final onset of death. For this auspicious purpose, Buddhists chant the *Satipatthana Sutta* beside the deathbed. This sutta is, as discussed in chapter 8, the Pali canon's most detailed exposition of the method of insight meditation. The scripture is rich in expressive mnemonic repetitions, the rhythm of which is easy and uplifting to listen to.

Visions of Rebirth in the Process of Death

I once attended a death ritual in a hermitage in southern Sri Lanka. The chanting took place beside the deathbed for several hours each day for several weeks, and this practice continued after the dying person, who was a bhikkhu of high seniority in the order, had lost consciousness. Apart from the general psychophysiological weakening in the dying process, in which perception nevertheless occurs (just like in the dream state), there are two conditions that can contribute to the disorientation of the dying person. One is that accumulated karma will come to fruition in a series of oversized symbol-contents (*kamma-nimitta*) in the process of death. The other is that the fruition occurs in the form of a so-called rebirth sign (*gati-nimitta*), which is a vision of the potentially coming rebirth plane. These visions may be of an expansive paradisiacal or hellish nature, according to the ethical quality of the karmic pattern that is surfacing as fruition. But regardless of whether wholesome or unwholesome fruition is involved, and unless the dying person is of an unusually meditative disposition, the structural ignorance and desire-thirst of the unenlightened person are activated in the final phase of the death process, either as clinging to pleasure or as hatred and fear of unpleasantness. The karma pattern can be just as psychologically nuanced as in the normal waking perception process. The formative karma activities of the last reaction become decisive for the subsequent "reconnection" of the stream of consciousness on any plane of existence in sangsara.

Relinking Consciousness

For the sake of simplicity, it is assumed in the following example that the rebecoming takes place from and to a human existence. In terms of development, this must be considered normal. The dying person's last karmic pattern comes to fruition in a karmic-ethical corresponding station of existence, in this case in a human womb. It can be understood in this way: At the same time as the conditions for life arise from the union of an egg and sperm cell at the new station of existence, the phenomenon of "relinking consciousness" arises.[10]

Relinking consciousness is the united egg and sperm cell's first moment of germinal consciousness under life-consolidating conditions. Relinking consciousness has one function of cross-connecting—it is a common constituent of consciousness that lasts only one moment and leaves a causal imprint in "the substream of becoming" (*bhavanga-sota*).[11] It is technically a karmic fruit and the entire previous life's sum of accumulated karmic patterns—and thus all past-life fetters and merits—is transferred to the relinking consciousness. And, this fruition is supported by the karmic accumulation of the future parent couple—whose physiological equivalent for a modern understanding must be the genome—as well as the general life-consolidating conditions in the situation, all of which form supportive conditions for the deceased's relinking to the new station of existence.

In the transition between the two stations of existence in a stream of consciousness, the consciousnesses of death and relinking are thus related partly through the specific conditions of the reproductive-karma relation and its specific support, which determines the ethical quality of the rebecoming. And it happens partly through the universal relation, which is a general supportive condition that, in principle, potentially cross-connects all carriers of consciousness in the sangsaric cycle of rebirths. Regardless of the distance between the two stations of existence, which in principle may be on opposite sides of the globe, death and relinking consciousness are instantly cross-linked where all the supportive conditions for maturation of the deceased's reproductive karma are present. But apart from this, the cross-connecting relinking consciousness arises with the same flowing regularity as any other moment of consciousness in relation to a previous and subsequent process at any point in the single stream of consciousness in this present life. Dipa Ma perceived all these details of the rebirth-relinking process when she meditated on retrospection in pairs of reconnection links and moments of death—both her own and others; she said it was like leafing through the pages of a book.

16 | In Tathagata's Footsteps

The description of the night of enlightenment in the suttas easily gives the impression of the ease with which Siddhattha had become a buddha after the failed period of asceticism. In several later suttas, to encourage the disciples in their endeavors, we get glimpses of Siddhattha's own struggles with fear and other anguish while he was meditating alone in the forest at night. When Siddhattha became overcome with fear at the sound of a branch snapping in the night, he allowed himself to be flooded with fear, a modern therapeutic expression. He remained physically motionless until the agonizing states had passed—while intensely observing the thoughts and sensations his fear provoked instead of acting on them. In this way, he unlearned his disturbing convictions about the meaning of these anxieties as it turned out that nothing frightening happened. We may assume that there were many such nights and days before his enlightenment. Shortly before, he made a decision that expresses the utmost awe-inspiring form of spiritual urgency (*samvega*) in Buddhism: "Willingly, let only my skin, sinews, and bones remain, and let the flesh and blood dry up in my body, but I will not relax my energy so long as I have not attained what can be attained by manly strength, energy, and exertion."[1]

According to the mnemonic formulation used in many suttas, on the night of enlightenment, Siddhattha activated the first four jhanic absorptions he had learned from the munis (see chapter 2). He then developed the ability to recollect the past lives of other beings in the sangsaric treadmill of death and rebirth processes, and he retrospected his own past lives in this perspective. Finally, Siddhattha transitioned from samatha to vipassana and developed the insights in the four noble truths, culminating in the transcendence of the stream of consciousness in nibbana with the irrevocable elimination of polluting influxes (*asavas*).

The Ideal of Threefold Knowledge

The whole account spans one night and summarizes the ideal of "threefold knowledge" (*te-vijja*), which is expressed in a fixed sutta formulation that is often also used in the description of a disciple's enlightenment. Paranormal recollection and the celestial eye were the two paranormal skills that the Buddhists prioritized the most. Together with nibbana realization—that is, the direct understanding of the four noble truths—threefold knowledge constituted a desirable spiritual ideal. The order of knowledge does not express a hierarchical developmental process because regardless of how useful paranormal abilities may be, they do not lead to the irreversible elimination of the contaminating influxes (*asava*). Since the ideal is practically quite extensive, it could be thought that paranormal recollection and clairvoyance were formally included later in the description of the night of enlightenment to authorize the te-vijja ideal. But be that as it may, "threefold knowledge" was articulated as the footprint of the Tathagata, addressed as a recommendation for emulation by the best of his disciples, although only the elimination of the asavas—the enlightenment experience of the four noble truths—in general qualifies as the footprint of the Tathagata. But it's worth highlighting the importance that insights into paranormal memories of past lives are given.

The Buddha's Omniscience

Threefold knowledge also seems to have been the early Buddhism's definition of omniscience (*sabbannuta*).[2] "Gotama has the threefold true knowledge [*te-vijja*],"[3] the Buddha explained to the philosopher Vacchagotta, but clearly after having *denied* being "omniscient and all-seeing." Several of the gurus whose spiritual greatness the Buddha didn't acknowledge declared themselves to be "omniscient." This applied, among others, to Mahavira, the historical founder of Jainism, and the philosopher Puruna Kassapa, who denied the operation of the law of karma. They both considered themselves to be "omniscient, all-seeing, and in possession of infinite knowledge." This kind of declaration concerning spiritual excellence seems in those days to have been a cliché that, all in all, meant nothing. However, in several places in the suttas, it is declared or implied that the Buddha had also been omniscient.

> Bhikkhus, in this world with its devas, Mara, and Brahma, among this population with its ascetics and brahmins, its devas and humans, whatever is seen, heard, sensed, cognized, reached, sought after, examined by the mind—that I know.[4]

However, the statement should not be understood naively. The Buddha has a perfect understanding of the three universal characteristics—anicca, dukkha, and anatta—and the conditional nature of phenomena; in short, the generality of the stream of the universal norm. Therefore, it can be said of him that he understands everything in the past, the present, and the future. This and similar utterances in this abstract sense are not uncommon in the suttas. Samana Gotama's declaration of threefold knowledge seems authentic to a very early tradition in Buddhism because the ideal clearly marks a delimitation in relation to the notion of omniscience, because the tendency within all later schools of

Buddhism was precisely in the direction of perceiving the Buddha as omniscient on an increasingly exaggerated and grandiose scale.

A popular assumption was that the Buddha had known everything, down to the smallest trivial circumstance, that would ever happen in the infinite future. But the ability of foreknowledge (precognition) presupposes the fatalistic notion of predestination and is, as already explained, contrary to the Buddha's teaching, which asserts the freedom of the individual will to choose their future. As for the clairvoyant ability to intuit another person's future rebirth path, this isn't precognition—present perception of a future object—but the intuition of the future consequences of what a person has accumulated from a path of dominant habitual karma that has been mapped out. Essentially this intuition can be seen as a version of the understanding that the pre-Socratic philosopher Heraclitus expressed with the words, "The character of a man becomes his destiny."[5]

Past Lives of the Buddha

The development of a special category of the enlightened, the so-called perfect buddha (*sammasambuddhasa*)—whose spiritual career begins intentionally in distant past lives, is only hinted at in the suttas and lacks the doctrinal presentation in later scriptures, especially the postcanonical, which seriously gets the bodhisattva (Pali, *bodhisatta*; a future buddha) concept up and running.

The perfect buddha is a great teacher, in contrast to his followers, the more commonly enlightened arahants—of later schools also called the "hearer buddhas" (*savaka-buddhas*). But in this connection, it is nevertheless worth noting that "threefold knowledge" was, in early Buddhism, the spiritual common denominator for both Buddha Gotama and his most advanced disciple.

Paranormal memories are mentioned in several suttas, which also refer to other perfected buddhas who lived before Buddha

Gotama. The suttas describe the teaching as being like an ancient, ruined city rediscovered by Siddhattha in the rainforest, a place where the yogic tradition supposedly had once thrived. Among the earlier fully enlightened buddhas, Buddha Gotama specifically mentions Buddha Kakusandha, Buddha Konagamana, and Buddha Kassapa—the three most recent perfect buddhas—each of whom had established a monastic community, or sangha. The Buddha's extraordinary mental abilities were considered partly due to the lifetimes he had spent as a disciple of these great teachers. For example, when the Buddha and his disciple Ananda visited a site in Kosala where the previous perfect buddha Kassapa had lived, Buddha Gotama explained that during Kassapa's time, he had been reborn as a Brahmin named Jotipala, who became one of Kassapa's leading disciples. And the Buddha's ability to recall past lives was particularly remarkable because he had practiced this skill in previous lifetimes.

However, the systematized mention of the Buddha's memories of past lives is based on the presentation in the Jataka (rebirth biographies), which spans 554 of his past lives on various planes of existence. With these popularized accounts—in which the presentation of the law of karma reflects the popular understanding to a greater extent than the essential Buddha teachings that have been explained in this book—the foundation was laid for the formalized bodhisattva concept, which contributed strongly to a growing Buddha cult.

The Sphere of the Uplifted Ones

The suttas conceive of thirty-one different planes of existence for the rebecoming of consciousness, of which thirty are higher and lower, respectively, than the human sphere of consciousness.[6] While the plane closest to human consciousness is the lower world of the animals, the highest planes are identical with the states of jhana consciousness the meditator on the human plane enters in their own mind. The perception of time differs in these higher worlds—the span of a life can be eighty-four thousand cosmic cycles.[7] But essentially these worlds, too, are as transient as the dew on the grass. The structural ignorance and desire-thirst of sangsara are also latent in these states. However, the longer the life span is, the more difficult it gets for consciousness to develop liberating insight into momentary changeability.

In contrast, on the human plane—"the sphere of the uplifted ones" (*manussa bhumi*)—the life span is rarely over one hundred years. The leaves wither and fall from the trees at relatively short intervals. The brightness of youth slips only too soon into the incipient fading of old age. An immediate understanding of the reality of the universal norm of changeability and conditioning seems obvious. There are other benefits too. Life here is generally not so full of suffering that a person with some wholesome karma in their baggage doesn't have the surplus energy to withdraw from the pulverizing everyday life to seek existential orientation in deep insight meditation. On the other hand, human life is rarely so full of joy and peace that a wise person cannot feel impelled by spiritual urgency to do just this. Rebecoming a human being is therefore considered to be the most spiritually favorable condition in the vast cycle of sangsara.

The Endless Sangsara

And contrary to what you might think, the prospect of rebirth ad infinitum is no source of comfort and relief in the short time a single human life lasts.

> Meditators, this sangsara is without discoverable beginning. A first point is not discerned of beings roaming and wandering on hindered by ignorance and fettered by craving. What do you

> think, meditators? Which is more: the stream of tears that you have shed as you roamed and wandered on through this long course, weeping and wailing because of being united with the disagreeable and separated from the agreeable—this or the water in the four great oceans? . . . For a long time, meditators, you have experienced the death of a mother . . . the death of a father . . . the death of a brother . . . the death of a sister . . . the death of a son . . . the death of a daughter . . . the loss of relatives . . . the loss of wealth . . . loss through illness; as you have experienced this, weeping and wailing because of being united with the disagreeable and separated from the agreeable, the stream of tears that you have shed is more than the water in the four great oceans.[8]

It is thus only here, in the sphere of the uplifted ones, where the awareness of the stream of impermanency is so obvious that an especially motivated stream of consciousness in its development one day will culminate in *the perfect buddhahood* for the relief and joy of all beings.

The Bodhisattva's Vow

Originally the bodhisattva's mental continuum was nothing special. He is in no way "chosen," since Buddhism doesn't believe in the existence of a creator god. We see that in one of the higher worlds resides the Vedic-Brahminical creator-god Brahma, who is unaware that he himself is created and will therefore one day cease. Completely in the existential spirit of the dhamma, the bodhisattva must motivate himself for the great task. But in the life in which he makes up his mind and takes the so-called bodhisattva vow to become a teacher for all humanity, he must be a person of such an extraordinary spiritual carat that, according to the doctrinal view, he not only possesses all eight jhanas as well as paranormal abilities but is also able to gain arahantship in the self-same life if he strives for it.[9] However, he postpones this final achievement in favor of developing the potential, the ultimate development of which, together with the culminating arahantship, signifies the great teacher.

The Trials of the Bodhisattva

The bodhisattva is inevitably whirled into the most dramatic worldly entanglements, even though he mostly extricates himself from them again, but never resorts to violent behavior. Even in a life when his insane father, jealous of the bodhisattva's charisma, amputates his arms and legs, the great being's mind is devoted to compassion for the delusion of others, instead of hatred and condemnation. Nonviolence and moderation toward all sentient beings in sangsara are fundamental to him. On one occasion, the Buddha declared that in the whole universe he could not find anyone who was dearer to him than he was dear to himself. He went on to elucidate:

> Since each and every person is so precious to themselves
> Let the self-respecting harm no other being.[10]

In this way, the Buddha saw himself in all other beings—and saw each being's welfare in the concerns of his own welfare. The emotional culmination of this is "the great compassion (*maha-karuna*)," which includes all beings whatsoever and which is activated in the Buddha after his enlightenment in Bodh Gaya, when he decides "to help humanity aboard the ship of the universal norm . . . and thus ferry them to safety across the ocean of birth and death,"[11]—to the other shore, nibbana.

According to eighty-three of the rebirth biographies in the Jataka, the bodhisattva was reborn in many lives to a life as a teacher and guide to others. In one life, he renounced the right of succession to a kingship and wandered alone into the forests, having intuitively grasped the truth of universal impermanence by merely observing the trickle of a dewdrop from the tip of a blade of grass. The bodhisattva was reborn into a life as a king a total of eighty-five times. In between, he endured life as, among other things, a potter, blacksmith, dancer, and slave. He was reborn many times as the lord of the deva angels. Many other times he was reborn as a noble animal. No humiliations had spared him in the cycle of rebirths, but neither triumph nor joy were unknown to him either. All the while, he develops the ten bodhisattva virtues (*parami*), which include the perfection of generosity, wholesome conduct, renunciation, wisdom, energy, patience, truthfulness, determination, loving-kindness, and equanimity of mind.

The Interaction of Beings

Because of their karmic interaction with the bodhisattva, many beings were reborn again and again in the various planes of existence along with him. Thus, the disciple Ananda had developed his commendable loyalty to Buddha Gotama through many lives of unselfish actions in interaction with him. Ananda was one of the great "listeners" and one of the Buddha's cousins. During the last twenty-five years of the Buddha's life, Ananda served as the Buddha's right hand in all practical matters. In this capacity, he followed the Buddha everywhere and naturally played a key role when the first systematic collection of the memorized transmissions was made three months after the Buddha's death. All Siddhattha's family members—his mother, Mahamaya, who died the week after giving birth to Siddhattha; his father, Suddhodhana, who married his mother's sister, Mahapajapati; Siddhattha's cousin Yasodhara, whom he married when they were sixteen years old; and their son Rahula, who was born the same night when the twenty-nine-year-old Siddhattha had wandered out into "homelessness"—had all been together countless times in previous lives. In a similar way, the most prominent members of the monastic order had developed their character traits and spiritual orientation in interaction with the bodhisattva through many lives. The other two main disciples, Venerable Sariputta and Venerable Maha Moggallana, had developed their strong ties to Buddha through more than thirty existences, even often being brothers.

The Same in Living

The following sutta makes a heartwarming clue to how beings who engage with one another are likely to cross paths in later lives:

> Then, in the morning, the Blessed One (Bhagava)[12] dressed, took his bowl and robe, and went to the residence of the householder Nakulapita, where he sat down in the prepared seat. Then the householder Nakulapita and the housewife Nakulamata approached the Blessed One, paid homage to him, and sat down to one side. The householder Nakulapita then said to the Blessed one:
>
> "Bhante, since I was young, when the young girl Nakulamata was given to me in marriage, I do not recall ever transgressing against her even in thought, much less by deed. We wish, Bhante, to see one another not only in this present life but also in future lives."
>
> The housewife Nakulamata in turn said to the Blessed One: "Bhante, since I was a young girl given to the young householder Nakulapita in marriage, I do not recall ever transgressing against him even in thought, much less by deed. We wish, Bhante, to see one another not only in this present life but also in future lives."

> [The Buddha said,] "Householder, if both husband and wife wish to see one another not only in this present life but also in future lives, they should have the same faith, the same virtuous behavior, the same generosity, and the same wisdom. Then they will see one another not only in this present life but also in future lives."[13]

These loving spouses who, according to the commentary to the sutta, had been parents to the Buddha in a past life, aren't predestined to meet again in their future lives, but across existences their acts of love toward each other form dominant supporting conditions for their life paths, enabling them to be attracted to each other in relationships repeatedly.

The bodhisattva's rebirth path is a trans-sangsaric event that inevitably influences large streams of beings with karmic prerequisites to understand the teaching of the universal norm. They are reborn in the same time frame when the bodhisattva's consciousness culminates in the perfect buddhahood to again interact with him and thereby be exceptionally favored by the fulfillment of his wisdom.

The Universal Norm of Buddhas

We still live in the spiritual sphere of Buddha Gotama, where his interpretation (*sasana*) of the universal norm is available to all who are interested. Although the Buddha's teachings on universal impermanence are themselves impermanent, one should not worry because in this "happy cosmic cycle" (*badda kappa*) another bodhisattva will culminate in the perfect buddhahood.[14] His name is Metteyya (The Loving One), and he is currently dwelling in his penultimate existence on one of the lower celestial worlds.[15] In enlightenment, the future Buddha—like Buddha Gotama and other buddhas before him—will transcend the cycle of sangsara forever. Then boundlessly freed from ignorance, desire-thirst, and hatred, Buddha Metteyya will enter this world with its mountains and valleys for the rest of his life span to help humanity aboard the vessel of the good teaching that will ferry them safely across the ocean of birth and death.

In the future arc of cosmic cycles, Buddha Metteyya, according to this profound understanding, is but one out of an infinite series of perfect buddhas, arising and ceasing as day after night in the dynamic process of the universes in accordance with the stream of consciousness. Their arising is neither arbitrary nor miraculous; it is the natural flowering of the dhamma, the universal norm that pulses through the fabric of existence.

17 | The Formative History of the Sangha

The remaining forty-five years of Buddha Gotama's life after enlightenment are closely linked to the spread of the Buddhist monastic order, the Sangha, in the lush spiritual life of northern India, whose currents and geographical centers are reflected in the Pali scriptures with the Buddha as a central figure. The history of the Sangha and the rules for its regulation are handed down in the Vinaya Pitaka, the third collection of writings in the Pali canon. The time-bound aspect of the dhamma belongs to the practice of the Vinaya (discipline), which in a historical sense has secured the teachings as a living spiritual tradition down to the present day. The Vinaya collection, which is generally less known in the West than the suttas, is also unique in that it contains the canon's oldest chronological account of the events immediately following the Buddha's enlightenment. Later, however, chronology is abandoned for the sake of presenting the subject matter in the set of rules, which is instituted as the order grows. In some cases, there are detailed accounts of the events that led to a rule, and in this connection, you get surprisingly down-to-earth glimpses of the Buddha figure. Apart from the biographies of rebirth, and in addition to the Buddha's self-narrative, the early biography of the Buddha is based on these accounts from the period after his enlightenment, when he appears as a public figure—a period that he no longer talks about chronologically.

The Buddha in Rajagaha

One of the Vinaya writings begins with the events that have been elucidated in the previous chapters. Thus, we hear again at length of the Buddha's enlightenment, his hesitation to make the teachings known, his walk to the Seers' Park at Sarnath, and his first two speeches delivered there. After the episode of the five ascetic kinsmen's gain of arahantship, there follows an account of fifty-five other arahants in Sarnath. This scripture also contains a record of the First Council immediately after the Buddha's death, when the tradition of the doctrine was systematized; and of the Second Council, one hundred years after his death, when the order was first split into different schools. Another Vinaya script is a kind of register that classifies all the monastic rules. They are still used punctually by the monastic order. Some of the rules have undoubtedly been instituted in the post-Buddha era and are just formally attributed to an origin with the Buddha's intervention. On the other hand, it is difficult to imagine that the extensive monastic organization that the Buddha left behind, spread over a large area of northern India, could have existed at this time without many guidelines for its existence.

The movement that took shape around the Buddha's missionary activities was never called anything other than the Sakya samanas (*samana sakyapuytiya*) during his lifetime—Sakya being the name of the clan of the Buddha.[1] This was even though the movement included members of all walks of life and population groups in North India. The movement had from the beginning a missionary aim. It was in keeping with the time and is also clear from the Buddha's invitation to the first sixty arahants in the Seers' Park in Sarnath:

> Go wandering, monks, for the benefit and happiness of humanity, out of compassion for the world, for the good, benefit, and happiness of gods and humans. . . . Proclaim the Teaching that is good in the beginning, good in the middle, and good in the end.[2]

The Monastery in Bamboo Grove in Rajagaha

After sending out the first missionary arahants, the Buddha returned alone to the area around Bodh Gaya, where he established a thousand samanas in arahantship. Together they went with the Buddha to Magadha's capital, Rajagaha, where they took up residence in a palm grove outside the city. The following wording reached King Bimbisara:[3]

> That good Gotama has a fine reputation. . . . He has a Teaching that's good in the beginning, good in the middle, and good in the end. It has a true goal and is well articulated. He sets out a perfectly complete and pure spiritual life. It's good to see such perfected ones.[4]

Together with a large retinue, the king seeks out the Buddha, who instructs him in the four noble truths. Shortly afterward, the king donated his pleasure garden, Bamboo Grove, outside Rajagaha, to the order's first permanent residence. Jivaka, the king's physician, who was living under the orders of the king to take care of sick bhikkhus, donated another grove to the growing order. Gradually several monasteries sprang up in Rajagaha. Later, the king publicly declared himself the patron of the order while remaining the patron of the Jain monastic order, which rivaled the Buddhists. This tolerant gesture was common in those days in India. The presence of the Buddha and his disciples in Bamboo Grove quickly becomes the talk of the town. Many men are subsequently attracted to the order, including the two "great listeners," Venerable Sariputta and Venerable Maha Moggallana, who had previously been disciples of a wandering philosopher. However, at a certain point, this rapid growth of the order was bound to cause displeasure in parts of the population, and the following saying began to spread: "*The Samana Gotama gets along by making us childless; the Samana Gotama gets along by breaking up families. The Samana Gotama gets along by making us widows.*"[5]

The Buddha Returns to Kapilavatthu

After the events in Rajagaha, the Buddha returned for the first time after his enlightenment to his homeland in the Sakya clan south of the lower Himalayas. The clan was one of the smaller ones in the border area between present-day Nepal and India. The early Indo-European clans in North India experimented with democracy just like their contemporary counterparts in Greece, and there is much to suggest that Siddhattha's father was elected as clan leader. He likely held the position until the Buddha returned to Kapilavatthu for the first time. The account in the Vinaya Pitaka neither mentions that the father was a king nor at that time clan leader, but it provides an interesting insight into Siddhattha's family situation.

Strong family feelings often followed in the wake of the order's progress, and Buddha's own family was no exception. The Buddha's son Rahula had come into the world when Siddhattha had left home seven years earlier and thus had never seen his father. On the Buddha's return, Yasodhara, his meditation widow, so to speak, points to the Buddha and says to Rahula, "This is your father, Rahula / Go and ask for your inheritance."[6] There is another telling example in the Vinaya Pitaka where a woman sends her child to her now-ordained husband with the words, "This is your son, samana, now get him some food." The undertone of irony and perhaps bitterness can be sensed in Yasodhara's case too. Moreover, this is the first time that the Buddha's son is mentioned in the canon.

> Then the boy Rahula approached the Lord; having approached, he stood in front of the Lord, and said: "Pleasant is your shadow, Samana." Then the Lord, rising up from his seat, departed. Then the boy Rahula, following close behind the Lord, said, "Give me my inheritance, Samana. Give me my inheritance, Samana." Then the Lord addressed the Venerable Sariputta, saying, "Well then, Sariputta, let the boy Rahula go forth."[7]

But the Buddha's father, Suddhodhana, urges the Buddha that children and young people under the age of twenty are not ordained in the future without parental permission. The Buddha satisfies this request with the rules for the ordination of novices that are instituted on this occasion. Rahula, however, remained in the order—a conventional father-son relationship never arose between the Buddha and his boy. In turn, the chief disciple, Sariputta, became the boy's spiritual guide, and several of the Buddha's sermons are spoken directly to Rahula. The result of all this favor wasn't absent. At only twenty years old, Rahula achieved enlightenment. And when the order of nuns later came into existence, Yasodhara joined it and achieved enlightenment. So, everything ended well.

Debate Pavilions and Parks of Philosophers

Sometimes in the Pali canon, the mention of the Buddha by the public is referred to as "the wandering philosopher Gotama." Although the Buddha did not consider himself a philosopher, after enlightenment he joined the philosophers' custom of wandering among the spiritual centers on the Ganges Plain to participate in exchanges of ideas with anyone who was interested. These spiritual centers were often located outside cities and towns, where wealthy citizens and rajas (kings and clan leaders) had built "debate pavilions" (*kutuhalasala*). The spiritual elite could summon each other and debate under the greatest possible public attention—and where anyone who had something to dispute could take the floor.

Many of Buddha's suttas were spoken from the pavilions, which also framed the era's other great spiritual movement, which included munis (yogis) and ascetics who resided in the "philosophers' resorts" (*aramas*) often located near the debate pavilions and were scenic areas reserved for wandering philosophers, ascetics, and yogis. The Resort of the Seers in Sarnath, where the Buddha delivered his first two suttas, was one of the most famous aramas. The suttas were often addressed to either yogis, ascetics, or Vedic priests (brahmins) in these resorts around the Ganges Plain, and several monasteries were established here in the Buddha's time.

For the first twenty years after enlightenment, the Buddha had no permanent residence anywhere. The wanderings and life in the debate pavilions are the overarching narrative frameworks for his speeches. Many suttas are spoken in the debate pavilions in dialogue with laypeople, brahmins, wanderers, or samanas of various observances. The suttas are mainly spoken in the eastern Ganges Plain, but also as far west as the land of the Kurus near present-day Delhi, where the Discourse on the Four Foundations of Mindfulness (*Satipatthana Sutta*) took place.

The Regulation of the Sangha

The Buddha was continuously instituting rules for the distribution and use of clothing, mats, utensils, food, and medicine; guidelines for ordination, rainy season stays, the relationship between supervisor and student, and much more. He also gave practical hints on nail clipping, the five advantages of chewing antiseptic wood (which is still a common way of brushing teeth in rural India), and the five disadvantages of not doing so. Apart from the formalities of ordination, early Buddhism was devoid of initiation rites, as Theravada still is. A novice, or a fully ordained bhikkhu who is a student, has the right to choose his own spiritual guide, with whom he should live for at least five years. But for the sake of his meditation, the student may well live alone, far away from the monastery, even before then. There were, and still are, no strict criteria for admission to the order. An ordained person could (can) leave the order at any time again and perhaps later be reordained. This was the case, for example, with Bhikkhu Cittahattha, who became an arahant after returning to lay life a total of six times.

The Buddha's Teachings Spread

At a certain point in the order's early history, one of the Buddha's greatest lay benefactors, the multimillionaire Anathapindika, turns up and achieves stream entry. In Savatthi (in the region bordering present-day Nepal), Anathapindika donated an attractive grove to the order, which became the setting for the Jetavana monastery, where many of the Buddha's speeches were later held. In Savatthi, the order also received a great benefactor in Visakha, also known as Migaramatta, who also achieved stream entry. She became known for permanently furnishing two thousand dining places for the order in her home. And she donated the funds for the construction of the Eastern Monastery, which was also located in Savatthi. It is a common misconception in the academic study of religion in the West that early Buddhism was reserved for monastics and did not address the laity. This is contradicted by many accounts in the canon and is underlined by the fact that the teachings were, as the Buddha said, "an open hand" that addressed everyone.

And, of course, especially the debate pavilions gave the Buddha's teachings a wide interface with the people of the Ganges Plain. As a result of their association with the Buddha or his enlightened disciples, several laypeople gained the buddho-meditative gains without then "going from home to homelessness." This was the case for the wife and parents of Yasa, one of the first arahants in Sarnath; the father of the Ugga family, who was one of the order's greatest benefactors in Vesali; the father of the Dighvu family; and the father of the Citta family, who is singled out by the Buddha as the one among the male disciples who excellently taught others the dhamma. Among the female lay disciples, Khujjuttara, "the hunchback," was especially possessed of great wisdom. She guided and induced many laywomen to achieve realizations, often stream entry.

The Early Enclaves

In several places in the Vinaya Pitaka, we hear of the Buddha's wanderings between the early enclaves of monastic communities, mainly around Rajagaha, Vesali, Savatthi, Kapilavatthu, and Kosambi,[8] sometimes accompanied by 500 or 1,250 disciples who might in turn be accompanied by enthusiastic laypeople with bullock carts full of provisions. All these monastic communities are settings for many of the discourses in the Sutta Pitaka. Many of the monastics, individually or in small groups, also spent part of the year outside the rainy season wandering between the monasteries, with detours to various centers where ascetics and munis resided. But each member formally belonged to a particular monastic enclave, to which they returned to spend the rainy season. In the later part of his life, the Buddha spent a total of nineteen rainy seasons at the Jetavana monastery in Savatthi. At this time, the monasteries functioned as self-governing collectives, and all internal affairs were decided collectively according to democratic guidelines continuously instituted by the Buddha.

A Free Intellectual Life

The members of the order were trained to dispute with opponents in the large assemblies on the debate pavilions. Among the monastics themselves there was always a lively debate. There was a free intellectual life within the monastic community, with disputes arising from the inception of the order. The disputes were kept at a reasonable level during the Buddha's lifetime but eventually threatened to split the order. A serious dispute arose while the Buddha was staying at the Ghosita monastery in Kosambi, where a bhikkhu admitted to contravening a Vinaya rule but denied it. The Buddha did not settle the conflict with his authority but assumed the role of mediator, urging both sides to show restraint in interpreting the rules instituted by the Buddha himself.[9] However, both sides were uncompromising, leading to a scuffle between the bhikkhus after which the Buddha left the monastery without a word. In the following months, he lived alone under a tree in the company of an elephant in the forest. The dispute ended with the transgressor admitting his transgression, but it was a harbinger of the friction that would eventually split the order into separate schools and give rise to the richness of scriptural developments within the schools, especially within the Abhidhamma.

All disputes, both regarding Vinaya and doctrinal issues of dhamma, should ultimately be decided by the stance of each monastic member in the monastery. If the matter became complicated, the dispute could now be settled by vote, either open or secret, where bamboo "ballots" were distributed. The decision of the majority then stood.[10] The democratic decision-making procedure was no doubt copied from the council halls of the Sakya clan, of which the Buddha's father, Suddhodhana, had allegedly been the elected leader for a while. Similar experiments with initiatives for democracy sprouted in several of the other Buddhist clan states—for example, the Land of the Free Clans (north of present-day Patna in Bihar), where the Second Council (ca. 380 B.C.E.), after the death of the Buddha, took place and which for the first time split the order in two. The elders (*theras*) became the source of eleven other schools, plus the elders' own school, Theravada, which was largely what remained of the mainstream tradition.[11]

The Great Listeners

Many of the members of the monasteries had a past as samanas, munis, or wandering philosophers before encountering the Buddha's teachings. Many were highly gifted and had great personalities. Among them was an inner circle of "great listeners" who had no small share in keeping the growing organization on its feet and later ensuring that the systematization of the Buddha's teaching was handed down to posterity. Sariputta and Maha Moggallana, the two chief disciples who were both prominent figures in the Sutta Pitaka, didn't survive the Buddha, nor did Rahula. But Ananda, the Buddha's cousin and personal secretary for twenty-five years, as well as Upali, the former barber who became the order's foremost Vinaya expert, and the highly ascetic Mahakassapa came to occupy the leading roles at the First Council, when the chanted recitations for dhamma and Vinaya were systematized immediately after the Buddha's death. Other notable figures who no doubt also had something to say on that occasion were the clairvoyant Anuruddha, also a cousin of the Buddha; Punna and Mahakappina, two dhamma speakers highly praised by the Buddha; Mahakotthita, who was praised for his expertise in logical analysis; and Mahakaccana, who was praised for his long, articulate expositions of brief summaries (i.e., sutta threads). All these venerable bhikkhus, as well as many others, achieved enlightenment. The vast majority were "double liberated"—that is, meditation experts in every aspect of samatha and vipassana. They express opinions in several discourses in the Sutta Pitaka, either in dialogues on weighty subjects with the Buddha or sometimes as main speakers.

The Establishment of the Order of Nuns

At a certain point, while the Buddha was staying in Vesali, the women were given permission to go forth from home into homelessness under the patronage of the order. It happened at the urging of the Buddha's stepmother, Mahapajapati, with Ananda as her empathetic advocate. Already from the first days in the Resort of Seers, there were women among the lay disciples who won stream entry. The fact that women were capable of spiritual perfection, which was the logical justification in Vesali for the establishment of the Order of Nuns, cannot therefore have caused any great surprise. Nevertheless, the nuns caused quite a stir, and they were not put on the same level as the bhikkhus. For example, nuns were required, regardless of their seniority in the order, to stand up to greet even a junior bhikkhu, whereas the bhikkhus had no duty to greet the nuns at all. This and other unreasonable rules were explained by the fact that such were the conditions within other sects. But the reasoning hardly comes from the Buddha, who clearly didn't consider how rival sects—the Jains, for example—organized themselves. On the contrary, several other extra rules for the nuns show an unusual understanding of feminist issues. It quickly became a problem that unmarried women in stages of unwanted pregnancy joined the order. In this connection, the order instituted a rule—and here, if anything, we hear the enlightened voice of the Buddha—that a bhikkhuni (nun) who had become pregnant before ordination could remain in the order if she wished, give birth to the child under the auspices of the monastery, and live with it until it could take care of itself.[12] How old the child had to be then is not mentioned, but a child could be ordained when it was old enough "to chase crows away from a field." In any case, the rule can be said to be very liberal for an order of nuns. Women over the age of twenty could also, under special circumstances, be ordained in their home via a messenger if they were unwillingly prevented from leaving home.

A group of the thirteen most prominent bhikkhunis are praised by the Buddha for their wisdom, meditative special skills, and abilities as excellent instructresses. Some even speak for themselves in the Sutta Pitaka, although far less often than the bhikkhus. Especially the nuns Dhammadinna and Khema are highlighted as inspiring speakers. According to the account, Khema had previously been married to the bodhisattva in a past life. Several of the women became known for their paranormal abilities, such as "the curly-haired" Bhadda, the clairvoyant Sakula, and Bhadda Kaccana. The bhikkhuni order flourished alongside the bhikkhu order within the monasteries, and nuns had their own so-called *patimokkha* assemblies, where they collectively, just like the monks, resolved various conflicts. The collection *Therigatha* (*Verses of the Elder Nuns*) contains seventy-three poems by the enlightened bhikkhunis, with the custom being to declare the attainment of arahantship before the Buddha. In comparison, *Theragatha*, which is for the bhikkhus, contains 107 poems of arahants. Considering that the women often had to overcome gender-specific obstacles before their ordination, the number of female arahants must be said to be quite impressive. Both the Buddha's stepmother, Mahapajapati, and, as mentioned, his former wife, Yasodhara, became bhikkhunis and attained arahantship.

The Last Days of Buddha's Life

The Auspicious One (Bhagava) continued his tireless wanderings between the monastic communities of the Ganges Plain until his last days. He spent the last rainy season in Beluva, near Vesali. Here he had a serious attack of what was probably dysentery. But he recovered, and the venerable Ananda, who had feared the worst, expressed his joy that the Buddha would not leave this world until the order had received final instructions.

> Now I am frail, Ananda, old, aged, far gone in years. This is my eightieth year, and my life is spent. Even as an old cart, Ananda, is held together with much difficulty, so the body of the Tathagata is kept going only with supports.
>
> Therefore, Ananda, be islands unto yourselves, refuges unto yourselves, seeking no external refuge; with the Dhamma as your island, the Dhamma as your refuge, seeking no other refuge.[13]

Buddha's final speech highlights the fundamental principle of the practice of his teachings: the individual's essential responsibility to take ownership of their spiritual journey. Through continuous, absorbed observation of the objects within the four foundations of mindfulness, the meditator becomes their own island, their own light, and their own refuge, "seeking no other refuge." These were among the Buddha's final words.

The Ending in Kusinara

After the rainy-season stay, the Buddha and Ananda went on a journey with many stays in the monasteries north of Vesali. At a certain point, the Buddha's weakened health was aggravated by acute food poisoning. With his samadhi, he suppressed the pain, and the journey continued to the region around Kusinara (near present-day Nepal). Here they arrived in the spring, now together with five hundred bhikkhus, all established in one of the four degrees of arahantship. After arriving during the spring full moon (Vesak), the assembly took up residence in a grove of flowering sandalwood trees outside the town. In a body position with outstretched legs called the lion pose, in which the Buddha was in the habit of resting, he lay down attentively on one side between two enormous sandalwood trees. And still, in the third vigil of the night, he spoke to the assembled.

> "Behold now, monastics, I exhort you. Impermanent are all elements of being! Strive with urgent earnestness (*appamada*)."
>
> This was the last word of the Tathagata.
>
> And the Bhagava entered the first jhana. Rising from the first jhana, he entered the second jhana. Rising from the second jhana, he entered the third jhana. Rising from the third jhana, he entered the fourth jhana.[14]

In this way, the dying Buddha entered and ascended in flowing succession, up through the hierarchy of jhanas to the eighth formless jhana. The exceptionally clairvoyant Anuruddha, who was present in the assembly, viewed the Buddha's stream of consciousness, and then in reverse order through the absorptions to the first jhana—and from there again up through the hierarchy to the second jhana—to the third jhana—and to the fourth jhana, which had been the bodhisattva's foundation jhana for the attainment of the perfect buddhahood forty-five years earlier during the spring full moon of Vesak.

> And rising from the fourth jhana, the Bhagava immediately passed away.[15]

Tathagata's Footprints

Buddhism in various schools spread all over East and South Asia and is today also a growing, inspiring spiritual factor in our part of the world. But it is beyond the scope of my account to enter a discussion of the developments of later Buddhism. It suffices to record that they were no less literarily prolific and sectarian branching than those of the early period. But we must not forget that the Buddha's dhamma is in the strict sense not a theory but a journey into the mind. Like the early period, the basis for the development of later Buddhism has been the subjective source of the understanding of reality, which is intuited in samadhi-developed states of consciousness. The broadest common features of expression of the Buddha's dhamma have been its vital humanity and personal freedom of spirit, the firmament of buddho-meditative spirituality (which isn't fixed anywhere in the mind or the universe), and the dazzling guiding star of enlightenment's transcendental clarity and wisdom as the goal of realization and liberation from suffering. The Thus-Arrived-or-Gone, the Tathagata, the Untraceable, left very distinctive tracks after all.

APPENDIX:

Cultural, Textual, and Metaphysical Context of Buddhism

This appendix provides supplementary background information that, while not the central focus of this book, is nevertheless important for understanding the roots of the Buddhist tradition.

1. The Three Collections in the Pali Canon

The Pali canon has been handed down in three large collections, called Tipitaka (Three Baskets) (see Bibliography of Pali Texts). The largest collection consists of the Sutta Pitaka (Basket of Discourses), which contains mainly the discourses of the Buddha but also those of several of his most prominent disciples, both male and female. In addition, there are several separate books, including the legends about the Buddha's rebirth biographies (Jataka). The second collection, Vinaya Pitaka (Basket of Discipline), contains the set of rules for monastic life and many accounts from the order's formative history, as well as the canon's oldest systematized presentation of events in the Buddha's life after his enlightenment. The third collection, the Abhidhamma Pitaka (Basket of the Higher Doctrine), contains extensive analyses and expositions of the theorems in the Sutta Pitaka.

The term *basket* refers to the wicker baskets with the prepared palm leaves on which the first written traditions of the canon's recitatives were stored in Sri Lanka from around the beginning of the Common Era. The Three Baskets have been accompanied by a steady stream of commentaries and extracanonical books, of which the Indian bhikkhu Buddhaghosa's fifth-century meditation manual, *Visuddhimagga* (The Path of Purification), is the most significant. Very little is known about Buddhaghosa from Bodh Gaya, despite his great importance to Theravada Buddhism. He was a very nerdy scholastic whose doctrinarian dissections and digressions can exhaust a modern reader. Nevertheless, his principal work, the *Visuddhimagga*, must be regarded as one of the great works of spiritual world literature. It incorporates a wide range of valuable sources that circulated in the early meditative environment of Buddhism.

2. Upanishad Teachings

In the history of Indian scriptural developments, the meditative notions of sangsara, karma, and the self first emerge in the assimilation of Vedic Brahmanism in a dozen Upanishadic texts around 600 B.C.E. The texts were composed by various unknown *rishis*, "seers," and signify a shift from the sacrificial cult teachings of the Vedas. The main theme of the Upanishads is the identification of the individual's immortal core, atman (the soul or self), with Brahman, the universal force that the Vedic priests believed they could control through their ritual sacrifices to the gods. Most likely inspired by subcultural yoga practices, the Upanishadic seers reinterpreted the universal force, Brahman, as the cosmic ground of being, which is both transcendent and immanent—and gradually, Brahman became identified with the creator god Brahma. Very little technique of meditation is explained by the Upanishads, but the seer's used Vedic mantras as objects of meditation to promote states of samadhi, where the meditating Atman became one with Brahma. Thereafter, the illusion of karma and sangsara was assumed to cease, and the soul was considered liberated. As the seers of the Upanishads renounced the significance of the Vedic sacrificial cult, their teachings were esoteric and communicated in secrecy to initiates in the forests, in contrast to Buddha's "open hand" that poured forth the new era's teachings from the debate pavilions, which served as forums for the democratization of spiritual life during the Buddha's time. The Buddha regarded the notions of Atman and Brahman as illusions, and he did not perceive the changing world of conditioned phenomena as an illusion but as the realities of *thusness*. Historically, the traces of Buddhist teachings presumably have some common roots with the yoga of the Upanishads and likely go back to the Indus civilization, which predates the arrival of Indo-European populations in the region. This early yogic tradition extended probably into what is now northern India, where meditative practices persisted within smaller communities until the Buddha's time. These techniques of concentrated meditation and personal insight gained popularity during the Buddha's era as many individuals in India grew disillusioned with the declining relevance of Vedic rituals and the perceived corruption of the priestly class. The teachings of the Upanishads eventually came to be known as Vedanta, meaning "the culmination of the Vedas," symbolizing the apex of Vedic philosophical thought.

3. Patanjali's *Yoga Sutras*

Hinduism's oldest systematic presentation of yoga and meditation formally sees the light of day with Patanjali's *Yoga Sutras*, the dating of which varies between the years 300 B.C.E. and 500 C.E. However, Patanjali is a compiler from a very ancient tradition, and as a person, he is unknown. The writing consists of 195 mnemonic sentences (Skt. *sutra*), which in book form don't take up more than half a dozen pages. Subsequently, knowledgeable yogis have been authorized by tradition to add copious expositions and explanations. These expositions are easier to date because of their polemics against late Buddhist schools. The most significant expositions are thus from the years 600 C.E. and 800 C.E.[1] Both the sutras and the later expositions are, apart from basic yoga technique, connected to Kapilamuni's Samkhya teaching, which together with the teachings of yoga was adopted by the later developed Hinduism (as we know it today) as two of its "six orthodoxies." In the commentary on Patanjali's *Yoga Sutras*, Kapilamuni is declared to have been one of the fathers of this yoga system. Kapilamuni believed that the observable world of phenomena and the mind were based on a kind of material primordial substance (Skt. *prakriti*). Behind this primordial matter radiates an eternally unchanging monad-soul (Skt. *purusha*). As a result of karma and ignorance, the soul is entangled in primordial matter and the cycle of rebirth. The soul is therefore constantly confused with the primordial matter by uneducated people. But through the jhanic absorptions, the soul is isolated and liberated by wise people. Patanjali's *Yoga Sutras* are recognized as the foundational text of all later yoga-based schools of Hinduism. According to Patanjali, consciousness is a core entity due to the immanence of the immortal soul. In the exposition of book 1, sutra 32, on concentration on consciousness as a unity, the two classical exponents Veda Vyasa and Vachaspati Micra are given the opportunity to polemicize against the Buddhist view of the coreless stream of consciousness. If consciousness is a stream, they argue, it would be impossible to concentrate consciousness. The Buddhists are therefore called "momentists" and "destructivists."

4. Jainism

Another major school of thought that arose in the sixth century B.C.E. in opposition to the Vedic culture is the Jain teaching. The founder of the teaching, Mahavira, was contemporaneous with the Buddha and is often mentioned in the Buddha's speeches. According to the Jainist tenet of animism, both organic and inorganic phenomena right down to the microscopic level were the bearers of an individual, immanent but obscured monad-soul, "turning around" in the cycle of rebirths and basically striving for transcendental purity in meditatively concentrated "isolation." Jains linked rudimentary yoga with rigid forms of self-punishing asceticism and very extensive moral prohibitions. Jainism's concepts, including the perception of ignorance and karma as a kind of matter with which the soul's purity is entangled, point back to influences from Samkhya philosophy or bear witness to a common subcultural background. In Jain's oldest canon, there are clear, although highly legendary, references to the pre-Indo-European spiritual tradition from presumably the Indus Valley culture.

5. Matter

The aggregate of matter includes the body and the objects of the senses and is described using the four symbolic elements of earth, fire, air, and water, the understanding of which aims to break down misperceptions of matter, especially with a view to overcoming mental attachments to the senses. The exposition of matter is therefore often designed as a guide to meditation on the elements in the thirty-two parts of the body, according to ancient Indian anatomy.[2] The symbolic elements can be meditated upon as individual states, element by element (according to the suttas), or as compositions in perception of the characteristics of all four elements (according to the Abhidhamma). We follow the latter interpretation here.[3] The element of earth includes extension, solidity, and form. The element of fire is the generic element of temperature (heat or cold) that separates organic matter from inorganic matter. The element of air constitutes all movement and wave vibration. In the Abhidhamma, these elements are said to be "tangible," whereas the element of water is "intangible." Water is the element of binding force that binds the other elements into definite patterns of matter. For example, in the perception of the water in a lotus pond, the volume of the water is the earth element, the temperature of the water is the fire element, and any movement is the air element, while the element of water holds the elements together in precisely the form of water. The elements co-occur with or without four secondary elements: colorant, odorant, flavoring, and nutritional substance. The Abhidhamma's commentators (approx. eighth century C.E.) developed an atomic theory based on what they perceived as the smallest analyzable constituent of matter, called *param-anu*. There are 501,147,137 *param-anus* in the width of a finger. The param-anu is the smallest possible composition of the characteristics of the symbol-elements, and like all other composite phenomena (*sankhara-dhamma*), the param-anu is characterized by the three universal characteristics (anicca, dukkha, and anatta).

6. A Great Cosmic Cycle

A great cosmic cycle, or eon (*mahakappa*) according to Buddhist cosmology, spans four subcycles during which the physical universe begins what is called (1) "the contraction," continues with (2) the process that culminates in chaos and destruction, after which (3) a new universe begins its "expansion," that then (4) continues until the next great cosmic cycle begins with "the contraction" of the existing universe. The mahakappa thus comprises two successive universes, with a typically Buddhist emphasis on precisely the tendency toward the dissolution of everything. Each universe consists of many world systems, each with its own terrestrial planets, sun, moons, stars, and upper and lower planes of existence. But since some of these planes of existence consist solely of streams of consciousness without appendages of matter, they aren't influenced by the cycles of the physical universe. The perception of how many world systems exist in each universe varies between one thousand and ten million small, medium, and large ones. The number is also under steady acceleration through the commentary literature. However, one thing is clear: The Buddhists didn't make the mistake of assuming our Earth was the center of the universe as was done in Western culture, until Copernicus demonstrated the misunderstanding. In every universe, perfect buddhas arise. In this universe, six perfectly enlightened ones have flourished, while a final and seventh, Buddha Metteyya, is on the way in his development. Thus the Buddhist teachings are discovered and repeated as universes arise and cease.

As a curiosity, it is relevant to compare the cosmology of Buddhism with modern astrophysics' perception of the universe, which is thought to be about ten to fifteen billion years old and in the process of expanding, and perhaps in several billion years will begin to contract. According to astrophysics' understanding, the universe—which includes billions of galaxies with an immeasurably large number of solar systems—began with a "big bang" and may possibly end in a reverse bang, after which a new bang will result in the beginning expansion of a new universe—for the same not entirely clarified reason as the previous time. Basically, the Buddha was not interested in cosmological speculations.

7. The Thirty-One Planes of Existence in Sangsara

The order of these planes is ethical-psychological and not topographical. The planes are divided at the top of the formless sphere that mentally corresponds to the formless (*arupa*) jhanic consciousnesses. Below follows the sphere with form that corresponds to the jhanic consciousnesses with form (*rupa*). The two upper spheres are called "the world of the gods," where the brahmas, or the higher devas, are assumed to dwell. Often in the Pali canon, these beings from the higher worlds receive teachings about the causal conditioning of their minds, impermanence, potential suffering (*dukkha*), and the coreless self, which is a novelty for them. On these occasions, the brahmas are depicted with Vedic mythological attributes. This was one of the ways in which the Buddhist scripture collectors later subordinated Vedic Brahmanism to the popular understanding of the Buddha's teachings. As consciousness matrices though, the planes are identical to the jhanic consciousness absorptions. The nonliberated meditator, who develops the jhanic dimension of consciousness but does not overcome structural ignorance, thus flows into the jhanic dimension of consciousness after biological death. A gradual transition of the lower jhana worlds is assumed to relate to the physical universe as light, whereas the higher formless jhanas exist independently as a kind of primal dimension of the stream of consciousness. Below the sphere with form begins the sensory sphere of the physical universe, which is divided at the top into seven happy planes, of which the first six are the existence planes of the lower devas (a kind of light angel). The seventh and lowest is the human plane, the sphere of the uplifted. Below here, one finds the unhappy planes of the sensory sphere: the world of animals, the world of spirits, the world of demons, and finally the sentient beings on the "downward path" (*niraya*)—or if you will, on the decline. (*Niraya* is most often translated as "hell.") The entire sensory sphere, with a certain transition of the lower jhana worlds, is dependent on the modality of the physical universe for their existence and therefore perishes with the "rolling up" of the great cosmic cycle. When all other conditions for the continuity of the stream of consciousness are suspended, the formless consciousness absorptions are the only supporting condition for the sangsaric continuity of sentient beings. Therefore, at the end of the universe, all structurally ignorant sentient beings spontaneously continue in the jhanic dimension of their streams of consciousness.[4] When the universe is again "unrolled," these expanded streams of consciousness continue and spread at various stations of existence in accordance with previously accumulated karma. For the sake of convenience, reference is made above to the systematized presentation in Abhi. Sang. 5.1–6. But the hierarchy of rebirth is mentioned in many places in the suttas—see, for example, Majj. Nik. 120. According to the suttas, the notions of sangsara's planes of existence and cosmology are based on clairvoyant investigation.

In continuation of the eighth jhana, there is another phenomenon that is neither a jhana nor an intuitive insight but involves the complete cessation of perception and feeling, resulting in a blank absence lasting up to seven days. It is called the "extinction of perception and feeling" (Ang. Nik. 9.34) and can only be achieved by an enlightened individual who has mastered all eight jhanas. The state represents the culmination of practicing the four bases of concentration in samatha, combined with attaining either non-return or full enlightenment. It is frequently mentioned in the Pali scriptures due to the high regard associated with mastering it. The samana who achieved this seemingly absurd control over consciousness was considered an expert, having mastered the full range of Buddhist meditative attainments. In many Western interpretations of Buddhism, this attainment is often mistakenly equated with the transcendental realization of nibbana, which is an incorrect understanding.[5]

8. The *Tibetan Book of the Dead*

According to the *Tibetan Book of the Dead* (*Bardo Thödol*), a tantric Mahayana Buddhist scripture, the consciousness of the deceased or the dying flows in observation of the karmic accumulations and their exaggerated projections in the so-called bardo (intermediate state). The bardo exists between the beginning of death and the moment of rebirth in the next station of existence. The duration of the bardo varies between a few days and seven times seven days, according to the mental purity of the deceased or dying person. According to Theravada, the transition between the two existences is immediate after the cessation of the last process of perception in this life. This interpretation is found throughout the Pali canon. Several of the early Buddhist schools, however, operated with the concept of an "intermediate state" that one could imagine continuing after the onset of brain death, where perception still occurs if consciousness is primary in relation to matter. The conventional perception of time is, in any case, a controversial concept in the context of consciousness phenomena in the death experience, as evidenced by accounts of near-death experiences by people in modern times who have been declared clinically dead and then awakened to consciousness.[6] From these considerations, there is no inconsistency between the interpretation of the death and rebirth process in early and later Buddhism, even though more details could be mentioned. *Bardo Thödol* is, however, first and foremost a tantric meditation manual, the content of which must be understood in the context of tantric Buddhism's highly symbolic yoga.

Abbreviations

Abhid-patth	Abhidhamma Patthana
Abhid-sang	Abhidhammattha Sangaha
AN	Anguttara Nikaya
Dhp	Dhammapada
Dhs	Abhidhamma Dhammasangani
DN	Digha Nikaya
Iti	Itivuttaka
Ja	Jataka
MN	Majjhima Nikaya
Mv	Mahavagga
Patis	Patisambhiddamagga
SN	Samyutta Nikaya
Skt.	Sanskrit
Ud	Udana
Vimm	Vimuttimagga
Vism	Visuddhimagga

Notes

Introduction

1. *Anagarika* means "the homeless one" and is an epithet for a Buddhist monk who has returned to secular life. The suffix *-ji* added to a proper name is a traditional Indian honorific. Vipassana (insight meditation) is one of Buddhism's two main forms of meditation.
2. This description is from the time I lived in Bodh Gaya. An eighty-foot-high Japanese Buddha that was erected in 1989 close to the Mahabodhi Temple is therefore not mentioned. Nor the many changes caused in recent times by an annual tourist flow of over half a million people.
3. Dhp 328. Gil Fronsdal, trans., *The Dhammapada: A Translation of the Buddhist Classic with Annotations* (Shambhala 2023).
4. Mental notes are used for sharpening attention during vipassana practice in the Mahasi Sayadaw tradition. The phenomenon is described in a later chapter. The example in the anecdote above is, of course, extreme.
5. AN 8.19. Bhikkhu Bodhi, trans., *The Numerical Discourses of the Buddha: A Translation of the Anguttara Nikaya* (Wisdom Publications, 2012).
6. Tulku Urgyen Rinpoche, *Vajra Speech: Pith Instructions for the Dzogchen Yogi* (Rangjung Yeshe, 2001), 62.
7. SN 45.63. Bhikkhu Bodhi, trans., *The Connected Discourses of the Buddha: A Translation of the Samyutta Nikaya* (Wisdom Publications, 2000).

1. The Thus-Arrived, Tathagata

1. Theravada Buddhist countries begin their chronology from the year of the Buddha's death according to a traditional dating that puts his life at 624–544 B.C.E. However, modern chronological understanding perceives 563–483 B.C.E. to be more realistic.
2. James Victor Kuhr, *Herakleitos fra Ephesos* (V. Pios Boghandel, 1917). The quote in English is translated from the Danish by me. Heraclitus, the father of process thinking in Western culture, was probably twenty years younger than Siddhattha Gotama.
3. AN 2.5. Bodhi, *The Numerical Discourses of the Buddha.*
4. MN 27. Bhikkhu Nanamoli and Bhikkhu Bodhi, trans., *The Middle Length Discourses of the Buddha: A Translation of the Majjhima Nikaya* (Wisdom Publications, 1995). It's often pointed out in translations that *tathagata* means both "the one who has thus arrived" and "the one thus gone," but for the sake of simplicity, I use "the one who has thus arrived," as the full wording does not change anything about the meaning of the epithet.
5. The concept of *tathata* (thusness) is a strongly ontologically charged concept in Buddhist teachings. The Thai Buddhist master Bhikkhu Buddhadasa explains the concept of *tathata* as follows: "When tathātā is seen, the three characteristics of anicca (impermanence), dukkha (suffering), and anatta (not-self) are seen, sunnata (emptiness) is seen, and idappaccayata (specific conditionality) is seen. Tathātā is the summary of them all—merely thus, only thus, not-otherness." (Buddhadasa, Bhikkhu, 1997). Translations from Pali to English often translate *tathata* as "reality" or "actuality," but I often prefer to use the literal meaning of the concept, "thusness," with its rich Buddhist connotations.
6. MN 22. Nanamoli and Bodhi, *The Middle Length Discourses of the Buddha.*
7. SN 12.65. Bhikkhu Bodhi, trans., *The Connected Discourses of the Buddha: A New Translation of the Samyutta Nikaya* (Wisdom Publications, 2000).
8. SN 12.65. Bodhi, *The Connected Discourses of the Buddha.*
9. See appendix section 1 for an overview of the Pali canon.
10. AN 3.25. Nyanatiloka, trans., *The Buddha's Path to Deliverance: In Its Threefold Division and Seven Stages of Purity* (Bauddha Sahitya Sabha, 1969).

2. Samana Gotama and His Self-Narrative

1. AN 3.39. Bodhi, *The Numerical Discourses of the Buddha.*
2. AN 3.39. Bodhi, *The Numerical Discourses of the Buddha.*
3. AN 3.39. Bodhi, *The Numerical Discourses of the Buddha.*
4. AN 3.39. Bodhi, *The Numerical Discourses of the Buddha.*
5. SN 12.28. Bodhi, *The Connected Discourses of the Buddha.*
6. AN 11.1. The phrase "as it actually is" or "as it really is" (*yathabhuta*) is a mnemonic stock phrase that refers to the intuitively penetrating way in which the insight meditator recognizes the true nature of the object, its thusness.
7. MN 26. Nanamoli and Bodhi, *The Middle Length Discourses of the Buddha.*
8. MN 26. Nanamoli and Bodhi, *The Middle Length Discourses of the Buddha.*
9. See appendix section 2 for an overview of the Upanishadic teachings.
10. See appendix section 3 for an overview of Patanjali's *Yoga Sutras.*
11. MN 36.
12. See appendix section 4 for a review of the Jain teachings.
13. MN 36. Nanamoli and Bodhi, *The Middle Length Discourses of the Buddha.*
14. MN 4. Nanamoli and Bodhi, *The Middle Length Discourses of the Buddha. Asavas* is most often translated into English as "taints," "corruptions," "cankers," "impurities," or "influxes." In the quote, I replace "taint" with "influx." A synonym for the *asavas* is the root conditions that activate unwholesome karma patterns that lead to the *kilesas* (defilements) of the mind. For clarity, I have inserted "(misperceived ego-) becoming" in the place of Nanamoli and Bodhi's "being" (*bhava*), which broadly refers to the cycle of rebirths always resulting from the clinging to a misperceived core self/ego in the present life.

3. The Core Teaching About Non-Core Self

1. SN 22.102. Bodhi, *The Connected Discourses of the Buddha.* Again, I have substituted Bodhi's use of "existence" (*bhava*) with "(ego-) becoming."
2. Sigmund Freud, *Das Unbehagen in der Kultur* (Grölls Verlag, 2022), 8. The quote in English is translated from the German by me.

3. SN 22.59, the Buddha's second discourse, known as the *Anatta-lakkhana Sutta*.
4. DN 16. Maurice Walshe, trans., *The Long Discourses of the Buddha: A Translation of the Digha Nikaya* (Wisdom Publications, 1995).
5. For an overview of the Upanishad teachings, see appendix section 2.
6. SN 12.15. Bodhi, *The Connected Discourses of the Buddha*. Cf. epigraph by Tulku Urgyen from *Vajra Speech* that opens this book.
7. Vism 17, sec. 167. Bhikkhu Nanamoli, trans., *The Path of Purification (Visuddhimagga): The Classic Manual of Buddhist Doctrine and Meditation* (Buddhist Publication Society, 1975).
8. AN 3.65.
9. T. W. Rhys Davids, trans., *The Milinda Panha* (Jazzbee Verlag, 2021).
10. Abhid-sang 1, sec. 27.
11. MN 38.
12. SN 12.44. Bodhi, *The Connected Discourses of the Buddha*. Again, I use "(misperceived ego-) becoming" instead of Bodhi's "existence."
13. MN 38. Bodhi, *The Middle Length Discourses of the Buddha*.
14. See appendix section 5 for a review of Buddhism's conception of matter.
15. See chapter 4, note 7.
16. *Dhamma* is often translated into English as "phenomenon" but also as "a mental object, thing, idea, principle," etc. I often prefer to retain the Pali term with its specific, subtle Buddhist connotations.
17. AN 3.136.
18. See appendix section 6 for an outline of the cosmology of Buddhism.
19. Ud 8.3. F. L. Woodward, trans. *The Minor Anthologies of the Pali Canon, Part II: Verses of Uplift (Udana) and As It Was Said (Itivuttaka)* (Pali Text Society, 1935).

4. Karma, Perception, and the Ethical Freedom of Will

1. AN 3.47. Bodhi, *The Numerical Discourses of the Buddha*. Though the quote here is unchanged, elsewhere, in the quoted English translations of Pali texts that translate *anicca* as "impermanent," I often change the translation to "momentary change" because the latter captures the phenomenologically fundamental insight in vipassana, which the Buddha always refers to by the concept of anicca. It's the first insight knowledge (or stage) in vipassana, and it is called "intuitive knowledge of rise and fall" (*udayabbaya-nana*).

2. MN 135. Nanamoli and Bodhi, *The Middle Length Discourses of the Buddha.*
3. Abhid-patth 1.
4. AN 6.63. Bodhi, *The Numerical Discourses of the Buddha.*
5. Abhid-sang 1 sec. 27; and 4. The theorem of the consciousness process (*citta vitthi*) in the Abhidhamma compendium (Abhid-sang shines a light on details of the perception process that are implicit in the central theorem of dependent origination found in the suttas. According to the theorem, many perception processes occur in the span of just a fleeting moment. The perception process is "repetition conditioned" with increasing or decreasing intensity many times when perceiving most objects. Between each process, moments of subconscious "becoming-link" (*bhavanga-citta*) flow. The first detailed theory of the perception process in the history of ideas was formulated by the Buddhists.
6. Vism 14, sec. 135. Nanamoli, *The Path of Purification.*
7. *Sankhara* is one of the five aggregates and a key term that apparently is difficult to translate. Etymologically, according to Bhikkhu Bodhi, *sankhara* means "things that act together in making other things." See Bodhi, trans., *The Connected Discourses of the Buddha.* The Pali Text Society translators switch between translations—volitional activities, formations, activities, compounds, activities-compounds, constructions, synthesis, etc. *Sankhara* is used in an ontological sense about all phenomena (except *nibbana-dhamma*, which is not a compounded phenomenon). *Sankhara* is also used in an ethical-psychologically delimited sense about karmically wholesome or unwholesome activities in the perception process. It is in this sense that I translate *sankhara* as "formative karma activities," to shine a light on their character as either *passively formed activities* in the receptive fruit phase of perception or as *actively forming activities* in the proactive phase of perception and in this sense counts as one the five aggregates (*sankhara khandha*) that are subject to clinging. When the term *sankhara* is used in the ontological sense of all phenomena (*sankhara-dhamma*), I use the translation "processes," "process activities," or "process phenomena." The further presentation will make the meaning clear.
8. The third root in each of these examples (respectively hate, non-hatred, craving, and non-craving) is a dormant condition in each example.

9. AN 3.61. Bodhi, *The Numerical Discourses of the Buddha.* Here I have replaced Bodhi's "ascetic" with the original Pali "samana."
10. AN 3.61. Bodhi, *The Numerical Discourses of the Buddha.*
11. Abhid-patth 1. Twenty-four categories of causes or relations, or conditions (*paccaya*) are enumerated, of which the karma cause constitutes one category, while another is the karma fruit effect. The remaining categories support either one or the other phase of the perception process on different relational surfaces. Previously I have mentioned "repetition conditioning" and "decisive support conditioning." In the following, for the sake of simplicity, I merely apply "support conditioning" to all supportive paccaya. All supporting conditions are implicit in the theory of "dependent origination" but are fully conceptualized for the first time in Abhidhamma theorems.
12. DN 33. The dukkha inherent in conditioned phenomena may also be translated as "suffering of the compounded."
13. SN 56.11. Bodhi, *The Connected Discourses of the Buddha.*
14. AN 10.60.
15. AN 4.77. Bodhi, *The Numerical Discourses of the Buddha.*
16. For example, AN 10.176.
17. The five silas that are normative for laypeople and explicated in many suttas are: abstaining from taking life, taking what is not given, sexual activity that causes harm, lying, and the use of intoxicants.
18. AN 2.9.
19. Vimm 11, sec. 1. N. R. M. Ehara, Ven. Soma, and Ven. Kheminda, trans., *The Path of Freedom (Vimuttimagga)* (Buddhist Publication Society, 1961).
20. AN 4.232–239. Bodhi, *The Numerical Discourses of the Buddha.*

5. Ignorance, Desire-Thirst, and Hatred

1. AN 4.77. The subject matter corresponds to the Christian problem of original sin, which in the meditative culture of India was an unknown and strange concept. The Buddha takes a strictly rational approach to the existential aspect of the question.
2. See appendix section 1. Ven. Buddhaghosa is the most important ancient commentator of Pali Buddhism.
3. AN 4.49.
4. Vism 17, sec. 242.

5 Vism 14, sec. 162. Nanamoli, *The Path of Purification.*
6. MN 22. Nanamoli and Bodhi, *The Middle Length Discourses of the Buddha.*
7. MN 44. The structure of the analysis is a fixture in many accounts of the unenlightened person's self-perception in the suttas. The unenlightened believes or perceives that (1) the self/ego is the object; (2) the self/ego owns the object; (3) the object is in the self/ego; or (4) the self/ego is in the object. *Sakkaya* literally means "own body" in the sense of one's "own collection"—i.e., of the five aggregates; when multiplied with the four distortions (*vippallasa*), twenty types of sakkaya-ditthi are obtained. *Ditthi* always refers to a wrongly conceptualized perception. *Sakkaya-ditthi* is thus a misinterpretation of the five aggregates that are subject to clinging.
8. MN 2. Nanamoli and Bodhi, *The Middle Length Discourses of the Buddha.*
9. SN 45.179–180.
10. SN 25.1.

6. The Noble Mindfulness with Clear Comprehension

1. SN 47.20. Nanamoli and Bodhi, *The Middle Length Discourses of the Buddha.*
2. SN 47.20. Nanamoli and Bodhi, *The Middle Length Discourses of the Buddha.*
3. SN 47.20. Nanamoli and Bodhi, *The Middle Length Discourses of the Buddha.*
4. SN 35.23–32.
5. AN 1.575. Bodhi, *The Numerical Discourses of the Buddha.*
6. MN 10. Nanamoli and Bodhi, *The Middle Length Discourses of the Buddha.* I replace Bodhi's original "full awareness" with "clear comprehension," a common alternative translation.
7. See MN 10.
8. Vism 14, sec. 141. Nanamoli, *The Path of Purification.*
9. Bhikkhu Bodhi, *Investigating the Dhamma: A Collection of Papers* (Buddhist Publication Society, 2015), 125. "Mindfulness in the context of satipatthana practice, always occurs as part of anupassana, a word that further clarifies its role. We usually translate anupassana as 'contemplation,' but it might also be illuminating to understand

it more literally as an act of 'observation.' The word is made up of the prefix anu, which suggests repetition or closeness, and the base -passana, which means 'seeing.' Thus, mindfulness is part of a process that involves a close, repetitive observation of the object."

10. MN 10. Nanamoli and Bodhi, *The Middle Length Discourses of the Buddha.*
11. A third overarching term for meditation in Pali is *jhe* (to think), which refers to jhanic meditation. What is interesting here is the indication of the ancient Indian conception of thoughtless cognition in deep samadhi as a form of thinking. However, in accordance with common practice, I apply the concept of meditation to both samatha and vipassana.
12. SN 47.19. Bodhi, *The Connected Discourses of the Buddha.*
13. SN 47.19. Bodhi, *The Connected Discourses of the Buddha.*
14. MN 10. Nanamoli and Bodhi, *The Middle Length Discourses of the Buddha.*
15. SN 48.12.
16. SN 35.95. Bodhi, *The Connected Discourses of the Buddha.*
17. Ledi Sayadaw, *The Manual of Light & The Manual of the Path to Higher Knowledge* (Buddhist Publication Society, 2007).
18. MN 141.
19. MN 77. Nanamoli and Bodhi, *The Middle Length Discourses of the Buddha.* I have replaced Nanamoli and Bodhi's "basis for spiritual power" with my preferred translation, "basis of accomplishment."
20. Patis 4, sec. 50. Bhikkhu Nanamoli, *The Path of Discrimination (Patisambhidamagga)* (Pali Text Society, 1982).
21. Bhikkhu Buddhadasa, *Mindfulness with Breathing: A Manual for Serious Beginners* (Wisdom Publications, 1996), 93.
22. Vism 14, sec. 143. Nanamoli, *The Path of Purification.*

7. The Development of Meditative Concentration

1. MN 7. Nanamoli and Bodhi, *The Middle Length Discourses of the Buddha.*
2. AN 3.65. Bodhi, *The Numerical Discourses of the Buddha.*
3. SN 54.9. Bodhi, *The Connected Discourses of the Buddha.*
4. SN 56.1. Bodhi, *The Connected Discourses of the Buddha.* Here I have replaced Bodhi's "things" with "the dhammas," reflecting the original Pali terminology.

5. Vism 14, sec. 139. Nanamoli, *The Path of Purification.*
6. MN 43.
7. MN 43. The five links of absorption are often mentioned with different translations in Western books on Buddhism. The metaphors I quote from Buddhaghosa's *Visuddhimagga* will clarify the way I translate them here.
8. Archaeological finds from the Indus civilization, a Bronze Age culture neighboring the Ganges Valley, contain religious symbols and phenomena prevalent in India today, including references to yoga. A soapstone seal from around the second millennium B.C.E. depicts a figure in this classical full lotus posture of yogic meditation. Sir John Marshall, *Mohenjo-daro and the Indus Civilisation* (Arthur Probsthain, 1931).
9. Alternatively, instead of using mental notes with words, count each breath in rounds of two, ten, or twenty. For example, count "one" as you inhale, "two" as you exhale, and continue up to ten before starting over. Avoid counting beyond twenty, as this may lead to drowsiness. The goal is to focus your attention on each phase of the breath as you count, helping you stay present and mindful.
10. Vism 4, sec. 89.
11. Antoine Lutz et al., "Long-Term Meditators Self-Induce High-Amplitude Gamma Synchrony During Mental Practice," *Proceedings of the National Academy of Sciences of the United States of America* 101, no. 46 (2004): 16369-16373.
12. Leigh Brasington, *Right Concentration: A Practical Guide to the Jhanas* (Shambhala Publications, 2015).
13. Vism 4, sec. 98. Nanamoli, *The Path of Purification.*
14. Vism 4, sec. 108. Nanamoli, *The Path of Purification.*
15. Patis 1, sec. 459. Nanamoli, *The Path of Discrimination.*
16. MN 140. Nanamoli and Bodhi, *The Middle Length Discourses of the Buddha.*
17. DN 1. See also appendix section 3 for an overview of the Hindu yoga according to Patanjali.
18. MN 52. See also the analyses of the jhanas in MN 111; Dhs, sec. 16; *The Expositor*, translation of *Atthasalini*, vol. 1, part 1-4.
19. For the sake of chronology in my personal narrative, I started out practicing pure vipassana the way Munindra-ji taught. Later, at retreats in the West under the competent guidance of Leigh Brasington, I practiced some of the jhanas out of curiosity.

20. In the suttas there is a mnemonic formula for four approaches to vipassana and samatha: (1) development of samatha before vipassana, (2) development of vipassana before Samatha, (3) development of samatha in coupling with vipassana, and (4) development of only vipassana (AN 4.170.) The short of it are the two approaches mentioned above: (1) vipassana with jhana; (2) vipassana without jhana—and beginning at many different levels of pre-jhanic samadhi, most often with breathing meditation at the outset, although other samatha meditations can be used as a vehicle for samadhi before the transition.
21. Vism 18, sec. 5.
22. Anagarika Munindra-ji in personal communication with the author.

8. The Four Foundations of Mindfulness

1. SN 47.4. Bhikkhu Bodhi, *Reading the Buddha's Discourses in Pali: A Practical Guide to the Language of the Ancient Buddhist Canon* (Wisdom Publications, 2020). I replace the translation "contemplation" with a phrase that conveys the meaning and etymological coloring of the Pali word, *anupassana*: "continuous absorbed observation," as I tentatively follow the clarifying recommendation by Ven. Bhikkhu Bodhi stated in chapter 6 note 9. I also replace Bodhi's "mind" with "mental states."
2. SN 47.51. Bodhi, *The Connected Discourses of the Buddha*. I have replaced Bhikkhu Bodhi's "establishments of mindfulness" with my preferred "foundations of mindfulness." Both are common translations of the Pali term *satipatthana*.
3. MN 10.
4. MN 10. Nanamoli and Bodhi, *The Middle Length Discourses of the Buddha*. Again, I substitute "continuous absorbed observation" for "contemplation" (*anupassana*).
5. The Pali word *dipa* means both "an island" and "a lamp." The latter translation is rarely used but stems from the pioneer translation of DN 16 by the founder of the Pali Text Society, T. W. Rhys David: "Therefore, O Ananda, be ye lamps unto yourselves. Be ye a refuge to yourselves." Rhys Davids is also the originator of the translation of *sati* as "mindfulness."
6. Vism 4, sec. 41.

7. MN 10. Nanamoli and Bodhi, *The Middle Length Discourses of the Buddha.*
8. MN 10.
9. MN 10. The enlightenment factors (*bojjhanga*) arise with the first insights into momentary impermanence. The factors comprise mindfulness, energy, intense interest, serenity, concentration, and equanimity of mind, while intuition has the status of the last factor, intuitive investigation of dhamma (*dhamma-vicaya*). For a detailed review of the seven enlightenment factors, see Joseph Goldstein, *Mindfulness: A Practical Guide to Awakening* (Sounds True, 2013).
10. Patis 13, sec. 41–43. Note that, oddly enough, the five spiritual faculties are not mentioned here, but they are part of the thirty-seven dhammas that lead to enlightenment.
11. MN 10. Nanamoli and Bodhi, *The Middle Length Discourses of the Buddha.* Again, I substitute the translation "contemplation" (*anupassana*) with "continuous absorbed observation." Also, in alignment with my use of nomenclature, I substitute "mental object" with the more meaningful original Pali concept "dhamma."

9. The Four Noble Truths

1. Mv 1. Bhikkhu Brahmali, *Theravada Collection on Monastic Law: A Translation of the Pali Vinaya Pitaka into English* (SuttaCentral, 2021).
2. SN 56.11. Bodhi, *The Connected Discourses of the Buddha.*
3. Mv 1. Brahmali, *Theravada Collection on Monastic Law.*
4. MN 138. Nanamoli and Bodhi, *The Middle Length Discourses of the Buddha.*
5. SN 22.60.
6. Mv 1.
7. Mv 1. Brahmali, *Theravada Collection on Monastic Law.* Where Bhikkhu Brahmali uses the terms "rebirth" and "existence," I favor the terms "renewed becoming" and "(distorted ego-) becoming." It is crucial to understand that the desire or craving for becoming inherently involves clinging to the misperception of ego during the process of perception. Conversely, the desire or craving for non-becoming reflects a rejection of the misperceived ego, tied to feelings of displeasure within the same process of becoming. Both the desire

for becoming and non-becoming ultimately lead to the misperception of ego-becoming and the cycle of rebirth.

8. MN 9. Nyanatiloka, *The Buddha's Path to Deliverance.*
9. Mv 1. Brahmali, *Theravada Collection on Monastic Law.* Where I use "mentality and the senses," Brahmali's original translation uses "name and form"; where I use "the six sense spheres of object stimulus," Brahamali's original uses "the six sense spheres"; and where I use "object stimulus," Brahmali's original uses "contact."

   Dependent origination is used everywhere in the Sutta Pitaka, both in its formal twelve-relations entirety and in several detailed analyses of dhammas, aggregates, elements, spheres, and the conditioning, interconnectedness, and becoming of the processes in the causal relation between this and that (*idappaccayata*) in relation to bondage or liberation. The theorem, which is the heartwood of Buddhist process thinking, underlines the conditioning of the six processes of perception, which are "empty of any selfhood susceptible to the wielding of power since it exists in dependence on conditions" (Vism 17, sec. 283). The Buddha explains dependent origination in ninety-three discourses in *Nidana Samyutta* in the Samyutta Nikaya. This analysis is expanded in the Abhidhamma Pitaka by the list of the twenty-four "dependencies" (*paccaya*) (see chapter 4 note 11) that includes the category of *supportive conditions* of the active and passive phases of perception, which can be explained by the theorem.
10. Mv 1. Brahmali, *Theravada Collection on Monastic Law.* Where Bhikkhu Brahmali uses the translation "craving," I prefer "desire-thirst"; where he uses "grasping," I prefer "clinging"; where he uses "existence," I prefer "(misperceived ego-) becoming." Note that feeling in the receptive phase is a supportive condition for the root condition of desire-thirst in the proactive phase and *not* a root condition for it (Vism 17, sec. 237), in which case there would not be space for free will and the elimination of suffering.
11. Mv 1. Brahmali, *Theravada Collection on Monastic Law.*
12. Mv 1. Brahmali, *Theravada Collection on Monastic Law.*
13. Mv 1. Brahmali, *Theravada Collection on Monastic Law.*
14. SN 22.59. Bhikkhu Bodhi, trans., *In the Buddha's Words: An Anthology of Discourses from the Pali Canon* (Wisdom Publications, 2005), 342. This is the Buddha's second speech in Sarnath. *Nibbida* is one of the Pali terms for

which many suggestions are found in Western translations. The English translators oscillate between "disillusionment," "disenchantment," "estrangement," "repulsion," "dispassion," "indifference," "waning," "revulsion," "disgust," "aversion," etc. Unfortunately, there has been a certain tradition of preferring the latter three variants, which are philologically correct but misleading in terms of meditative psychology. I prefer to use "disillusion" and "disenchantment" interchangeably to convey all cognitive and emotional aspects of the concept of *nibbida*. The term requires knowledge of insight meditation.

15. SN 56.11.
16. SN 56.11. Bodhi, *The Connected Discourses of the Buddha.*
17. Dhs. Thera Nynaponika, *Abhidhamma Studies: Researches in Buddhist Psychology* (Buddhist Publication Society, 1965), 31.
18. DN 16. Sister Vajira and Francis Story, trans., *Last Days of the Buddha: The Maha Parinibbana Sutta of the Pali Canon* (Buddhist Publication Society, 1964).
19. For example, Mv 1.
20. Mv 1. Brahmali, *Theravada Collection on Monastic Law.*

10. Enlightenment and Liberation

1. Vism 22, sec. 4. Nanamoli, *The Path of Purification.*
2. The sphere of consciousness or mind (*manayatana*) is a term for all forms of consciousness that has an object.
3. Vism 21, sec. 67. *The Path of Purification.*
4. Vism 22, sec. 5. Nanamoli, *The Path of Purification.*
5. MN 49. Bhikkhu Nanananda, *Concept and Reality in Early Buddhism* (Buddhist Publication Society, 1971), 61 et seq. According to Venerable Nanananda, all states of the stream of consciousness, even the eighth of the jhanas (the sphere of neither perception nor nonperception), have an object through which consciousness is "manifested"—in contrast to the objectless consciousness of nibbana that accordingly is "non-manifestative" (*vinnanam anidassanam*) and, as the case stands, is "infinite."
6. Vism 22, sec. 122. Nanamoli, *The Path of Purification.*
7. SN 43.14-43.
8. AN 3.55. Bodhi, *The Numerical Discourses of the Buddha.*
9. AN 3.47. Bodhi, *The Numerical Discourses of the Buddha.*

10. AN 3.32. Bodhi, *The Numerical Discourses of the Buddha.*
11. Ud 8.1. Woodward, *The Minor Anthologies of the Pali Canon, Part II.*
12. AN 9.34. Bodhi, *The Numerical Discourses of the Buddha.*
13. Nyanatiloka, *Buddhist Dictionary: Manual of Buddhist Terms and Doctrines* (Frewin, 1972).
14. MN 60.
15. SN 38.1. Bodhi, *The Connected Discourses of the Buddha.*
16. Dhs 1, sec. 576–582.
17. A common concept in the suttas and mostly translated as "supramundane." It implies both the transcendental nibbana as an ontological category and the nibbana element with residue left in the case of the living arahant. However, the concept of "being above the world" also encompasses the flow of the thirty-seven (psychological, moral, and spiritual) factors *leading to* enlightenment, and in this sense implies so many developmental gradients of the depth of the ocean of the dhamma. Ledi Sayadaw, *The Manual of Light & The Manual of the Path to Higher Knowledge* (Buddhist Publication Society, 2007).
18. Sayadaw, *The Manual of Light.*
19. SN 22.87. Bodhi, *The Connected Discourses of the Buddha.* Here I use the term *universal norm* where Bhikkhu Bodhi uses simply "Dhamma."
20. Vism 23, sec. 6 et seq.
21. Iti. 44.
22. Iti 44.
23. MN 72.
24. Mv 5. I. B. Horner, trans., *Book of Discipline, Vol. IV* (Pali Text Society, 1952).
25. MN 60.
26. Iti 38.
27. AN 8.19. Bodhi, *The Connected Discourses of the Buddha.*
28. SN 44.2.
29. MN 22.
30. MN 68.
31. SN 12.49. Bodhi, *The Connected Discourses of the Buddha.*

11. The Seven Purifications

1. MN 51. Nanamoli and Bodhi, *The Middle Length Discourses of the Buddha.*
2. SN 45.56. Bodhi, *The Connected Discourses of the Buddha.*

3. Erik Braun, *The Birth of Insight: Meditation, Modern Buddhism, and the Burmese Monk Ledi Sayadaw* (University of Chicago Press, 2013).
4. SN 35.23–32.
5. MN 24.
6. The nine intuitive "vipassana knowledges" (*vipassana-nanas*), or stages, are first outlined in Patis 1, sec. 283 et seq., and Patis 5, sec. 78 et seq. Formally, the first stage, "intuitive knowledge of rise and fall," according to this reckoning, is a designation *only* of the insight that is completely free from the side effects of concentration, as culminating in "the purification of the course of the practice." However, for the sake of convenience, I use the designation of the stage *also* about the beginning of the learning phase of vipassana. The stages are elaborated in various commentaries and Abhidhamma manuals and in Vism 20, 21, and 22; and Abhidsang 9, sec. 6 et seq. Furthermore, both in Patis and Vism (and elsewhere) lists of seven and eighteen vipassana knowledges are mentioned, respectively, which overlap with the nine stages of insight that are furthermore formulated as ten stages when the learning phase of the first stage (called "investigating knowledge") is reckoned as a separate stage. See Mahasi Sayadaw, *Practical Insight Meditation: Basic and Progressive Stages* (Buddhist Publication Society, 1971); *The Progress of Insight: A Treatise on Buddhist Satipatthana Meditation* (Buddhist Publication Society, 1973); and *Manual of Insight: Translated and Edited by the Metta Foundation Translation Committee* (Wisdom Publications, 2016).
7. Mahasi Sayadaw, *Practical Insight Meditation: Basic and Progressive Stages* (Buddhist Publication Society, 1971), 21. Physical processes—that is, the perception of the senses.
8. The commentary to Vism op. cit. in Vism 21, note 11.
9. MN 10. Nanamoli and Bodhi, *The Middle Length Discourses of the Buddha*. Here again I replace Bhikkhu Nanamoli and Bhikkhu Bodhi's "contemplating" with "continuous absorbed observation."
10. AN 7.71. Bodhi, *The Numerical Discourses of the Buddha*. Here again I have replaced Bhikkhu Bodhi's "taints" with "influxes," my preferred translation for the Pali *asava*.
11. MN 62. Thera Narada and Bhikkhu Mahinda, "The Great Exhortation to Rahula," in *Advice to Rahula* (Buddhist Publication Society, 1974).

12. Mahasi Sayadaw, *The Progress of Insight: A Treatise on Buddhist Satipatthana Meditation* (Buddhist Publication Society, 1973), 17 et seq.
13. Vism 21, sec. 24.
14. Vis. Mag. 21, sec. 35. Nanamoli, *The Path of Purification.*
15. AN 7.74. Bodhi, *The Numerical Discourses of the Buddha.*
16. MN 137. Nanamoli and Bodhi, *The Middle Length Discourses of the Buddha.*
17. Nyanatiloka, *Buddhist Dictionary: Manual of Buddhist Terms and Doctrines*, ed. Nyanaponika (Frewin, 1972).
18. MN 137. Nanamoli and Bodhi, *The Middle Length Discourses of the Buddha.*
19. Mahasi Sayadaw, *Progress of Insight*, 21.
20. Mahasi Sayadaw, *Progress of Insight*, 22.

12. Stream Entry

1. Patis 23, sec. 2.
2. Mahasi Sayadaw, *Practical Insight Meditation: Basic and Progressive Stages* (Buddhist Publication Society, 1971), 31.
3. See Vism 22.
4. MN Sutta 56. Nanamoli and Bodhi, *The Middle Length Discourses of the Buddha.*
5. SN 56.51-60.
6. SN 55.6. Bodhi, *The Connected Discourses of the Buddha.*
7. SN 55.1. Bodhi, *The Connected Discourses of the Buddha.*
8. SN 55.4. Bodhi, *The Connected Discourses of the Buddha.*
9. SN 55.10.
10. Mahasi Sayadaw, *Practical Insight Meditation*, 36 et seq.
11. MN 56. Nanamoli and Bodhi, *The Middle Length Discourses of the Buddha.*
12. MN 56. Nanamoli and Bodhi, *The Middle Length Discourses of the Buddha.*
13. Pe Maung Tin, trans. *The Expositor*, translation of *Atthasalini*, vols. 1-2 (1920-1921), 306. Buddhaghosa's commentary.
14. Vism 19, sec. 27.
15. SN 25.1. Bodhi, *The Connected Discourses of the Buddha.*
16. SN 25.1. Bodhi, *The Connected Discourses of the Buddha.*

17. Vism 19, sec. 27. Nanamoli, *The Path of Purification.*
18. Dhp, 113. Fronsdal, *The Dhammapada.*

13. Practicing Loving-Kindness

1. MN 7.
2. Joseph Goldstein, *One Dharma: The Emerging Western Buddhism* (HarperSanFrancisco, 2002), 107.
3. Vism 9, sec. 10.
4. Vism 9, sec. 10. Nanamoli, *The Path of Purification.*
5. In this category, you can also meditate on pet animals, but according to Buddhaghosa, you cannot use an animal as a benefactor.
6. Vism 9, sec. 12. Nanamoli, *The Path of Purification.*
7. MN 7. Nanamoli and Bodhi, *The Middle Length Discourses of the Buddha.*
8. Modern psychological studies show that meditation on loving-kindness increases our ability to develop emotional empathy for ourselves and others. Empathy enhances social connectedness and prosocial behavior, increases positive feelings in general, and reduces negative feelings, especially anger, anxiety, and depression. For this reason, the meditation has been incorporated into secular therapeutic mindfulness practices in Western psychology; for instance, mindfulness-based stress reduction, mindfulness-based cognitive therapy, and self-compassion therapy, even though there is a clear distinction between the secular and the spiritual application of the meditation, as indicated above. There is also a big difference in the levels of samadhi developed in Buddhism versus Western therapeutic mindfulness practices—and the catharsis of the meditation varies accordingly.

14. Other Samatha Meditations

1. Island Hermitage, near Dodanduwa, and founded by Western monks in 1911.
2. MN 119. Nanamoli and Bodhi, *The Middle Length Discourses of the Buddha.*
3. MN 10. They are also called the "impurity" (*asubha*) meditations.
4. See appendix section 5 for a review of the elements of matter.

5. MN 28; Vism 8 and 11. See appendix section 5.
6. Vism 11.
7. MN 140. See also Dhs 1, sec. 265–268.
8. MN 140.
9. D. J. Chalmers, "Consciousness and Its Place in Nature," in *Philosophy of Mind: Classical and Contemporary Readings*, ed. D. J. Chalmers (Oxford University Press, 2002).
10. Amy Schmidt has written a wonderful monograph on Dipa Ma. See *Dipa Ma: The Life and Legacy of a Buddhist Master* (Blue Ridge, 2005).
11. For the four basic elements or perceptual characteristics of matter, see appendix section 5.
12. Vism 4, sec. 31. Nanamoli, *The Path of Purification*.
13. For kasinas, see Vism 4 and 5 and MN 77.
14. Vism 12, 2 et seq. Buddhaghosa includes the four formless jhanas in the preparation for paranormal abilities, but for the sake of convenience, only the first four jhanas with form are mentioned above, as they are the minimum. Dipa Ma mastered all eight jhanas.
15. Schmidt, *Dipa Ma*.
16. MN 39.
17. MN 128. Anuruddha was one of the Buddha's cousins and one of the "great listeners"—that is, important disciples.
18. SN 21.3.
19. MN 39. Nanamoli and Bodhi, *The Middle Length Discourses of the Buddha*. I have replaced Nanamoli and Bodhi's original "divine eye" with my preferred translation, "celestial eye."
20. DN 2.
21. Vism 13, sec. 4. Nanamoli, *The Path of Purification*.

15. Knowledge of Recollection of Past Lives

1. This and other terms about death and rebirth in this chapter are from the postcanonical literature. See Abhid-sang. 5 and Vism 17, sec.163 and 19. However, these notions are implicit in the canon. Moreover, "rebecoming" (*punabbhava*) is the common canonical term for rebirth in the suttas, while "relinking" (*patisandhi*) is the preferred term in the postcanonical literature. Mind you, "reincarnation" (a Christian term) implies conceptually "a substance soul" and is therefore a term never used in authentic reviews of Buddhism.

2. Vism 13, sec. 22 et seq. *Patisandhi* (relinking); that is, a rebirth-linking moment of consciousness, which is technically the karmic fruition of the previous life's death process. It performs the function of causal reconnection of the stream of moments of consciousness from one existence to the next.
3. Vism 13, sec. 22 et seq.
4. Vism 13, sec. 22 et seq.
5. Vism 13, sec. 22 et seq. The quote within the quote is from the mnemonic sutta formula in DN 2 among other places. This is thus the canonical standard presentation of the direct knowledge of recollection of past lives. Buddhaghosa's account is an exposition of the sutta formula, which begins his account and is repeated here at the end of his review. An eon of world contraction and expansion is a great cosmic cycle; see appendix section 6.
6. See Ian Stevenson (1974, an American psychiatrist who investigated twenty cases of spontaneous recall of past lives by young children; and Bhikkhu Analayo, *Rebirth in Early Buddhism: Current Research* (Wisdom Publications, 2018). Bhikkhu Analayo investigated an amazing case in Sri Lanka. As well known in Western culture, the Greek philosopher Pythagoras claimed to have remembered his past lives. Also, Plato and Socrates believed in the existence of past lives. It's not an uncommon belief today in Asia and South America across different religious observations.
7. DN 1. Walshe, *The Long Discourses of the Buddha.*
8. This term and the following in this chapter are from the postcanonical literature. See Abhid-sang. 5, sec. 7; Vism 17, sec. 163; and Vism 19, sec.15. But these are implicit notions from the canon.
9. For a commentary on the *Tibetan Book of the Dead*, see appendix section 8.
10. Abhid-sang 5, sec. 11.
11. Abhid-sang 5, sec. 11. Cf. the principle of the process of death and rebirth in the template for dependent origination: Conditioned by ignorance is the reproduction karma. Conditioned by the reproductive karma (of the past life), relinking consciousness arises (in the next life). Conditioned by relinking consciousness is mentality and body—that is, the karma-fruit-related aspect of the embryonic process in a subconscious flow (*bhavanga-sota*)—until the conscious series of perception arises in the new life. But for the fully enlightened one, all ignorance is eliminated, and therefore no reproduction karma arises.

Consciousness is therefore terminated (*nirodho*) in the final nibbana (*parinibbana*). Note that "subconscious moments of becoming" (*bhavanga-citta*) also flow between the conscious processes of perception in contemporary life.

16. In Tathagata's Footsteps

1. AN 2.5. Bodhi, *The Numerical Discourses of the Buddha.*
2. MN 71.
3. MN 71. Nanamoli and Bodhi, *The Middle Length Discourses of the Buddha.*
4. AN 4.24. Bodhi, *The Connected Discourses of the Buddha.* Mara is a kind of a fallen deva angel.
5. James Victor Kuhr, *Herakleitos fra Ephesos* (V. Pios Boghandel, 1917).
6. For a review of the planes of existence, see appendix section 7.
7. For a review of Buddhist cosmology, see appendix section 6.
8. SN 15.3. Bodhi, *The Connected Discourses of the Buddha.*
9. In the above and following, reference is mainly made to the systematized presentation that can only be found in the postcanonical literature: the *Nidana-Katha* scripture (the so-called Buddha legend), which is added to the Jataka collection and the *Cariyapitaka* (The Basket of Conduct) as an introduction; also, the *Buddha-Vamsa* (The Lineage of the Buddhas) and the *Cariyapitaka* (The Basket of Conduct), furthermore, the *Madhuratthavilasini* (The Clarifier of the Sweet Meaning), which is the commentary on the *Buddha-Vamsa* and which collects all the threads of the bodhisattva concept under the Theravada point of view. According to the *Buddha-Vamsa*, Siddhattha had received instruction and confirmation from twenty-four previous highly perfected buddhas, but only seven are mentioned in the suttas.
10. Jack Kornfield, ed. *The Teachings of the Buddha* (Shambhala Publications, 2024), 122.
11. Ja, *Nidana-Katha*. E. B. Cowell, ed. *Stories of the Buddha's Former Births: Translation of the Jataka* (Pali Text Society 1895-1907).
12. The epithet *Bhagava*, here translated as "the Blessed One," is a spiritual courtesy title that is impossible to translate into Western languages. The title is still common in the mention of present-day spiritual figures in India. *Bhagava* is often translated as "the Divine

One," "the Blessed One," "the Auspicious One," "the Exalted One," "the Highly Honored One," and "the Lord," etc.

13. AN 4.55. Bodhi, *The Numerical Discourses of the Buddha.*
14. See appendix section 6 for a review of the cosmic cycles.
15. The Pali canon mentions Metteyya only once, as Buddha Gotama predicts his attainment of perfect buddhahood sometime in the future (DN 26). At that time, Metteyya was a bhikkhu in the order. However, there is a very brilliant hagiography about the future Buddha in postcanonical literature.

17. The Formative History of the Sangha

1. The Sakya clan still flourishes scattered over a large area in the lower Himalayas, from the Kathmandu valley to Kalimpong on the border of Sikkim, where the author has visited them. Unlike the rest of the area's population, who are either Hindus or Mahayana Buddhists, the Sakyas adhere to Theravada Buddhism.
2. Mv 1. Brahmali, *Theravada Collection on Monastic Law.*
3. Magadha (present-day Bihar) is the best known of the kingdoms of ancient and medieval India. The two largest empires in Indian history emanated from here: the Maurya dynasty in the third century B.C.E. and the Gupta dynasty in the fourth century C.E. King Bimbisara is also mentioned in both the Jain scriptures and the Hindu scriptures. He conquered the neighboring country of Anga and thus laid the foundation for the Magadha kingdom and its immeasurable riches, which were the target of Alexander the Great's campaign to India in the fourth century B.C.E.—a goal he, as is well known, didn't fulfill, as his soldiers refused to follow him farther than the Punjab in northwest India.
4. Mv 1, sec. 4. Brahmali, *Theravada Collection on Monastic Law.*
5. Mv 1, sec. 4. Brahmali, *Theravada Collection on Monastic Law.*
6. Mv 1, sec. 4. Brahmali, *Theravada Collection on Monastic Law.*
7. Mv 1, sec. 4. Brahmali, *Theravada Collection on Monastic Law.*
8. Kosambi was in the vicinity of present-day Allahabad.
9. Mv 10. sec. 4.
10. Cullavagga 4, vol. 5.
11. Abhidhamma Katha.

12. Cullavagga 10, vol. 5. Brahmali, *Theravada Collection on Monastic Law.*
13. DN 16. Vajira and Story, *Last Days of the Buddha.*
14. DN 16. Vajira and Story, *Last Days of the Buddha.*
15. DN 16. Vajira and Story, *Last Days of the Buddha.*

Appendix

1. James Haughton Woods, trans., *The Yoga-System of Patanjali* (Harvard University Press, 1914).
2. MN 28.
3. Abhid-sang 6, sec. 2 et seq.
4. AN 10.29.
5. Nyanatiloka, *Buddhist Dictionary: Manual of Buddhist Terms and Doctrines*, ed. Nyanaponika (Frewin, 1972), 108; Abhid-sang. 4, sec. 14.
6. Pim Van Lommel, *Consciousness Beyond Life: The Science of the Near-Death Experience* (HarperOne, 2010).

Bibliography of Pali Texts

This bibliography includes canonical and postcanonical texts of the Theravada tradition. The texts I reference most frequently are suttas from the Majjhima Nikaya (MN), the Anguttara Nikaya (AN), and the Samyutta Nikaya (SN) of the Sutta Pitaka. My quotations of these texts are mainly from translations by Ven. Bhikkhu Bodhi and Ven. Bhikkhu Nanamoli. Other translators are occasionally referenced, and their editions are listed below in the "Other Sources of Canonical Literature" section. This section also includes texts from the Khuddaka Nikaya, the Vinaya Pitaka, and the Abhidhamma Pitaka.

In the notes, direct quotations of the suttas include the sutta number as well as the translator's name and the title of the English edition of the source text. Paraphrases of and general references to suttas include only the sutta number. A sutta number combines the abbreviation of a sutta collection's title with a number corresponding to the sutta's location within the collection. For example, MN 10 is Majjhima Nikaya, sutta 10. See the abbreviations key for more information.

For other titles mentioned in the notes, see Bibliography of Secondary Sources and Sanskrit Texts.

Sutta Pitaka

Bodhi, Bhikkhu, trans. *The Connected Discourses of the Buddha: A New Translation of the Samyutta Nikaya*. Wisdom Publications, 2000.

Bodhi, Bhikkhu, trans. *The Numerical Discourses of the Buddha: A New Translation of the Anguttara Nikaya*. Wisdom Publications, 2012.

Nanamoli, Bhikkhu, and Bhikkhu Bodhi, trans. *The Middle Length Discourses of the Buddha: A Translation of the Majjhima Nikaya.* Wisdom Publications, 1995.

Walshe, Maurice, trans. *The Long Discourses of the Buddha: A Translation of the Digha Nikaya.* Wisdom Publications, 1995.

Other Sources of Canonical Literature

Aung, S. Z., and C. A. F. Rhys Davids, trans. *Points of Controversy (Katthavatthu).* Pali Text Society, 1915.

Bodhi, Bhikkhu, trans. *In the Buddha's Words: An Anthology of Discourses from the Pali Canon.* Wisdom Publications, 2005.

Bodhi, Bhikkhu, trans. *The Suttanipata: An Ancient Collection of the Buddha's Discourses Together with Its Commentaries.* Wisdom Publications, 2017.

Brahmali, Bhikkhu. *Theravada Collection on Monastic Law: A Translation of the Pali Vinaya Pitaka into English.* SuttaCentral, 2021.

Cowell, E. B., ed. *Stories of the Buddha's Former Births (Jataka)*, vols. 1-4. Pali Text Society, 1895-1907.

Fronsdal, Gil. *The Dhammapada: A Translation of the Buddhist Classic with Annotations.* Shambhala Publications, 2023 (second edition).

Horner, I. B. *Book of Discipline, Vol. 5.* Pali Text Society, 1952.

Horner, I. B. *Chronicle of the Buddhas (Buddhavamsa).* Pali Text Society, 1975.

Kornfield, Jack, ed. *The Teachings of the Buddha.* Shambhala Publications, 2024 (reissue).

Nanamoli, Bhikkhu. *The Path of Discrimination (Patisambhidamagga).* Pali Text Society, 1982.

Nanamoli, Thera. *Three Cardinal Discourses by the Buddha.* Buddhist Publication Society, 1972.

Narada, U, trans. *Conditional Relations (Tikapatthana, Dukapatthana)*, vols. 1-2. Pali Text Society, 1969.

Nyanaponika, Thera, ed. *Advice to Rahula: Four Discourses of the Buddha.* Buddhist Publicatin Society, 1961.

Nyanaponika, Thera, and Bhikkhu Bodhi, trans. *Anguttara Nikaya Anthology.* Buddhist Publication Society, 2007.

Rhys Davids, T. W., trans. *The Milinda Panha: Questions of Kind Milinda.* Jazzybee Verlag, 2017.

Rhys Davids, T. W., trans. *A Buddhist Manual of Psychological Ethics (Dhammasangani).* Pali Text Society, 1900.

Thera, Nyanatiloka, trans. *The Buddha's Path to Deliverance: In Its Threefold Division and Seven Stages of Purity.* Bauddha Sahitya Sabha, 1969.

Vajira, Sister, and Francis Story, trans. *The Last Days of the Buddha: The Mahaparinibbana Sutta.* Buddhist Publication Society, 1974.

Woodward, F. L., trans. *The Minor Anthologies of the Pali Canon, Part II: Verses of Uplift (Udana) and As It Was Said (Itivuttaka).* Pali Text Society, 1935.

Postcanonical Literature

Ehara, N. R. M., Soma Thera, and Kheminda Thera, trans. *The Path of Freedom (Vimuttimagga).* Buddhist Publication Society, 1961.

Geiger, Wilhelm, and Mabel H. Bode, trans. *The Great Chronicle of Ceylon (Mahavamsa).* Pali Text Society, 1980 (reprint).

Maha Thera, Narada, trans. *A Manual of Abhidhamma (Abhidhammattha Sangaha).* Buddhist Publication Society, 1975 (third revised edition).

Nanamoli, Bhikkhu, trans. *The Path of Purification (Visuddhimagga).* Buddhist Publication Society, 1975.

Saddhatissa, H., trans. *The Birth Stories of the Ten Bodhisattas (Dasabodhisattupattikatha).* Pali Text Society, 1975.

Tin, Pe Maun, trans. *The Expositor (Atthasalini)*, vols. 1-2. Pali Text Society, 1920-1921.

Bibliography of Secondary Sources and Sanskrit Texts

Adikaram, E. W. *Early History of Buddhism in Ceylon*. Puswella, 1946.

Analayo, Bhikkhu. *Perspectives on Satipatthana*. Windhorse Publications, 2013.

Analayo, Bhikkhu. *Rebirth in Early Buddhism: Current Research*. Wisdom Publications, 2018.

Analayo, Bhikkhu. *Satipatthana: The Direct Path to Realization*. Windhorse Publications, 2003.

Bareau, A. "Les sectes bouddhiques du Petit Véhicule et leurs Abhidharmapitaka." *Bulletin de l'Ecole rançaise d'Extrême-Orient* 44, no. 1 (1951): 1–11.

Bodhi, Bhikkhu. *Investigating the Dhamma: A Collection of Papers*. Buddhist Publication Society, 2015.

Bodhi, Bhikkhu. *Reading the Buddha's Discourses in Pali: A Practical Guide to the Language of the Ancient Buddhist Canon*. Wisdom Publications, 2020.

Brasington, Leigh. *Right Concentration: A Practical Guide to the Jhanas*. Shambhala Publications, 2015.

Braun, Erik. *The Birth of Insight: Meditation, Modern Buddhism, and the Burmese Monk Ledi Sayadaw*. University of Chicago Press, 2013.

Buddhadasa, Bhikkhu. *Mindfulness with Breathing: A Manual for Serious Beginners*. Wisdom Publications, 1996.

Buddhadasa, Bhikkhu. *The Natural Cure for Spiritual Disease: A Guide into Buddhist Science*. Dhammadana Foundation, 1997.

Buddharakkhita, Acharya, trans. "Karaniya Metta Sutta: The Hymn of Universal Love." In *Metta: The Philosophy and Practice of Universal Love*. Buddhist Publication Society, 1989.

Campbell, Joseph. *Oriental Mythology: The Masks of God*. Penguin Books, 1976.

Chalmers, D. J. "Consciousness and Its Place in Nature." In *Philosophy of Mind: Classical and Contemporary Readings*, edited by D. J. Chalmers. Oxford University Press, 2002.

Conze, Edward. *Further Buddhist Studies*. B. Cassirer, distributed by Luzac, 1975.

Conze, Edward, trans. *The Large Sutra on Perfect Wisdom*. University of California Press, 1975.

Conze, Edward, trans. *Selected Sayings from the Perfection of Wisdom*. Shambhala Publications, 1975.

Conze, Edward. *Thirty Years of Buddhist Studies*. Columbia University of South Carolina Press, 1968.

Conze, Edward, I. B. Horner, D. Snellgrove, and A. Waley, eds. *Buddhist Texts Through the Ages*. Bruno Cassirer, 1954.

Cranston, Sylvia, ed. *Reincarnation: The Phoenix Fire Mystery*. Theosophical University Press, 1994.

Dayal, Har. *The Bodhisattva Doctrine in Buddhist Sanskrit Literature*. Motilal Banarsidass, 1932.

Demiéville, Paul. "Sur la mémoire des existences antérieures." *Bulletin de l'École française d'Extrême-Orient*, vol. 27 (1927).

Dutt, Nalinaksha. *Early History of the Spread of Buddhism and the Buddhist Schools*. Luzac, 1925.

Dutt, R. C. *The Ramayana and the Mahabharata: Condensed into English Verse*. Dutton, 1969.

Eliade, Mircea. *A History of Religious Ideas*. Vol. 2. University of Chicago Press, 1982.

Eliade, Mircea. *A History of Religious Ideas*. Vol. 3. University of Chicago Press, 1985.

Eliade, Mircea. *Yoga Immortality and Freedom*. Princeton University Press, 1985.

Evans-Wentz, W. Y., ed. *The Tibetan Book of the Dead*. Oxford University Press, 1960.

Evans-Wentz, W. Y., ed. *The Tibetan Book of the Great Liberation*. Oxford University Press, 1954.

Evans-Wentz, W. Y., ed. *Tibetan Yoga and Secret Doctrines*. Oxford University Press, 1958.

Frauwallner, E. *The Earliest Vinaya and the Beginnings of Buddhist Literature*. Rome Istituto Italiano per il Medio ed Estremo Oriente, 1956.

Freud, Sigmund. *Das Unbehagen in der Kultur*. Grölls Verlag, 2022.
Giles, H. A. *The Travels of Fa Hsien*. Cambridge University Press, 1923.
Glasenapp, Helmuth von. *The Doctrine of Karman in Jain Philosophy*. Trustees, Bai Vijibai Jivanlal, 1942.
Goenka, S. N. *The Discourse Summaries*. Vipassana Research Publications, 2000.
Goldstein, Joseph. *Mindfulness: A Practical Guide to Awakening*. Sounds True, 2013.
Goldstein, Joseph. *One Dharma: The Emerging Western Buddhism*. HarperSanFrancisco, 2002.
Goldstein, Joseph, and Jack Kornfield. *The Path of Insight Meditation*. Shambhala Publications, 1995.
Grønbech, Vilh. *Buddha*. Thaning & Appel, 1952.
Hoernle, A. F. R., ed. *Manuscript Remains of Buddhist Literature found in Eastern Turkestan*. Vol. 1. Clarendon Press, 1916.
Ikeda, Daisaku. *Buddhism in the First Millennium*. Kodansha International, 1977.
Ireland, John D., trans. *Samyutta Nikaya: An Anthology*. Buddhist Publication Society, 1967.
Jacobi, H., trans. *Gaina Sutras*. Part l. Sacred Books of the East Series. Oxford University Press, 1887.
Jacobi, H., trans. *Gaina Sutras*. Part 2. Sacred Books of the East Series. Oxford University Press, 1895.
Jones, J. J., trans. *The Mahavastu*. Vol. 1. Luzac, 1949.
Jones, J. J., trans. *The Mahavastu*. Vol. 2. Luzac, 1952.
Jones, J. J., trans. *The Mahavastu*. Vol. 3. Luzac, 1956.
Joshi, Lal Mani. *Brahmanism Buddhism and Hinduism*. Buddhist Publication Society, 1970.
Kalupahana, David J. *Causality: The Central Philosophy of Buddhism*. University Press of Hawai'i, 1975.
Keith, A. B. *The Samkhya System*. Oxford University Press, 1918.
Kern, H., trans. *Saddharma-pundarika, or the Lotus of the True Law*. Sacred Books of the East Series. Oxford University Press, 1884.
Kirk, G. S. *Heraclitus, the Cosmic Fragments*. University of Cambridge Press, 1954.
Kornfield, Jack. *Living Buddhist Masters*. Buddhist Publication Society, 1977.
Knaster, Mirka. *Living This Life Fully: Stories and Teachings of Munindra*. Shambhala Publications, 2010.

Kuhr, James Victor. *Herakleitos fra Ephesos*. V. Pios Boghandel, 1917.

Law, B. E. *A History of Pali Literature*. Vols. 1-2. Bhartiya Publishing House, 1974.

Lévi, Sylvain. "Sur la récitation primitive des textes bouddhiques." *Journal Asiatique*, (May-June 1915).

Lutz, Antoine, Lawrence L. Greischar, Nancy B. Rawlings, Matthieu Ricard, and Richard J. Davidson. "Long-Term Meditators Self-Induce High-Amplitude Gamma Synchrony During Mental Practice." *Proceedings of the National Academy of Sciences of the United States of America* 101, no. 46 (November 16, 2004): 16369-16373.

Marshall, Sir John. *Mohenjo-daro and the Indus Civilisation*. Arthur Probsthain, 1931.

Mascaró, Juan, trans. *The Bhagavad Gita*. Penguin Books, 1965.

Mejer, Jørgen. *Filosofferne før Sokrates*. Munksgaard, 1971.

Mitra, Rajendralala, trans. *The Lalita-vistara* (The Exposition of Recreations). Vols. 1-3. Baptist Mission Press, 1881, 1882, 1886.

Minh Chau, Thich. *The Chinese Madhyama Agama and the Pali Majjhima Nikaya: A Comparative Study*. Motilal Banarsidass, 1964.

Muerti, T. R. V. *The Central Philosophy of Buddhism*. George Allen & Unwin, 1955.

Nanananda, Bhikkhu. *Concept and Reality in Early Buddhism*. Buddhist Publication Society, 1971.

Narasu, P. Laksmi. *The Essence of Buddhism*. Asian Educational Services, 1993.

Nyanaponika, Thera. *Abhidhamma Studies: Researches in Buddhist Psychology*. Buddhist Publication Society, 1965.

Nyanaponika, Thera. *The Heart of Buddhist Meditation*. Buddhist Publication Society, 1962.

Nyanaponika, Thera, and H. Hecker. *Great Disciples of the Buddha: Their Lives, Their Works, Their Legacy*, edited by Bhikkhu Bodhi. Buddhist Publication Society, 1997.

Nyanatiloka. *Buddhist Dictionary: Manual of Buddhist Terms and Doctrines*, edited by Nyanaponika. Frewin, 1972.

Nyanatiloka, Mahathera. *Guide Through the Abhidhamma-Pitaka: Being A Synopsis of the Philosophical Collection Belonging to the Buddhist Pali Canon*. Buddhist Publication Society, 1971.

Poppe, Nicholas, trans. *The Twelve Deeds of the Buddha: A Mongolian Version of the Lalita-vistara*. Cambridge University Press, 2009.

Price, A. F., and Wong Lou-Lam, trans. *The Diamond Sutra and the Sutra of Hui Ning*. Shambhala Publications, 1969.

Prior, C. Robert. "Anagarika Munindra and the Historical Context." In *Buddhist Studies Review* 23, no. 2 (2006): 241-248.

Przyluski, Jean. *Le Concile de Rājagṛha: Introduction à l'histoire des canons et des sectes bouddhiques*. Librairie Orientaliste Paul Geuthner, 1926-1928.

Radhakrishnan, S., trans. *The Principal Upanishads*. Allen & Unwin, 1953.

Rapson, E. J. *The Cambridge History of India*. Vol. 1, *Ancient India*. Cambridge University Press, 1922.

Rescher, Nicholas. *Process Metaphysics: An Introduction to Process Philosophy*. State University of New York Press, 1996.

Rhys Davids, T. W., trans. *Buddhist Birth-Stories*. Asian Educational Services, 1925.

Rhys Davids, T. W. *Buddhist India*. T. Fisher Unwin, 1911.

Rhys Davids, T. W. *The History and Literature of Buddhism*. Susil Gupta, 1962.

Russell, Bertrand. *History of Western Philosophy*. George Allen & Unwin Ltd., 1962.

Salomon, Richard. *The Buddhist Literature of Ancient Gandhara: An Introduction with Selected Translations*. Wisdom Publications, 2018.

Salzberg, Sharon. *Lovingkindness: The Revolutionary Art of Happiness*. Shambhala Publications, 1995.

Salzberg, Sharon. *Real Happiness: The Power of Meditation; A 28-Day Program*. Workman, 2011.

Sarathchandra, E. R. *Buddhist Psychology of Perception*. Ceylon University Press, 1958.

Sayadaw, Ledi. *The Manual of Insight: Vipassana Dipani and The Noble Eightfold Path and Its Factors Explained: Magganga Dipani*. BPS Pariyatti Editions, 1992.

Sayadaw, Ledi. *The Manual of Light & The Manual of the Path to Higher Knowledge*. Buddhist Publication Society, 2007.

Sayadaw, Ledi. *The Requisites of Enlightenment*. Buddhist Publication Society, 1971.

Sayadaw, Mahasi. *Manual of Insight: Translated and Edited by the Metta Foundation Translation Committee*. Wisdom Publications, 2016.

Sayadaw, Mahasi. *Practical Insight Meditation: Basic and Progressive Stages*. Buddhist Publication Society, 1971.

Sayadaw, Mahasi. *The Progress of Insight: A Treatise on Buddhist Satipatthana Meditation*. Buddhist Publication Society, 1973.

Schmidt, Amy. *Dipa Ma: The Life and Legacy of a Buddhist Master*. Blue Ridge, 2005.

Shankman, Richard. *The Experience of Samadhi: An In-depth Exploration of Buddhist Meditation*. Shambhala Publications, 2008.

Smith, Vincent A. *The Oxford History of India*. Oxford University Press, 1981.

Stcherbatsky, Th. *The Conception of Buddhist Nirvana*. Publishing Office of the Academy of Sciences of the USSR, 1927.

Stcherbatsky, Th. *The Central Conception of Buddhism and the Meaning of the Word Dharma*. Cambridge University Press, 2009.

Stevenson, Ian. *Twenty Cases Suggestive of Reincarnation*. University of Virginia Press, 1974.

Suzuki, D. T. *The Essentials of Zen Buddhism*. E. P. Dutton, 1962.

Suzuki, D. T. *Mysticism: Christian and Buddhist*. Harper, 1957.

Suzuki, D. T. *On Indian Mahayana Buddhism*. Harper & Row, 1968.

Tripathi, Chandrabhal, ed. *Fünfundzwanzig Sutras des Nidana Samyukta*. Akademie Verlag, 1962.

Urgyen Rinpoche, Tulku. *Vajra Speech: Pith Instructions for the Dzogchen Yogi*. Rangjung Yeshe, 2001.

Van Lommel, Pim. *Consciousness Beyond Life: The Science of the Near-Death Experience*. HarperOne, 2010.

Wallace, B. Alan. *Contemplative Science: Where Buddhism and Neuroscience Converge*. Columbia University Press, 2007.

Warder A. K. *Indian Buddhism*. Motilal Banarsidass, 1970.

Warder A. K. *Introduction to Pali*. Pali Text Society, 1984.

Warren, Henry Clarke, trans. *Buddhism in Translations*. Motilal Banarsidass, 1998.

Webb, Russell. *An Analysis of the Pali Canon*. Buddhist Publication Society, 1975.

Wheeler, Sir Mortimer. *Early India and Pakistan*. Thames and Hudson, 1959.

Williams, R. *Jaina Yoga: A Survey of the Mediaeval Sravakacaras*. Oxford University Press, 1963.

Woods, James Haughton, trans. *The Yoga-System of Patanjali*. Harvard University Press, 1914.

Credits

I wish to express my gratitude to translator David Young, who helped me with the English version of my book, which I originally wrote in both Danish and English.

I also wish to express my gratitude to my editor at Shambhala Publications, Peter Schumacher, for valuable assistance.

I express my gratitude for permission to use the following texts from these publishers:

Excerpts from *Reading the Buddha's Discourses in Pali: A Practical Guide to the Language of the Ancient Buddhist Canon*. Copyright © 2020 by Bhikkhu Bodhi. Reprinted with the permission of The Permissions Company, LLC, on behalf of Wisdom Publications, wisdompubs.org.

Excerpts from *Visuddhimagga, "The Path of Purification,"* translated by Ven. Nanamoli 1975. Reprinted with the permission of Buddhist Publication Society. Sri Lanka.

Excerpt from *Path to Deliverance*, translated by Ven. Nyanatiloka 1952. Reprinted with the permission of Buddhist Publication Society. Sri Lanka.

Excerpt from *The Great Exhortation to Rahula*, translated by Narada, Thera & Mahinda, Bhikkhu 1974. Reprinted with the permission of Buddhist Publication Society. Sri Lanka.

Excerpts from *Practical Insight Meditation*, by Mahasi Sayadaw 1971. Reprinted with the permission of Buddhist Publication Society. Sri Lanka.

Excerpts from *The Progress of Insight*, by Mahasi Sayadaw 1973. Reprinted with the permission of Buddhist Publication Society. Sri Lanka.

Excerpts from *Last Days of the Buddha: The Maha Parinibbana Sutta of the Pali Canon*, translated by Sister Vajira, 1974. Reprinted with the permission of Buddhist Publication Society. Sri Lanka.

Excerpts from *Theravada Collection on Monastic Law: A Translation of the Pali Vinaya into English Vol 4-5*, by Bhikkhu Brahmali 2023: Published by SuttaCentral. Dedicated to the public domain via Creative Commons Zero (CC0).

Index